Guide to

Chinese Buddhism

中国佛教

Written by Zheng Lixin

Translated by Ling Yuan
English text edited by Sara Grimes

Foreign Languages Press Beijing

First Edition 2004

Home Page:
http://www.flp.com.cn
E-mail Addresses:
info@flp.com.cn
sales@flp.com.cn

ISBN 7-119-03334-4

Published by Foreign Languages Press
24 Baiwanzhuang Road, Beijing 100037, China

Distributed by China International Book Trading Corporation
35 Chegongzhuang Xilu, Beijing 100044, China
P.O. Box 399, Beijing, China

Printed in the People's Republic of China

Contents

Buddha's Tooth Pagoda in Lingguang Temple, Western Hills, Beijing

A replica of an ancient Buddhist statue given to the Chinese Buddhist Association by Buddhists in Sri Lanka

The White Pagoda in Tayuan Temple, Mount Wutai, Shanxi Province

Statues in the Yungang Grottoes, Datong, Shanxi Province

A Panoramic view of Xuanzhong Temple , Jiaocheng City, Shanxi Province

The Big Wild Goose Pagoda in Ci'en Temple, Xi'an, Shaanxi Province

The 1,000-handed Guanyin in Xiangguo Temple, Kaifeng, Henan Province

Shaolin Temple in Dengfeng, Henan Province

The dagoba in Qixia Temple, Nanjing, Jiangsu Province

The jade statue of Buddha in Yufu (Jade Buddha) Temple, Shanghai

The Mahavira Hall of Lingyin Temple in Hangzhou, Zhejiang Province

The Mahavira Hall in Donglin Temple in Lushan, Jiangxi Province

Guanyin (Avalokitesvara) Cave on Mount Putuo, Zhejiang Province

The Beamless Hall in Wannian (Ten-Thousand-Year) Temple on Mount Emei, Sichuan Province

The Giant Stone Buddha in Leshan, Sichuan Province

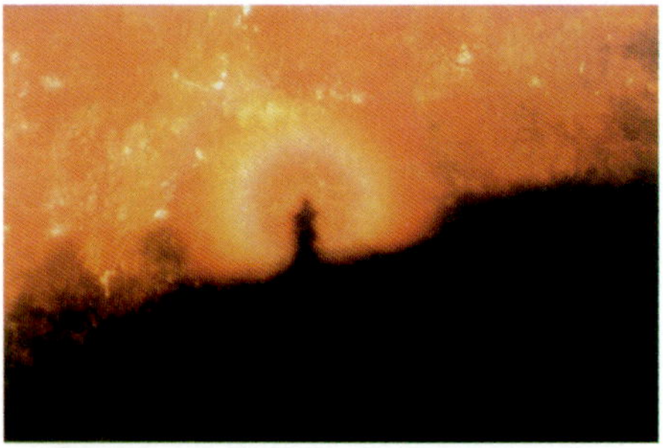

"Light of the Buddha", a natural phenominon often seen on Mount Emei

Statues in the Dazu Grottoes of Baodingshan Mountain, Sichuan Province

Buddhist Pagodas in Ruili City, Yunnan Province

Buddhist statues in the Mogao Caves at Dunhuang in Gansu Province

Potala Palace in Lhasa, Tibet

The Gilded Laughing Buddha in the Tashilhunpo Monastery, Tibet

A Tangkha painting

Preface

Buddhism was first introduced to China some 2,000 years ago and features three language-family branches introduced into the country at different times — Han, Tibetan and Pali Buddhism, all different in form and content. Because of this, Chinese Buddhist literature and art is perhaps unparalleled in the world. China Tour Guide: Chinese Buddhism, written by Zheng Lixin, emphasizes Han Buddhism, the Buddhism of the Chinese language. He gives a brief introduction to the history, schools and relationships between Han and other forms of Buddhism, the temples, the four famous Buddhist mountains in China, monks' societies and organizations, the classic scriptures, grotto arts, Buddhist festivals, major Buddhist activities and Buddhist societies and organizations. The book is not only suitable for tourists at home and abroad, but also worth reading for anyone who wants to know about Chinese Buddhism. The book is written in an easy and fluent style with accurate historical records and some interesting legends and stories.

Dao Shuren

Vice-president of the
Buddhist Association of China

Introduction

This book provides information on Chinese Buddhist beliefs, history, art, architecture, organizations, activities, festivals and holidays to help visitors better enjoy the many people, places and things in China associated with Buddhism. These include world famous historical and cultural sites like grottoes with treasure-troves of Buddhist carvings; sacred Buddhist mountains; temples, pagodas, and monasteries; statues and calligraphy of Buddhist sutras translated for centuries into Chinese from the original Sanskrit and other Indian languages; Buddhist emperors and other prominent Buddhists in Chinese history as well as the many Chinese monks, nuns and lay people who are practicing Buddhists today.

There are three forms of Chinese Buddhism: Han, Tibetan and Pali. These are distinctions based on the language system each religion employs to interpret and follow the teachings of Sakyamuni the Buddha who preached in India in the 6th century BC, or some 500 years before Buddhism began to make inroads into China. Han Buddhism and Tibetan Buddhism are Mahayana, a later form of Indian Buddhism that honors Sakyamuni but holds that there are a lot of Buddhas and a lot of heavens and other spiritual realms as well as a Universal Salvation. Mahayana is the Buddhism practiced in most northern countries in Asia, including Korea and Japan. Pali, also known as Southern Buddhism or Theravada Buddhism, is practiced by the Dai people and other ethnic groups in Yunnan Province of China, as it is in most southern Asian countries, including Cambodia and Sri Lanka. This is the earlier form of Buddhism, (also called Hinayana) that honors Sakyamuni and holds more to his original teachings on how a person can break the bonds of suffering. Brief introductions to Tibetan Buddhism and Pali Buddhism are included here, but the emphasis in this book is on the Buddhism of the Chinese language, or Han Buddhism that was introduced to China since the Han Dynasty around the 1st century BC-1st century AD.

An important religion in most Asian countries, Buddhism arrived in the majority Han-inhabited areas relatively late in the history both of China, which has a recorded history of some 5,000 years, and of Buddhism which traces its origins to Siddhartha Gautama (ca. 500 BC) born in Lumbini in Nepal. After first becoming Prince Siddhartha of Kapilavatthu, a tiny kingdom of India in ancient times, Siddhartha renounced wealth and position to embark on a religious life. The Brahmanic beliefs of his times held that endless cycles of reincarnation were based on karma, a good deed producing a good effect and a bad one an evil one, determining the fate after death of a good or evil destiny. Siddhartha wanted to understand how to break free of this cycle. Through the practice of a series of austerities in northern India near the Himalayan foothills, he achieved his goal at 35 years of age, under a bodhi tree, and became Buddha (Sanskrit for "Enlightened One") by realizing how to break the chain of rebirth and death. To explain this to his followers, he developed the Four Noble Truths and the Eightfold Noble Path (See Appendices V: Buddhist Terms) and spent some 45 years traveling and preaching, in the process founding a community based on poverty, chastity, and insight or meditation that became known as Buddhism. He was also called Sakyamuni, meaning "Sage of the Sakya people." Sakyamuni the Buddha died in his 80s around 483-487 BC to attain Nirvana, the Final Release.

Meanwhile, while Sakyamuni the Buddha and his disciples were preaching in India, near contemporaries in China like the great philosopher Confucius (551-479 BC) and Mencius (372-289 BC) and others, such as the Daoist philosopher Zhuangzi (369-286 BC), were helping to establish early Chinese ways of thinking. Daoism, based in ancient religious beliefs in China around the worship of heaven and ancestors, is the only major religion that came exclusively from Chinese roots to grow into maturity in Chinese soil; Confucianism is not a religion but rather an ethical system that is fundamental to Chinese society. After Buddhism arrived in China some time around the beginning of the Christian era, it took another some 600 years of major changes in both the spiritual and material life within Han Buddhist temples and monasteries before Buddhism came into its own in the Chinese cultural environment. While basic creeds remained largely intact, Buddhism changed in China in ways conductive to its dissemination and development in a foreign land, including some merging with Daoist and Confucian thinking. An old Chinese saying has it that the vast majority of people in China "wear a Confucian crown, a Daoist robe, and a pair of Buddhist sandals."

Just before the time Buddhism began to spread to the Han-inhabited areas of China, the basic split occurred around the 2nd century BC among followers of Buddha into the two branches, Theravada (Hinayana), the branch that remained closer to the earliest forms of Indian Buddhism and Sakyamuni, its founder; and Mahayana, the branch that embraced a spiritual journey that includes not just the individual and Sakyamuni Buddha but all beings and many Buddhas. Basically, the original Buddhism held that one must find the root of suffering, eradicate it and find Enlightenment through following certain rules that guided meditation and spiritual discipline. Mahayana brought the idea of a Universal Enlightenment and promised individual practitioners the help of Bodhisattvas, highly spiritual beings who choose to forsake Buddhahood to help others perfect themselves. While both branches of Buddhism spread to China, it was the Mahayana branch that took root and prospered in the Han-inhabited regions. As Buddhism reached its height in the Sui-Tang dynasties (581-907) — when almost all the emperors were adherents or supporters of Buddhism — new schools of Buddhism arose tailored to Chinese needs, all of them Mahayana. Over the generations, Buddhism became a part of Chinese culture itself, with a strong popular appeal and ideas that had an impact on Chinese philosophy, morality, literature, art and many other fields of learning. After Buddhism waned in India, China became its second cradle and the source of various schools in many other countries and regions.

Chapter 1 examines the basic creeds of Buddhism; the origins of Buddhist writings in India; the translation work into Chinese associated with these writings by scholars in India, China and elsewhere; and the composition of the *Tripitaka,* the Buddhist canon or doctrine that is a collection over centuries of writings —

including the *sutras* or teachings of Buddha. Diligent work over two millennia created a mass of Buddhist writings that are part of the *Dharma* or law, one of Buddhism's *triratna* (three treasures, the other two being the Buddha and the *Sangha* or community of believers). These writings also are treasures of Chinese cultural heritage.

Chapter 2 looks at the spread of Buddhism in China with an emphasis on Han Buddhism but also including brief descriptions of Tibetan and Pali Buddhism.

Chapter 3 gives a brief account of the origin of each of the major schools of Han Buddhism, its founders, tenets and ancestral hall or founding temple. After Buddhism became established in China around the 6th century, different schools began to emerge. The first was the Tiantai, followed by Sanlun, Huayan, Ci'en, Chan or Zen, Vinaya, Jingtu or Pure Land and the Esoteric or Tantra. These schools reached their height in the Tang Dynasty and thereafter went into decline or merged with others. Today the most common form of Buddhist practice for lay people in China is individual rather than congregational and integrates the meditation of the Chan School and the chanting of the Pure Land School. Chapter 3 also describes influence of each school on other countries, particularly Korea and Japan.

Chapter 4 takes a look at the Han Buddhist temple, its architecture, layout and interior design and offers brief descriptions of some of the major Buddhist temples in China. For those travelers wishing a ringside seat on what's happening inside a Chinese monastery, Chapter 4 includes information on Buddhist festivals and ritual celebrations, such as those surrounding the birthday of Sakyamuni Buddha. It also answers a series of questions about the organizational setup of monasteries connected with these temples including commandments and prohibitions, sources of income, and monastic daily life.

Chapter 5 introduces five major Buddhist grottoes a traveler may wish to see — Mogao Caves at Dunhuang, Maijishan Grottoes, Yungang Grottoes, Longmen Grottoes, and Dazu Grottoes. Creating and worshiping images of Buddhas, Boddhisatvas and celestial lands became important early in the history of Buddhism in China, and perhaps the most striking display of Buddhist sculpture and painting in China can be seen in her world-famous grottoes. Dunhuang Grottoes is the oldest example of Buddhist cave temple art, with a history of 1,600 years beginning in the Eastern and Western Jin dynasties (265-420). It compares favorably with the famous Ajanta Caves of India in terms of the scope of its engineering and the artistic level of its sculptures and murals — an impressive testimony to the skills of the working people of ancient China.

Chapter 6 offers a tour of China's four sacred Buddhist mountains — Mount Wutai, Mount Putuo, Mount Jiuhua and Mount Emei. A saying in China goes, "All the famous mountains under heaven are home to Buddhist monks." Dotted with monasteries and temples, these four Chinese mountains also are blessed with a truly "heavenly" landscape that makes them major tourist attractions particularly attractive for those visitors who are Buddhists.

Chapter 7 acquaints the reader with the centuries-old ties that Buddhists in China have had with Buddhists of other countries including India, Sri Lanka, Nepal, Myanmar, Cambodia, Thailand, Indonesia, Korea and Japan. This history has enabled Chinese Buddhists to act on their religious beliefs not only at home but also abroad by promoting cultural exchanges that have helped create and maintain goodwill between China and the rest of the world.

Chapter 1

Buddhist Scriptures

1. The Origins

Buddhism means following the teachings of Buddha — all of which were passed on through the recollections of his disciples in the form of *sutras* that usually begin with the words: "Thus have I heard ..." Sakyamuni himself left no written records of his lectures. The great Buddhist canon or doctrine, known as the *Tripitaka*, contains the sutras developed over many years into a mammoth combination of *sutra-pitaka* (the holy words of the Buddha), *vinaya-pitaka* (the discipline the Buddha laid down for his followers) and *Abhidharma-pitaka* (treatises written by disciples of different generations on their research into the Buddha's doctrines). Historical records are unavailable on the dates of the emergence of the various books in the *Abhidharma-pitaka* although it is estimated that they first appeared during the period of 3rd century-1st century BC. As for the *sutra-pitaka* and *vinaya-pitaka,* their origins are traced to the first anniversary of Sakyamuni's nirvana when his 500 disciples — worried that the Buddha's teachings would fall into oblivion if they were not collected in time — held the First Samgiti (Council) in Rajagrha. This gathering was lead by Buddha's disciple Mahakasyapa (Kasyapa). During the meeting, the disciple Ananda recited the *sutra-pitaka,* and the disciple Upali recited the *vinaya-pitaka* before the audience. Ananda recalled what the Buddha had said, where and to whom. The audience then discussed Ananda's recollections, filled in what he had forgotten and corrected his errors until consensus was reached on the final version. To indicate that each sutra was verified after Sakyamuni's death, each sutra was preceded by the words, "Thus have I heard ..." In very much the same fashion Upali's recollections of each and every commandment of Buddha, his reasonings behind it, and where he established it, were subjected to the audience's perusal before they were accepted as the official version of *vinaya* or commandments.

No written records were kept of the *sutra-pitaka* and *vinaya-pitaka* thus collected and verified, rather they were disseminated by word of mouth through the following generations in the many different monastic orders that developed among the Buddha's followers. In the first century BC, Buddhists — faced with inconsistencies in oral accounts — began to write down the sutras and commandments, with different Buddhist orders writing down their respective sutras and commandments. [The British Library has 57 fragments of Buddhist manuscripts on birch bark scrolls, written in the Kharosthi script and the Gandhari (Prakrit) language believed to be the earliest surviving Buddhist text. It is believed they are part of the long-lost canon of the Sarvastivadin School of Buddhism that dominated Gandhara — modern north Pakistan and east Afghanistan — that was instrumental in Buddhism's spread into central and east Asia.]

Around the first century, a major split occurred that divided Buddhism into the Mahayana and Hinayana branches or vehicles, with "Hinayana" the name given to the earlier school with beliefs that concentrated on the life of the Buddha and the individual's goal of achieving enlightenment, that is attaining nirvana — release from rebirth into non-being. The term Hinayana, originally a pejorative term used by Mahayana adherents, means "lesser vehicle;" Mahayana means "greater vehicle." Of the Hinayana schools, only Theravada also known as Pali or Southern Buddhism — remains today. The Buddhism practiced in China is primarily Mahayana, the Buddhism that advocates the gradual salvation of all with the assistance of Bodhisattvas. With all the differences among the followers of the Buddha, tremendous differences in his teaching are contained in the Buddhist classics.

2. The Scriptures in Chinese

The monumental task of translating Buddhist scriptures into Chinese began in the 1st century and continued for about a thousand years through the 11th century. The earliest translators faced formidable problems. As John King Fairbank, the American historian wrote in *China, A New History*:

"The Buddhist teachings were set forth in the great Buddhist canon or *Tripitaka*. Translation of sutras from this canon became the chief work of the first Buddhist monks in China. They and their followers faced enormously complex linguistic as well as intellectual problems — how to translate from Sanskrit, which was polysyllabic, highly inflected, and alphabetic like English and other Indo-European languages, into the monosyllabic, uninflected, ideographic script of China; how to convey in that rather terse and concrete medium, the highly imaginative and metaphysical abstraction of Indian mysticism."

But as large numbers of sutras and commandments and theories about them were translated into Chinese, these writings became a major part of Chinese cultural heritage. Most of the translations were done during the Tang Dynasty (618-907); few translations followed that time although some classics were translated in the Song Dynasty that followed the Tang.

Translation of *sutra-pitaka* and *vinaya-pitaka* started sporadically at best in the early days. Only after a period of time did some people begin to register the books they had translated, and because many of the translations were not signed, the names of the translators remain unknown to this day. By the Eastern Jin , Shi Dao'an (314-385) began collecting catalogues and books, and after many years of efforts, he came up with the *Catalogue of Miscellaneous Scriptures*, which provides a general record of the scriptures translated. (For more on Shi Dao'an, see Chapter 2.)

By the Southern and Northern dynasties, something akin to the *sutra-pitaka* appeared in the catalogue, *All the Scriptures Available*, but it fell short of being a streamlined classification. At the time, printing had not yet been invented, and all the translated sutras and commandments were hand-copied and bound in separate volumes. A person who specialized in copying was known as "sutra copier," a job that became fashionable. For instance, Emperor Wudi of the Chen of the Southern Dynasties once ordered 12 copies made of *All the Scriptures Available*; and his successor, Emperor Wendi, ordered 50 copies made. The same happened in the Northern Dynasties as well. Emperor Daowu (in reign 386-408) of the Northern Wei once issued an instruction on the copying of the *All the Scriptures Available*. In 560, Emperor

Xiaozhao of the Northern Qi had 12 collections of scriptures copied for his father. The court officials followed the example of the emperors, picking up the writing brush one after another to copy sutras. Sutra copying became even more prevalent during the Sui and the Tang.

The *Catalogue of Miscellaneous Scriptures* by Dao'an in the Eastern Jin Dynasty was followed by a series of other sutra catalogues. Among the better known are the *Collected Records of the Tripitaka* by Sengyou of the Liang Dynasty, *Catalogue of Scriptures during the Wei Dynasty* by Li Kuo of the Northern Wei Dynasty, *Catalogue of Scriptures of the Qi Dynasty* by Monk Fashang of the Northern Qi Dynasty, *Records of the Three Treasures (Triratna) of Various Dynasties* by Fei Changfang of the Sui Dynasty, *Records of Internal Classics of the Tang Dynasty* by Daoxuan of the Tang, and *Kaiyuan Records of Mahayana Buddhism* by Zhisheng of the Tang Dynasty. Among these, the *Kaiyuan Records of Mahayana Buddhism* by Zhisheng is the best in classification.

The following timetable of translations is based on Zhisheng's report in *Kaiyuan Records:*

Zhisheng divided the translated sutras and commandments into two sections: Mahayana Buddhism, and Hinayana Buddhism. In the section for Mahayana Buddhism are 515 titles of sutras in 2,173 volumes that were contained in 203 cloth slip-cases; 26 titles of commandments in 54 volumes put in five cloth slip-cases; and 97 treatises in 518 volumes in 50 cloth slip-cases. In the Hinayana section there are 240 sutras in 618 volumes in 48 cloth slip-cases, 54 titles of commandments in 1,446 volumes in 45 cloth slip-cases, and 36 treatises in 689 volumes in 72 cloth slip-cases. These, in addition to a collection of works by sages and wise men and writings by eminent monks of various dynasties, add up to 1,076 titles in 5,048 volumes. And a 1,000-word verse was compiled to facilitate reference. With its scientific classification, the *Kaiyuan Records* became the standard for all versions of *Tripitaka* classics following the Tang and the Song dynasties.

The invention of printing technology during the Song rendered hand-copying of Buddhist canons obsolete. Woodblock printed and movable-type printed versions of the *Tripitaka* began to appear. Following is a list of the printed versions during various dynastic periods:

Dynasty	Year	Number of translators	Number of classics translated	Number of volumes translated	Notes
Late Han	67-220	12	292	395	Translators unknown for 141 classics in 158 volumes
Wei	220-265	5	12	18	
Wu	222-280	5	189	417	Translators unknown in Wei and Wu for 87 classics in 261 volumes
Western Jin	265-316	12	333	590	Translators unknown for 58 classics in 59 volumes
Eastern Jin	317-420	16	168	468	Translators unknown for 40 classics in 48 volumes
Former Qin	351-394	6	15	197	
Later Qin	384-418	5	94	624	
Western Qin	385-431	1	56	110	Translators unknown for 41 classics in 86 volumes translated during the 317- 431 period
Former Liang		1	4	6	
Northern Liang	401-?	9	82	311	Translators unknown for 53 classics in 75volumes
Song	420-479	22	465	717	Translators unknown for 307 classics in 340 volumes
Qi	479-502	7	12	33	
Liang	502-557	4	39	93	
Chen	557-589	3	40	133	
Northern Wei	396-550	12	83	274	
Northern Qi	550-577	2	8	52	
Northern Zhou	557-581	4	14	29	
Sui	581-618	9	64	301	
Tang	618-830	21	263	1962	
Total		156	2,233	6,730	

The Song Dynasty:

1) The Shu Version of the *Tripitaka* of the Kaibao Reign, known for short as *Kaibao Tripitaka* or *Shu-Version Tripitaka.*
2) *Tripitaka* of the Kauyuan Temple of Wuzhou in present-day Jinhua, Zhejiang Province, which is not extant today.
3) Khitan version of *Tripitaka*, printed in the Liao Dynasty, and known as *Khitan Tripitaka* or Liao-Version of the *Great Tripitaka.*
4) *Tripitaka* of the Eastern Temple of Fuzhou of the Song Dynasty, known as Chongning Wanshou *Grand Tripitaka*, or Eastern Temple Version of *Tripitaka* of Fuzhou.
5) *Tripitaka* of the Kaiyuan Temple of Fuzhou of the Song Dynasty, known as *Vairocana Tripitaka* or *Fuzhou Tripitaka.*
6) *Tripitaka* of the Zifu Temple of Sixi in Anji Prefecture of the Song Dynasty, known as *Sixi Tripitaka* or *Huzhou Tripitaka.*
7) Tianning Temple *Tripitaka* of Xiezhou (present-day Xiexian County, Shanxi Province) of the Song Dynasty, generally known as *Jin Tripitaka* or *Zhaocheng Tripitak*a.
8) Qisha Yansheng Temple *Tripitaka* of Pingjiang Prefecture (present-day Wuxian County, Jiangsu Province) of the Song Dynasty, known as *Qisha Tripitaka* or *Yanshengsi Tripitaka.*

The Yuan Dynasty:

1) Great Puning Temple *Tripitaka* of Yuhang County, Hangzhou Circuit of the Yuan Dynasty, known as *Puning Tripitaka* or *Yuan Tripitaka.*
2) Hongfa Temple *Tripitaka* of Yandu of the Yuan Dynasty, which is probably the *Golden Tripitaka*, but needs to be verified.
3) Yuan-dynasty copper-block printed *Tripitaka.* Historical records mention this version, but its existence has not been confirmed.

The Ming Dynasty:

1) *Tripitaka* of the Hongwu version of the Ming Dynasty, i.e., the original version for the *Southern Tripitaka* of the Ming Dynasty, abbreviated as *Kenan Tripitaka.*
2) Southern Version of *Tripitaka* of the Ming, popularly known as *Southern Tripitaka.*
3) Northern Version of *Tripitaka* of the Ming, known as *Northern Tripitaka.*

4) Wulin Fangche Classical *Tripitaka* of the Ming, which no longer exists but is recorded in history books.
5) Classical Version of *Tripitaka* of the Lengyan Temple of Jiaxing of the Ming, also missing but recorded in history books.

Today few versions of *Tripitaka* prior to the Ming Dynasty are extant. Buddhism was suppressed twice by the emperors of the Northern Wei and Northern Zhou dynasties in 446 and 574. And during Emperor Wuzong's suppression of Buddhism during the Huichang reign (841-846) in the late Tang Dynasty, most Buddhist scriptures and treatises in Chinese were destroyed. In the early days, some Chinese versions of the *Tripitaka* found their way into Korea and Japan to be converted into local versions. These include the *Koryo Tripitaka* of Korea and the *Taisho Shinshiu Taisokyo* (*Revised Taisho Edition of the Tripitaka*) in Japan, both of which are printed in Chinese characters and stand testimony to the influence of the Chinese-version of *Tripitaka*. According to *A Dictionary of Buddhist Terms* (See Appendices VII: Suggested Readings) the Korean Tripitaka is the oldest extant Tripitaka in the world. In Tibet and Yunnan Province are versions of the *Tripitaka* in Tibetan and Pali languages. In China, Han Buddhist temples today feature a Qing - dynasty Chinese version of the *Tripitaka*, known as the *Dragon Tripitaka*. However, there is one place in China where visitors can see earlier Buddhist scriptures: The Yunju (Cloud Dwelling) Temple outside Beijing. (See 9. Major Han Buddhist Temples, Chapter 4). There visitors can see Buddhist scriptures engraved on 14,278 stone slabs dating back a thousand years to the Sui and Tang dynasties. The project was begun by the monk Huisi (See 1. Tiantai School, Chapter 3) to assure the survival of the scriptures on something more solid than silk and skins that were easily destroyed. Huisi's work continued through disciples into the 17th century, assuring the survival in China of written Buddhist scripture.

3. The Scripture Translators

Although different theories exist about how Buddhism first arrived in China, scholars are unanimous in considering An Shigao, who arrived in China in the mid-2nd century from Parthia (present-day Iran), as the first translator of Buddhist scriptures in China. Arriving shortly afterwards was Lokasema from Indo-Scythae (Scythia was an ancient country lying north and northeast of the Black Sea and partly east of the Aral Sea.). It is said that An Shigao translated classics of Hinayana Buddhism, while Lokasema worked Mahayana Buddhism. More monks arrived from the Western Territory and India during the Three Kingdoms period (220-280), the Eastern and Western Jin dynasties (265-420), the Southern and Northern dynasties (420-589), the Sui (581-618) and the Tang (618-907) dynasties. Meanwhile, many Chinese monks made pilgrimages westward and brought scriptures back to China to be translated.

The four major translators in Chinese Buddhist history are:

Kumarajiva (344-413), born in Kuqa in today's Xinjiang Autonomous Region in the west of China in a family of Indian descent. His translations of the Three Classics helped found the Sanlun School.

Tipitakacariya Paramartha (491-569), an Indian monk and scholar, who preached Buddhism in what is present-day Cambodia before he arrived in present-day Guangdong in China in 546.

Xuanzang (602-664), the Tang Dynasty pilgrim monk and scholar celebrated in both India and China, who became abbot of Ci'en Temple, the birthplace of the Ci'en School. His travels west — some 1373 years ago — in search of sutras inspired many myths and folk tales that were gathered some 400 years ago into *Journey to the West*, a book that became one of the great classics of Chinese literature.

Amoghavajra (705-774), an Indian born of the Brahman caste who arrived in China as a child and became a major founder of the Esoteric School.

For his tremendous contributions to the Sino-Indian cultural exchange, Kumarajiva in the Northern Wei Dynasty is regarded as the foremost of the four major sutra translators in the history of Chinese Buddhism, followed by Xuanzang whose remarkable accomplishments in the Tang Dynasty are recorded here in the next chapter.

As for Kumarajiva, he showed a religious vocation as a child and early on established a name for himself for his erudite knowledge of Mahayana and Hinayana classics. In 382 he was captured by the Eastern Jin general Lu Guang who had been dispatched by King Fu Jian of Former Qin (350-394) on an expedition against Kuqa, and was brought by the Chinese army to Liangzhou in present-day Wuwei, Gansu Province. During the 17 years he spent in Liangzhou, Kumarajiva learned local customs and habits and the Chinese language and prepared himself for a career as a Buddhist scriptural translator. In 401, he arrived in the Northern Wei metropolis of Chang'an (Xi'an) and won the respect of the emperor. With his arrival, Chang'an became one of the Buddhist centers of north China, and Kumarajiva became the leader of a team of Chinese and foreign scholars who translated large numbers of major scriptures, commandments and treatises into Chinese, thereby vastly replenishing the Buddhist literature in Chinese and opening up a new chapter in the development of Chinese Buddhism. Professor Shen Fuwei reported in *Cultural Flow between China and the Outside World throughout History*, published by the Foreign Languages Press in 1996, that from 402 to 413 Kumarajiva's team of some 800 Chinese and Indian scholar-translators translated 94 sets of scriptures in 425 volumes, surpassing in size and variety the later works of the noted translator, Xuanzang, in the Tang Dynasty.

To this day, the scriptures translated by Kumarajiva and Xuanzang remain the favorites among Chinese Buddhists.

Chapter 2

The Spread of Buddhism in China

1. Han Buddhism
汉语系佛教 (Hànyǔ Xì Fójiào)

Han Buddhism emphasizes the existence of many Buddhas — those who have attained enlightenment and are in heaven — and Bodhisattvas — those who have attained enlightenment but continue to live in the world to rescue others. The chief Buddha among the pantheon of Han Buddhist deities is Sakyamuni, the historic Buddha, but Mahayanists believe there were Buddhas before him and one who will come later, Maitreya, the Buddha of the Future. The most popular deity in China is the Avalokitesvara or Guanyin, the Goddess of Mercy whose image with a thousand eyes and hands is present at many Chinese Buddhist sacred sites. Other significant Buddhas and Bodhisattvas besides Sakyamuni, Maitreya and Guanyin include Amitabha, the Buddha of Immeasurable Splendor, who is worshiped in the Pure Land School; Samantabhadra, the Bodhisattva of Universal Benevolence; Manjusri, the Bodhisattva of Wisdom; Mahasthamaprapta, the Bodhisattva representing the Buddha-wisdom of Amitabha; Ksitigarbha, the Bodhisattva who protects children and travelers and saves people from hell; and Bhaisajyaraja, the Buddha of Healing and Medicine.

Theories vary on how Buddhism was introduced into the regions of China inhabited by the majority Han people. A theory popular among Buddhists themselves holds that the roots of Han Buddhism, the Buddhism translated into the Chinese or Han Language, can be traced to the arrival in Luoyang, China, of two Indian monks, Kasyapamatanga and Dharmaranya during the Eastern Han Dynasty (25-220). It is said that one night in 64 AD,

Eastern Han Emperor Mingdi dreamed of a golden man with halo flying over his palace. At the morning court the following day, he asked his ministers for an interpretation. One of the ministers named Fu Yi replied:

"In the West there is a god called Buddha. The golden man Your Majesty saw in your dream sounds like him."

The emperor then dispatched an 18-member mission to the west in search of the Buddhist doctrine or dharma. In 67 AD, the Chinese mission arrived in Indo-Scythae, where they came across Kasyapamatanga and Dharmaranya. These two monks returned with the mission to Luoyang, then the Chinese capital, in today's Henan Province. They brought with them Buddhist scriptures and sculptures, and began to translate the *Forty-two Chapter Sutra* in the White Horse Temple, considered the oldest Buddhist temple in China. Thus the first of the tens of thousands Han Buddhist monasteries and temples was originally built as a studio for Kasyapamatanga and Dharmaranya to do their translations of *sutra,* or the preachings attributed to Buddha. From the time of the Han Dynasty until Buddhism reached its heyday during the Tang Dynasty, translators worked on Buddhist scriptures in the White Horse Temple in Luoyang. (See 9. Major Han Buddhist Temples, Chapter 4)

However, the story about Kasyapamatanga and Dharmaranya has always been controversial, and remains so today. Some have gone so far as to allege that the *Forty-two Chapter Sutra* is not a translation at all but something concocted by some Chinese. Another main theory is the one favored by scholars: Buddhism was brought to China in 2 BC in the Western Han Dynasty when Yi Cun arrived from Indo-Scythia to dictate Buddhist scriptures to a man named Qin Jingxian. Whatever the truth of these two theories, given the narrow gap of 70 years between them, they both indicate that Buddhism first made its inroads into China during the interregnum between the Western and Eastern Han dynasties. Chinese Buddhist circles in 1998 held a grand ceremony to celebrate the 2000th anniversary of the introduction of Buddhism to China, acknowledging 2 BC in the reign of Emperor Aidi of the Western Han Dynasty as the year when Buddhism found its way into China.

At first, Chinese regarded the Buddha as a god from some

alien land on the same level as the Yellow Emperor, the legendary ancestor of the Chinese nation, and Laozi, the ancient philosopher traditionally said to have been born in 604 BC on whose philosophy Daoism is based. Daoism is the indigenous religion of China and its oldest cultural principle. However, Buddhism soon acquired a following among ordinary people in China, despite the absence of canonical texts. Not until the mid-2nd century did monks like An Shigao begin to arrive from the West Territory. As more and more scriptures were translated into Chinese, Buddhism gradually presented itself to the Chinese not only as a source of spiritual solace but also as a profound philosophy that played an important role in the development of civilization.

In the Three Kingdoms period (220-265), Buddhism was practiced in the kingdoms of Wei and Wu, but remained little known to the kingdom of Shu in the remote southwest part of the country. The history of Buddhism in the kingdom of Wei was marked by two major events: The arrival in 250 AD of Dharmakala, the first Indian monk to lecture Chinese monks on commandments and prohibitions, and the beginning of westbound pilgrimages by Chinese monks in search of Buddhist doctrines. In 260, the Chinese monk Zhu Shixing obtained certain scriptures in Khotan (a region in Turkistan in Central Asia) during a tour of the West Territory. His success inspired a wave of westward pilgrimages among Chinese monks during the Western and Eastern Jin dynasties (265-420).

During the Western and Eastern Jin dynasties, Buddhism spread to a fairly large part of the country. Many Buddhist classics were translated into Chinese and more and more temples and monasteries were built. With more Chinese translations of Buddhist scriptures came a new discipline of learning in China designed to rediscover the truth of Buddhism at a time when thinking of Laozi and Zhuangzi, the founders of Daoist thought that emphasized the relationship between humankind and nature, was in vogue. Quite a few Buddhists were also versed in Daoism, so Buddhist knowledge was often a mixture of both the preaching of the Buddha and the thinking of Laozi and Zhuangzi. The Eastern Jin Dynasty (317-420) was ensconced in south China, with the natural barrier of the Yangtze River keeping the Sixteen Kingdoms up north at bay. Mount Lushan and the city of Jianye (present-day Nanjing) emerged as two centers of Buddhism in the south, where many monks were engaged in the translation of Buddhist scriptures.

Many famous monks, scholars and teachers emerged during this period of the Western and Eastern Jin dynasties. They include:

Dharmaranya, an Indo-Scythian who lived with his family in Dunhuang in today's Gansu Province, was the most prolific Buddhist translator of the Western Jin (265-316). He translated 175 Buddhist scriptures into Chinese. Dharmaranya traveled to many kingdoms in the West Territory, mastering 36 languages along the way. Dharmaranya returned to Dunhuang and then to Chang'an, the capital, with a heavy load of Buddhist sutras and dedicated the rest of his life to translating. After Dharmaranya, copies of the Buddhist scripture were available in both Luoyang and Chang'an.

Fotucheng, a Buddhist monk from Kuqa, arrived in Luoyang in 310 AD in the Western Jin Dynasty at a time of war and turmoil. According to Volume III of the *Biographies of Preeminent Monks*, he had extraordinary powers with which he gained the confidence of General Shi Le who became the founder of the kingdom of Later Zhao (319-351) with a reign that lasted for 14 years. When Shi Le died, he was succeeded by his son, Shi Hong, before the power was usurped by Shi Hu, who also was advised by Fotucheng. It is said that he alone had tens of thousands of followers and more than 800 temples built under his influence.

Shi Dao'an (314-385), a disciple of Fotucheng was a native of Fuliu in Changshan northwest of present-day Quyang, Hebei Province. After establishing a following of several hundred monks, Shi Dao'an settled in Xiangyang in present-day Hubei Province as a lecturer and writer who won the esteem of Emperor Xiaowu of the Eastern Jin, and of Fu Jian, who made himself king of the Former Qin (350-394) in Chang'an. In 379, after his son's army conquered Xiangyang, Fu Jian had Shi Dao'an moved to the Wuchong Monastery in Chang'an where his reputation grew wider still. Kumarajiva, living in the West Territory at the time, held Shi Dao'an in high esteem, calling him the "Sage of the East."

Faxian (c.337-c.422), one of the most accomplished of the many pilgrim monks, became a monk while still a child in his native Pingyan in Shanxi Province. In 399, when he was 62,

Faxian started off with a group of disciples from Chang'an (Xi'an) on an 11-year journey to more than 30 kingdoms in search of commandments and scriptures. In India, the group paid homage to Buddhist sites and obtained a number of scriptures and commandments. In Sinhala (Ceylon, present-day Sri Lanka), Faxian was moved to tears when he saw local merchants offering Chinese-made silk fans to the Buddha as sacrifices. Two years later, he became so homesick that he boarded a ship in Sinhala and braving life-threatening adventures on the sea, returned to China in 412 AD. A year later, working together with the Indian monk Buddhabhadra (359-429), he translated six scriptures and treatises in Jiankang (present-day Nanjing in Jiangsu Province). Based on his travels in more than 30 countries, he wrote the classic *Faxian's Pilgrimage to India.* Faxian died at the age of 85 in Jiangling of Hubei Province.

All the emperors of the Southern Dynasties — Song (420-479), Qi (479-502), Liang (502-557) and Chen (557-589) — supported Buddhism, and the number of Buddhist temples as well as their inhabitants increased considerably. According to Volume Three of *Apology for Buddhist Truth* by the eminent Tang monk Falin, the cities of Luoyang and Chang'an during the Western Jin Dynasty (265-316) hosted a total of 180 temples, a number that snowballed to an amazing 1,768 during the Eastern Jin Dynasty (317-420). It kept growing in the ensuing Southern Dynasties, reaching 1,913 during the Song (420-479); then 2,015 during the Qi (479-502) and 2,954 during the Liang (502-557). The number might be even greater during the Northern Dynasties. Among the emperors, the most ardent supporter of Buddhism in the Southern Dynasties was Emperor Wu of the Liang, originally a Daoist before announcing at a meeting of 2,000 monks and laymen in 504 his decision to give up Daoism for Buddhism. Devoting himself to the study of Buddhist philosophy, he had monasteries built and Buddhist statues sculpted and enshrined. Major translators at the time included Gunabhadra (394-468) and Paramartha (499-569), an Indian monk who preached Buddhism in Funan (present-day Cambodia) before he arrived in Nanhai in present-day Guangdong in 546. Two years later, he went to the capital of the Liang Dynasty (502-557) in present-day Nanjing, Jiangsu Province, where he soon won the favor of Emperor Wu. However, a mutiny launched by General Hou Jing left Paramartha homeless and having trouble making ends meet. Despite the hardships, he translated large numbers of Buddhist scriptures and treatises and became one of the four major translators of Buddhist scriptures in the history of Chinese Buddhism.

In the Northern dynasties — that is, the Northern Wei (386-534), Eastern Wei (534-550), Western Wei (535-557), Northern Qi (550-577) and Northern Zhou (557-581) — development of Buddhism was more uneven. This period saw great accomplishments but also great losses. Most monarchs of these dynasties believed in Buddhism. Under their rule, construction of temples and translation of sutras flourished more than before, and the number of monks and nuns reached an all-time high of over 2 million. The world-famous Yungang and Longmen grottoes, and the unparalleled Yongning Monastery, the cradle of the Pure Land School, were built during this period, remaining to this day a part of China's precious cultural legacy. However, in the midst of this prosperity, Buddhism suffered two campaigns to eliminate Buddhism in what Buddhists refer to as "Disasters of the Dharma." One campaign was launched by Emperor Taiwu of the Northern Wei in 438, the other by Emperor Wu of the Northern Zhou in 574. Neither campaign lasted long, but both inflicted colossal losses on Buddhism.

During his days as prime minister of the Northern Zhou, Yang Jian, father of the Sui Dynasty that immediately followed Northern Zhou, worked to resurrect Buddhism from the destruction wrought in 574 by the Northern Zhou Emperor Wu (not to be confused with Emperor Wu, the devout Buddhist, of the earlier Liang Dynasty). Like Yang Jian, almost all the emperors in the Sui (581-618) and Tang (618-907) dynasties were adherents or supporters of Buddhism. (The lone exception was Emperor Wuzong of the Tang Dynasty, a Daoist, whose campaign against Buddhism had devastating effects.) After Yang Jian took the throne, he helped mastermind the renaissance of Buddhism in China during the Sui Dynasty. When Sui was later overthrown by the Tang Dynasty, Buddhism continued to grow during the reign of Emperor Taizong, Li Shiming, the founding father of the Tang Dynasty, and beyond.

So, the golden age of Han Buddhism came during the Sui and Tang dynasties (581-907). New generations of outstanding personages emerged in Buddhist circles, and an unprecedented number of Buddhist books were translated into Chinese.

The celebrated monk Xuanzang (600-664) alone during the Tang Dynasty produced 75 scriptures in 1,335 volumes in Chinese to become one of the four major translators of Buddhist scriptures in the history of Chinese Buddhism. Beginning in 629, Xuanzang traveled to the India where he lived for many years. He stayed in the Nalanda Monastery, the Buddhist and cultural center of India, and established an outstanding reputation throughout India. For example, upon the invitation of a prince of central India, Xuanzang presided over the sixth Buddhist congress in December 642 in the Indian city of Kanauj that was attended by 18 Indian princes and more than 6,000 Buddhist and Brahman monks and priests. Xuanzang eventually returned to China with a huge load of Sanskrit classics, some of which he translated into Chinese. In 646, Xuanzang finished writing his *Records of the Western Regions in the Tang Dynasty*, an important contribution to Chinese literature in 12 volumes about the 110 countries he visited during his 17 years of travel abroad. Xuanzang also translated Laozi's *Dao Te Jing* into Sanskrit, and the *Mahayana-sraddhotpada-sastra* by the Indian philosopher Asvaghosa from Sanskrit into Indian, thereby making historic contributions to Sino-Indian Buddhist exchanges. Xuanzang became the abbot of Ci'en Temple, the cradle of the Ci'en School, when it was the largest of its kind in Chang'an (Xi'an). (See Chapter 3. Major Schools of Han Buddhism)

Yijing (635-713), a native of Fanyang in present-day Zhuoxian, Hebei Province, was second only to Xuanzang for his achievements in the Tang Dynasty with some 239 volumes and 61 titles of translations and works. Yijing also traveled west, setting off in 671 from Yangzhou and boarding a ship at Panyu, Guangdong, for India where he arrived two years later. After roaming the country to see famous Buddhist sights, he settled in the Nalanda Monastery as a student. Eleven years later, having studied various schools of Indian Buddhism and collected 400 or so Sanskrit versions of Buddhist literature, he began his journey home. In 695, he arrived at Luoyang to the personal welcome of the Empress Wu Zetian and organized a new translation drive of Buddhist scriptures.

Major translators from outside China included Siksananda

(652-710) from the West Territory, and Amoghavajra (705-774), a northern Indian (although some say he was from Saharatta) born of the Brahman caste who arrived in China as a child with his uncle. In 742, Amoghavajra lead a 37-member Chinese delegation on a pilgrimage to Saharatta, where his studies covered both the open and Esoteric Sects of Buddhism. At the end of the journey, which also brought him to India, he returned to Chang'an, put together a workshop to translate large numbers of Sanskrit Buddhist scriptures and treatises into Chinese, most of which were Esoteric classics, thereby emerging as one of the four major translators in Chinese Buddhism history. (See Chapter 1 and 8. Esoteric School, Chapter 3)

Following its first in-roads into China during the Han Dynasty and after about six centuries of repeated adaptation to the local environment, the work of all the eminent translators during the heyday of the Tang helped enriched the collection of Buddhist sutras in the Chinese language to the point that they became a component part of Chinese culture. Buddhism completed its process of domestication during the Sui-Tang period to become a Chinese religion in form and essence with the emergence of the eight schools.

However, toward the end of the Tang Dynasty, Buddhism went into a decline after a crackdown on Buddhism in 842 during the 841-846 reign of Emperor Wuzong. Huge numbers of sutras were burned, monasteries were shut down, and monks were forced to return to secular life. Many schools ceased to exist as separate movements. Buddhism survived but never again enjoyed the kind of prosperity it had during the Sui-Tang period in China.

During the early Song Dynasty (960-1279), Emperor Huizong (1101-1125) of the Song was at first opposed to Buddhism but later changed his views. Development of Buddhism during the Song was characterized by the prosperity of a single sect, the Chan, although the Tiantai sect gained as well. The prevalent form of Buddhism in the Song Dynasty combined both the Chan (Zen) School's practice of meditation in a crossed-legged sitting posture and the Pure Land (Jingtu) School's practice of chanting the name of the Buddha. The Mongolian rulers of the Yuan Dynasty (1279-1368) supported Tibetan Buddhism (Lamaism). A number of eminent monks emerged during the Ming (1368-1644) and Qing (1644-1911) dynasties. Quite a few eminent Buddhist personages also emerged during the Republican period (1912-1949). These included the monks Dixian (1858-1932), Yuexia (1858-1917), Taixu (1889-1947), Hongyi (1880-1942), Xuyun (1840-1959), Yuanying (1878-1953), and Yinguang (1861-1940), and the lay Buddhists Yang Wenhui (1837-1911), Ouyang Jingwu (1871-1943), and Han Qingjing (1884-1949), whose hard work and dedication inspired hope for the revitalization of Buddhism.

After the founding of the People's Republic of China in 1949, China's Constitution guaranteed the basic rights and interests of citizens, including the right of religious belief. This has enabled Buddhists in China to enjoy freedom of religion while devoting themselves to the prosperity of both the country and Buddhism. After 1949 in China, buildings, sites, objects and relics sacred to Buddhists, such as copies and woodblocks of Buddhist scriptures, images and the famous Dunhuang, Longmen and Yungang cave-shrines, came under state protection. Temples were restored and refurbished, including the Ci'en Temple where Xuanzang once translated Buddhist works and the Xingjiao Temple where Xuanzang's body is entombed, both of which are in Xi'an, Shaanxi Province; the Guangji Temple in Beijing; the Lingyin Temple in Hangzhou; and the White Horse Temple in Henan Province, considered the oldest Buddhist temple in China. However, during the "cultural revolution" (1966-1976) these temples, like other Buddhist places and artifacts throughout China, suffered serious vandalism. Following the "cultural revolution", major state funding went into restorations, helping to lead to recognition around the world of the importance as Han Buddhist sites were added to the UNESCO World Heritage List. As of this writing, Buddhist-related World Heritage Sites include Mount Emei Scenic Area, including Leshan Giant Buddha Scenic Area, in Sichuan Province; Mount Wuyi in Fujian Province, the home to Daoists and Zen Buddhists for over 2,000 years; the Mogao Caves, also known as One-Thousand-Buddha Caves, seated on a cliff at the eastern foot of the Mingsha Mountain, Dunhuang City, Gansu Province; the Dazu Stone Carvings in Dazu County, Chongqing; Longmen Grottoes of Luoyang City, in Henan Province; and Yungang Grottoes near Datong City, Shanxi Province.

2. Tibetan Buddhism

藏语系佛教 (Zàngyǔ Xì Fójiào)

The Tantric (also known as Esoteric) Buddhism introduced into Tibet from India in the 7th century was a form of later Indian Buddhism, so like Han Buddhism is Mahayana. The founders of Tantric Buddhism ("gsang-sugags" in Tibetan meaning "the mystic truth") believed they were the recipients of profoundly secret doctrines of the Mahavaircona, or the Dharmakaya Buddha (Buddha in the body of the law) that constituted a true teaching that had not been revealed in the doctrines preached in public by Sakyamuni. All other schools of Buddhism are called "Exoteric" because their doctrines are based on what Sakyamuni openly said. Although Tantric Buddhism also incorporates the preachings of Sakyamuni, followers believe Tantric Buddhism is "the essence of the sacred religion," representing the highest and most difficult stage of monastic study.

Having originated in India, Tantric Buddhism evolved into what might be called Tibetan Tantric Buddhism but is referred to as Tibetan Buddhism to distinguish it from the Esoteric (Tantric) School of Han Buddhism (See 8. Esoteric School, Chapter 3) that is no longer practiced in China but still has followers through the Eastern Esoteric Buddhism in Japan. After Tibet became part of China during the Yuan Dynasty (1271-1368), the Yuan emperors were all pious followers of Tibetan Buddhism. The religion fell out of favor in Ming Dynasty (1368-1644), but by the Qing (1644-1911), for political purposes, the imperial court again held Tibetan Buddhism in high esteem. During the Republican years, Tibetan Buddhism spread far and wide in rural areas of western China, where it is still widely practiced.

The first stage of Tibetan Buddhism (called "Earlier Propagation") lasted about 200 years, beginning in the 7th century under the wise and far-sighted king Songtsan Gampo who worked to expand his territory and unify the tribes on the Qinghai-Tibet Plateau. The second stage (Latter Propagation) began in the mid-10th century . (Because monks are known as lamas in the Tibetan language, Tibetan Buddhism is also known as "Lamaism.")

Prior to the 7th century, Tibetans did not have a written

language. To create a written language for issuing orders and conducting exchanges with neighboring countries, Songtsan Gampo chose a group of children of noble families and sent them to Kashmir for study. Among them was Thonmi Sambhota, who returned home after excelling in linguistic studies to become the inventor of the grammar and written language of Tibet. The written language encouraged Songtsan Gampo to step up the introduction of Buddhism into Tibet. Under his leadership, translators teamed up to work on the scriptures. Statues of the Buddha and other deities in the Buddhist pantheon, introduced from neighboring countries, were enshrined for local worshipers. To show goodwill to these countries, Songtsan Gampo married Princess Bhrkuti of Nepal in the west and Princess Wencheng of the Tang court to the east. The Potala Palace was, for instance, first built by Songtsan Gampo to welcome Princess Wencheng. Both brides brought Buddhist statues to Lhasa, for which temples were constructed. Songtsan Gampo also formulated laws according to the principles of Buddhism to run state affairs. Visitors to Lhasa today can see statues of Songtsan Gampo, Princess Wencheng and Princess Bhrikuti Devi at the Jokhang Monastery, first built in 7th century, located in Barkor Street in the center of Lhasa. The Tang-Tubo [Han-Tibetan] Alliance Monument still stands in the square in front of the monastery.

Several generations after the death of Songtsan Gampo, Buddhism also made strides under the rule of Tride Tsugtan (reigned 704-755), who married Princess Jincheng of the Tang Dynasty. Tride Tsugtan sent people to study Buddhism in the hinterland of China who brought back many Buddhist scriptures. But at the same time, Buddhism in Tibet suffered setbacks at the hands of stubborn followers of an indigenous religion, Bon. [Over the ages, Tibetan Buddhism slowly adopted some of the Bon rites. Bon took on some Buddhist teachings and eventually disappeared.] Only after Tride Tsugtan's son, Trisung Detsan (reigned 755-797), took the throne did Tibetan Buddhism revive. Many Indian sutras were translated into Tibetan, and Tibetan Buddhism reached the zenith of its first stage of development. From 762-766, the renowned Samye Monastery was built. In 767, the first Buddhist service ceremony in the history of Tibet was held at which 12 Indian *bhiksus (*mendicants) were invited to lecture on Buddhist doctrines. During Trisung Detsan's reign the compilation of the *Tripitaka* was basically completed, a project in which many Indian and hinterland Chinese scholars joined Tibetan counterparts in the translation of this colossal Buddhist work. This concerted effort left a precious cultural legacy for the Tibetan people.

However, in 841, the Tibetan King Lang Darma (?-842), masterminded a purge of Buddhists that inflicted tremendous losses on the religion. For a little more than a century monks virtually disappeared from the land of Tibet — they took refuge in the safety of the Kham region [eastern Tibet]. The persecution of Buddhism ended in the early 10th century, when Tibetans began to arrive in Kham to learn the doctrines, and Tibetan Buddhism staged a slow comeback that marked the beginning of its second stage of development.

In 1042, the Tibetans invited Mahanayaka Atisa (982-1054) from India to preach on Buddhism. Atisa, translated as "Shusheng" in Chinese, was actually not the real name of the man, the second of three brothers of the royal family of a tiny Indian kingdom. It was an honorary title bestowed on him by a king of Ngari (a region in Tibet). Translation and preaching were the tasks of Atisa's mission to Tibet, where he was supposed to stay for three years. However, after the road of his return to India was blocked by war in the border region of Nepal, Mahanayaka Atisa remained in Tibet. In 1046, Atisa settled in Nyetang, where he died at the age of 72. During his lifetime, Atisa translated more than a hundred Buddhist writings, replenishing the literature of Tibetan Buddhism. As an important figure in the later stage of development of Tibetan Buddhism, his academic ideas exerted a far-reaching influence on the later development of Lamaism.

During the Yuan Dynasty (1271-1368), Kublai Khan appointed the celebrated Lama Phags-pa of Tibet imperial patriarch and entrusted him with the task of creating a written form of the Mongolian language. As a result, Tibetan Buddhism reached its acme , and it spread throughout Mongolia.

The Ming Dynasty (1368-1644) saw the emergence of another famous personage in Tibetan Buddhism, Tsong Khapa, a native of Qinghai who began studying Buddhism in Lhasa after he was ordained as a monk. He wrote prodigiously, was dedicated to promoting Tibetan Buddhism, acquired quite a following and eventually emerged as the guru of Lamaism in its later stage of development. He revamped the religious system of Tibet to cope with rampant corruption and to safeguard the integrity of Buddhism. He eventually convened a grand assembly and established the Gelugpa School, or Yellow Hat School because all the members wear yellow hats. The Gelugpa is now still the dominant School of Tibetan Buddhism because it has the largest number of followers and runs most of the lamaseries in Tibet.

In the course of five centuries of development since it first spread into Tibet in the 8th century, Tibetan Buddhism has branched out into more than ten schools, including Kadampa, Kagyupa, Sakyapa, Jonangpa, Shichepa, Kotrapa, Shangpa Kagyupa, Shalupa, Nyingmapa, and Gelugpa.

The *Tripitaka* of Tibetan Buddhism consists of two parts. The first part is *Kanjur*, or *The Section of the Buddha*, which includes the holy words of the Buddha and the commandments and secret incantations he formulated. The second part is *Tanjur*, or *The Section of Ancestors*, which is a collection of eulogies to historical Buddhist figures and Tibetan kings, as well as enunciations of sutras and incantations. Totaling more than 4,000 volumes, the Tibetan *Tripitaka* is an essential part of the world's cultural heritage.

Figuring prominently among the religious leaders of Tibetan Buddhism have been the Panchen Lama and the Dalai Lama, both regarded as reincarnations of Tsong Khapa, the reformist leader of Tibetan Buddhism. The current Panchen, who lives in Lhasa, is the 11th reincarnate; and the current Dalai, who went into exile in India during his 1959 rebellion in Tibet, is the 14th.

The first Panchen Lama was Khedrub Je (1385-1438) born in the village of Chewo in Latu Toshong near Tibet, with Xigaze as its chief city. He became a novice and began learning the Buddhist doctrines while a child. At 18, he showed talent for writing. At 23, he became a disciple of Tsong Khapa. In 1431, he became the abbot of the Ganden Monastery. In 1438, he died at the age of 54, ending a life as a famed Buddhist scholar with a wealth of writings to his credit. The late generations of the Panchen Lama were said to be his reincarnates. The current 11th Panchen Lama was born in Tibet in 1990.

The first Dalai Lama was Gedun Truppa (1391-1474), born at the Shabtu Pasture near the Sakya Monastery. The son of a poor family, he grazed cattle for other families while a young child. He began his monkhood at the age of seven. At 25 he attended lectures of Tsong Khapa. In 1426 he became a preacher of Buddhism, and after he turned 40 he began to write. In 1447, he built the Tashilhunpo Monastery. In 1474, he died at the age of 84, going down in Tibetan history as a preeminent Buddhist scholar and author of many religious writings. It is said that the later generations of the Dalai Lama were Gedun Truppa's reincarnates, including the 7th Dalai Lama who oversaw in the 1740s the construction of Norbu Lingka, or "Treasured Garden" in the Tibetan language, as a summer resort for Dalai Lamas of later generations.

Of all architectures of Tibetan Buddhism, the Potala Palace (Potala in Sanskrit means "Sacred Place of Buddhism"), Jokhang Monastery and Norbu Lingka in Lhasa are on the UNESCO World Heritage List, with the Potala Palace being listed in 1994; Jokhang Monastery, in 2000; and Norbu Lingka, in 2001.

The best-known lamaseries in other regions of China include the Kumbum Lamasery of Qinghai, the Labrang Lamasery of Gansu, the Wudang Lamasery of Inner Mongolia and the Yonghe Lamasery of Beijing.

3. Pali Buddhism

巴利语系佛教 (Bālìyǔ Xì Fójiào)

Pali Buddhism is popular in Southeast Asian countries as well as in areas of Yunnan Province of China inhabited by the Dai ethnic group. Pali Buddhism — also known as Southern Buddhism or Southern Theravada — is the only surviving Hinayana branch of Buddhism, the closest to the earliest Indian Buddhism. A local dialect of ancient India, the Pali language did not have a written form. So, Pali was spelled out in other languages in different ways. Thus the Pali scriptures of Buddhism in Sri Lanka, Thailand and Myanmar are written variously in the alphabets of these countries, but they are pronounced largely the same.

Opinions differ as to when it found its way into Yunnan. An analysis of different history books leads to the conclusion that Pali Buddhism first spread from Myanmar to the present-day Xishuangbanna, Dehong, Simao, Lincang, and Baoshan areas of Yunnan some 1,300 years ago, roughly between the 6th and 7th century. Besides the Dai, this school of Buddhism also is popular among the De'ang's, Blang's, and some of the Va's.

Southern Buddhism in Yunnan fell into two stages of development. The first stage, from the 7th to the 12th century, saw the spread of this school of Buddhism from Burma. The first temple of the Southern Buddhism, called "Wabajie", was built in Xishuangbanna in 615. Some simple prayer rooms also emerged at the time. During this period there was no written form for the Dai language; Buddhist sutras were passed from mouth to mouth then and memorized by rote. The population of adherents was small. They stayed together indoors during the rainy season, and went preaching in other seasons.

Large-scale war broke out between the Pagan court of Burma and Thailand in the 12th century. The war forced the inhabitants of Xishuangbanna and neighboring areas to flee home, leaving their farmlands in waste. Along with the way, Buddhism went into a decline. The 12th century marked the end of the first stage of development of Southern Buddhism in Yunnan.

Buddhism staged a comeback in Xishuangbanna after the 12th century. But the source of the comeback was not Burma, but Chiengmai of present-day Thailand. The preachers brought Lannathai editions of scriptures, and began construction of temples, thereby enabling Buddhism to mingle with the local culture. A ritual system was formulated as well. Local scholars translated and annotated large numbers of Pali scriptures into the Lannathai language, which gained popularity among people who spoke the Dai, Lolo, and Lao dialects.

Southern Theravada consists of four major schools: Run, the most influential school in Yunnan Province; Baizhuang or "monastic school" in the Dai language; Duolie, a Burmese word meaning "stop it' referring to a legend surrounding its establishment, and Zuodi, the Chinese transliteration of a Burmese word that means sincerity.

The monasteries of Theravada Buddhism in Yunnan are

administered at three levels. At the top level is the general temple of an administrative area, such as the general monastery of Xishuangbanna. At the middle level are the central monasteries of "banna's" and "meng's" (administrative divisions), and at the bottom level are village temples. For a long time these temples served as both religious sanctuaries and cultural centers where monks taught local people how to read and write. With the establishment of schools, temples changed back to serve as religious sanctuaries and the living quarters for monks, but they remain as centers for traditional culture of the ethnic communities, and as such retain their popularity among the local people. During Buddhist and folk festivals, followers make it a point to assemble in local temples to worship and celebrate. Different from their counterparts elsewhere in China, temples in Yunnan keep only the statues of Sakyamuni.

People living in those areas in Yunnan where Theravada Buddhism is popular follow more or less the same customs as in Myanmar, Thailand and the Laos. For example, boys are obliged to spend some time in a monastery before returning to secular life. The minimum stay is three months, but a boy may choose to stay in a monastery for a lifetime, which means he has to forsake marriage and dedicate himself to the Buddha for the rest of his life. Few people today make this choice. As elsewhere, monks in Yunnan belong to two categories: *sramaneras* (novices) and *bhiksu* (mendicants). In modern times, a tiny number of *sramanerikas* (female novices) have joined the local religious ranks. There are as many as ten monastic or honorary titles for eminent *bhiksus* and abbots.

The Theravada's canonical classics are known as *Pali Tripitaka* and consist of scriptures, commandments, and treatises. Although the *Pali Tripitaka* has the same title as does the canonical classics of Han Buddhism, the content is vastly different. The *Pali Tripitaka* furnishes valuable material for a study of primitive forms of Buddhism and Sectarian Buddhism and for comparative study of Han and Tibetan Buddhism. Since ancient times quite a few scholars of the Dai-inhabited areas have been transliterating, translating and annotating books in the *Pali Tripitaka* into their native language, leaving behind a major cultural heritage that, if sorted out, could be of major importance for academic research and international cultural exchange.

The Demenglong Fota Pagoda in Xishuangbanna and the monastery at Ruili, both in Yunnan Province, are fine examples of Pali Buddhist temples.

Chapter 3

The Major Schools of Han Buddhism

Introduction

All of the eight major schools of Buddhism reached their height in the Tang Dynasty, then went into decline to merge with each other and more or less disappear as individual schools in China except for the Chan and Pure Land, schools that remain strong in China today. However, the history and beliefs of each school remain important in Buddhist studies, and several of the schools are active today thanks to followers in other countries and regions, particularly Korea and Japan. In the Sui-Tang era many Japanese monks studied in China, and as they returned home the Yogacara, Huayan, Chan, Pure Land, Tiantai, Esoteric Schools were established one after another in Japan. The one exception was the Vinaya School, which was founded in Japan by the Chinese monk Ganjin (See Appendices II: Who's Who in Han Buddhist History). Monks from Korea — which then consisted of the three separate countries of Koguryo, Shinla and Baekje — also arrived in China in the Tang to study and to return to establish versions of each of the Han Buddhist schools. The following descriptions of the major schools of Han Buddhism include for each an introduction of at least one temple in China recognized as its "ancestral hall" or place of origin. Thanks to the spread of Buddhism to China's immediate neighbors and beyond, these temples today welcome pilgrims from all over the world.

1. Tiantai School 天台宗 (Tiānt ái Zōng)

In Brief: The earliest school to emerge in Han Buddhism, Tiantai

Zhiyi, the founder of the Tiantai School
of Han Buddhism

was founded by the prestigious monk, Zhiyi (538-597), during the interregnum between the Chen (557-589) and Sui (581-618) dynasties. The name of the Tiantai School of Buddhism in China honors Zhiyi, posthumously honored as Grand Master of Tiantai for the long years he spent practicing austerities on Mount Tiantai in present-day Tiantai County, Zhejiang. Zhiyi — who is said to have had double pupils in each of his eyes — synthesized various theories and practices that helped guide Han Buddhism into its own form, especially through his book *Insights into the Lotus Sutra*. The guiding philosophy for the Tiantai School is "The Great Chiliocosm or Universe exists in one mind." The ancestral hall is Guoqing Temple, about 100 miles south of the city of Ningbo in Zhejiang Province. Another early Tiantai temple is Yuquan Temple in Dangyang, a town about 25 miles east of the city of Yichang in Hubei Province. Today in China, many people study Tiantai, but few claim to be members. However, Guoqing Temple includes an ancestral memorial hall dedicated by the South Korean Tiantai School, and the temple is also popular with Japanese visitors for its ties to Buddhism in Japan.

Background: The Tiantai School derives its major doctrine from the *Lotus Sutra (Saddharmapundarika sutra),* the sutra or teachings of Buddha considered among his most accessible teachings. Tiantai became extremely popular during its early days, but by the mid-Tang it was in decline as other schools emerged. During the persecution of Buddhism during the reign of Tang Emperor Wuzong (841-846), most Tiantai writings were damaged or lost. Thanks to the efforts of some followers during the period that encompassed the Five Dynasties (907-960) and the Song Dynasty (960-1279), some of the lost documents were retrieved from Korea and Japan, and the Tiantai School showed some signs of revival. Towards the end of the Ming Dynasty (1368-1644), a monk by the name of Zhixu (also known as Ouyi) delved into the study of the Tiantai School. However, he was not a follower, and his studies covered the philosophies of the other Buddhist schools. During the interregnum between the Qing (1644-1911) and the Republic (1912-1949), the monk Dixian (1858-1932) made a name for himself as a self-styled advocate of the Tiantai School.

Founder: Zhiyi, a native of Huarong (present-day Jianli), Hubei Province, was 18 when he became a novice under the tutelage of Monk Faxu of the Guoyuan Temple in Xiangzhou (present-day Changsha), Hunan Province, and began learning the commandments from another monk by the name of Huikuang. Two years later he was initiated into the *Complete Commandments* (*Upasampana*). With a penchant for meditating on the dharma door (*dharmaparyaya*), he arrived at Dasu Mountain in Guangzhou (present-day Guangshan County, Henan Province) in 560, where he soon won the favor of his master, Monk Huisi. In 567, Zhiyi settled down in the Waguan Temple [no longer extant] of Jinling (present-day Nanjing, Jiangsu Province), where he preached the way of meditation (*dhgaya*) and began writing. In 575, he arrived on Tiantai Mountain in Zhejiang Province for his own meditation sessions. In 585, the last emperor of the Chen Dynasty, Chen Shubao, honored Zhiyi by sending for him to lecture in the Hall of Supreme Being in Jinling. After the downfall of the Chen Dynasty, Zhiyi arrived at Mount Lushan in present-day Jiangxi Province. In 591, he was invited to Yangzhou to initiate into the *Bodhisattva Sila* (*The Precepts of Bodhisattva*) Yang Guang, the son of Emperor Wen of the Sui, who had just been crowned the King of Jin, with Yangzhou as his fiefdom. A year later he returned from Yangzhou to his native town of Jingzhou, where he built the Yuquan Temple on Yuquan Mountain in Dangyang. After the temple was completed, he lived there for two years as a preacher. In 595, he visited Yangzhou once again at the invitation of Yang Guang, and returned to Mount Tiantai in the 9th lunar month of that year. Zhiyi died in 597.

Beliefs: The philosophy of the Tiantai School originated in the teachings of Huiwen, a Buddhist monk of the Northern Qi (550-577). From his research of the *Mahaprajnaparamita-sastra* and the *Madhyamika-sastra,* Huiwen derived the theory that the three kinds of wisdom — earthly, spiritual and the supreme wisdom of the Bodhisattvas and Buddhas — can be achieved through one's own mind. Further, three ways can be followed to achieve enlightenment: The study of all as void, the study of all as temporary — or a middle approach to both. Huiwen's philosophy was inherited by his disciple Huisi, and when Zhiyi learned it from Huisi, he developed the theory that "the Great Chiliocosm or Universe exists in one mind," which became the guiding principle of the Tiantai School. Following the theory of the *Lotus Sutra*, the

Tiantai School divided the life of Sakyamuni into five periods, with different sutras associated with different periods. (The *Garland Sutra* [*Buddhavatamsaka-mahavaipulya-sutra*] came first; the Lotus and Nirvana Sutras were preached in the Buddha's last days.) Tiantai further divides the teaching itself into eight different kinds. Historical records indicate that Zhiyi had the indispensable assistance of a disciple, Guanding (561-632), who took notes on all his lectures and remarks and compiled them into books to serve as the canons for the school. The most important of these is *Insights into the Lotus Sutra.*

Ancestral Hall: Guoqing Temple is sequestered in the rural and scenic beauty of Mount Tiantai in Zhejiang Province. After Zhiyi's death in 597, his follower, Yang Guang, the Prince of Jin of the Sui Dynasty, carried forward Zhiyi's wish to have the Guoqing Temple built on Mount Tiantai. In the Tang Dynasty, the temple was one of the four major Buddhist temples in China. The buildings as they stand in the temple today were constructed in the Qing Dynasty, including 14 halls and pavilions and chambers and 600 rooms. Along the temple's axial line are the main halls — the Maitreya Hall, the Yuhua Hall, and the Mahavira Hall. The Maitreya Hall is flanked east and west by the Bell and Drum towers. In the Mahavira Hall, a 13-ton bronze statue of Sakyamuni sits in the company of 18 arhats carved out of *nanmu* hardwood. Along the eastern line are the canteen, the abbot's residence, the Yingta (Greeting the Pagoda) Chamber, the Xiuzhu Studio, the Meditation Chamber, and the Jingguan Hall. Along the west line are an array of ancillary rooms, including the Anyang Chamber, the Guanyin Hall, the Artifact Display Room, and the Miaofa Chamber that has the Tripitaka library on the second floor and the meditation hall downstairs. A plum tree in the compound, reportedly planted during the Sui Dynasty by Guanding, Zhiyi's disciple who compiled his books, is more than 1,400 years old. Standing in front of the temple is a nine-tiered hexagonal stupa about 240 feet or 59.3 meters in height. Seng Yixing, a Tang-dynasty astronomer, once paid a visit to the Guoqing Temple to learn arithmetic from a hermit who had become a monk there. Legend has it that the hermit, who had an inkling of the impending visit, told his disciple that Seng would arrive by the time the stream in front of the temple began to flow west. A stele at the site is inscribed with the line, "The arrival of Yixing caused this stream to flow westward."

2. Sanlun School 三论宗 (Sānlùn Zōng)

In Brief: The Sanlun School of Buddhism, also known as the school of "Three Classics" or "Dhamma Pakati," had its heyday when it was first created by the monk Jizang (549-623) in the Tang Dynasty. Its decline began after the mid-Tang following the emergence of the Huayan (Avatamsaka), Ci'en and other schools. The guiding philosophy of the Sanlun School is "All things are void." The ancestral hall is the Qixia Temple in the Qixia Mountain in the suburbs of Nanjing, Jiangsu Province, which was also known for its grottoes and cliff sculpture. Caotang Temple in Huxian County 36 miles southwest of Xi'an is also a primary Sanlun temple, and Jiaxiang Temple in the city of Shaoxing in Zhejiang Province is also one of the earliest temples of the Sanlun School. A lack of successors to Jizang contributed to the decline of the Sanlun School — something that might be attributed to its main theory of "an unattainable void" being so absolute that people either found it unacceptable or were simply frightened of it. As a matter of fact, over the years many have studied the Sanlun School philosophy, but few have regarded themselves as followers. The situation remains to this day.

Background: The Sanlun School is based on the three classics or three "*sastras*" — the *Mulamadhyamaka-karika* and the *Dvadasamukha-sastra*, which were works of a major scholar of Mahayana Buddhism of India, Nagarjuna (c. 3rd century. See also Chapter 3), and the *Sata-sastra*, the work of Nagarjuna's disciple, Aryadeva (3rd century) — as translated into Chinese by Kumarajiva (344-413), the celebrated monk from Kuqa. After Kumarajiva translated the "three classics," most of his disciples dedicated themselves to disseminating the doctrines contained in them. However, only one of the disciples, Sengzhao, was able to inherit Kumarajiva's ideas and safeguard the purity of the theories of the three books. The books first circulated in the north, then found their way south of the Yangtze River to a mountain then known as Mount Sheshan (present-day Qixia Mountain) in the suburbs of Nanjing through a monk from north China, Senglan, who became abbot of Qixia Temple. In 512 during the Liang Dynasty, the devout Buddhist Emperor Wu dispatched ten monks to the temple to learn the "three classics" from Senglang. The top student among these ten monks, Sengquan, later became the master of a monk named Falang, who eventually rose to fame and acquired a large following of his own. But none of Falang's followers could compare with Jizang (549-623), who founded the Sanlun School by drawing on the quintessence of the "three classics." Jizang's new interpretations of the three ancient books were later dubbed "New Three Classics."

Founder: Jizang was born in 549 in Jinling (present-day Nanjing), and his name was given him by Paramartha (499-569), the great Indian Buddhist monk and scholar who was in Jinling then translating Buddhist scriptures. Jizang was a descendent of a man who fled his native land of Pathia (present-day Iran) because of a family feud, and first arrived at Nanhai (in present-day Guangxi) before settling in Jinling. When Jizang was a child, his father often brought him to lectures given by Falang (507-581) at the Xinghuang Monastery. At seven, Jizang was tonsured as a novice under the tutelage of Falang. In Jizang's youth, the country was being torn apart by war between the falling Chen Dynasty and the rising Sui Dynasty. Buddhist temples were abandoned and monks became homeless. During the turmoil, Jizang furthered his studies of Buddhist literature by collecting works from the ruins of the monasteries. By 19, he showed unusual talent in reciting Falang's lectures, showing that he had progressed in his study of the "three classics." After the Sui restored peace to the Baiyue region (present-day Zhejiang and Fujian provinces), Jizang arrived at Huiji (present-day Shaoxing, Zhejiang Province), and settled in the Jiaxiang Temple, where he was respectfully addressed as "Master Jiaxiang," as he lectured in Buddhist doctrines that were often attended by more than a thousand. In 606 during the Sui Dynasty, Emperor Yang summoned Jizang to Yangzhou and set him up at the Huiri Temple. Later, Jizang went to Chang'an (present-day Xi'an), where he was warmly received by the royal family, and was settled into the Riyan Temple. His lecturers in Chang'an attracted people from all over the country. In 618, when Li Yuan entered Chang'an as the founding emperor of the Tang

Dynasty, Jizang was one of the ten eminent monks the emperor invited to conduct Buddhist affairs for him. Incomplete data show that Jizang wrote 91 volumes on 21 subjects, most of which were about the doctrines of the Sanlun School. Jizang died in 569.

Beliefs: The Sanlun School divides the teachings of Sakyamuni into two collections or three wheels of dharma. The two collections refer to the Sravaka Canon that belongs to the Hinayana doctrine and to the Bodhisattva Canon that belongs to the Mahayana doctrine. The three wheels represent a chronology of the Buddha's teachings: The fundamental wheel of dharma is the first sermon the Buddha delivered; the incidental wheel of dharma means all other teachings of the Buddha over 45 years; and the from-the-incidental-to-the-fundamental wheel of darma is the Buddha's final sermon before entering Nirvana. The Sanlun School's theories boil down to the belief that the multitude of things in the universe, both material and spiritual, came into being because of *hetupratyaya*, that is, internal and external causations. Only when all the necessary conditions become available can a thing come into existence. Otherwise nothing could happen. For the same reason, all things owe their existence to the availability of various conditions, and their own identities are empty and unattainable.

Ancestral Hall: During the Tang Dynasty, the Qixia Temple was one of the four major Buddhist temples of the time. Originally, the temple was built some time in the Jianyuan reign (479-482) of the Southern Qi of the Southern and Northern Dynasties as the hermitage of Ming Sengshao who later converted the hermitage into a temple. During the Tang Dynasty, the Qixia Temple, with 49 halls, chambers and pavilions, was one of the four major Buddhist temples of the time. In 1855 during the Qing Dynasty, the temple was razed during war and turmoil. The buildings of the temple today — including the gatehall, the Hall of Heavenly Kings, the Vairocana Hall, the Tripitaka Pavilion, and the Shicui Pavilion — were mostly reconstructed in 1908 in the Qing Dynasty. More additions were made during the Republican years. When one enters the gatehall and passes the Maitreya Hall, the visitor comes into a spacious enclosed courtyard with four sides lined with other halls and anterooms. The Vairocana Hall perches high above the courtyard on the mountain. The artifacts in the collection of Qixia Temple include stone sculptures of the Southern Dynasties and stone inscriptions of the Five Dynasties. The stupa standing about 45 feet or 15 meters tall beside the Qixia Temple was built in 601 in the Sui Dynasty, a four-layered octagonal structure of white stone engraved with exquisite patterns. Jizang, the founder of Sanlun Buddhism, actually never visited Qixia Temple. But the temple is considered the birthplace of the Sanlun School because of its history of promoting Jizang's theory on the "three classics" and because Jizang's master, Falang, is a major figure in the religious school of Qixia Temple. Following the work of Senglang and Falang, the Qixia Temple emerged as the central bodhimandala of the Sanlun School for the region south of the Yangtze River.

3. Huayan School 华严宗 (Huáyán Zōng)

In Brief: The Huayan School of Buddhism, also known as Xianshou or Avatamsaka, is based on interpretations of the *Garland Sutra (Buddhavatamsaka-mahavaipulya-sutra)* by the monks Du Shun (557-640), his disciple, Zhiyan (602-668) and Zhiyan's disciple, Fazang (643-712). Fazang is considered the founder of the Huayan School for his summarizing the earlier *Garland Sutra* interpretations. Established during the Tang Dynasty, the school spread extensively but was cut short by Emperor Wuzong's persecution of Buddhism toward the end of the Tang Dynasty. All the literature of this school was lost at that time, though some of it later was retrieved from Korea and Japan during the Song Dynasty. The Huayan School's guiding philosophy is "One is all, and all is one, and the relationship between all things is one of harmony and mutual incorporation, with no distinction made between them." A monk from Korea, Uisang, studied the *Garland Sutra* in the Zhixiang Temple as a classmate of Fazang. After Uisang returned to his country, he became the patriarch of the Huayan School of the East Sea. The ancestral hall is Huayan Temple in Chang'an County, Shaanxi Province, near the city of Xi'an. In modern times, the monks Yuexia (1858-1917) and Yingci (1873-1965) promoted the Huayan School. In 1914, Yuexia established Huayan University in Shanghai and Hangzhou, and made

Fazang, the founder of the Huayan School
of Han Buddhism

contributions to the Huayan School by training a contingent of successors.

Background: Although Fazang is considered the founder of the Huayan School, the ideas behind it belong to the monk Du Shun, an expert of *dhyana* and *samadhi*. Legend has it that he had certain divine skills. To show his respect for Du Shun, Emperor Taizong bestowed on him the title "Heart of the Emperor." Du Shun classified the teachings of Sakyamuni into five divisions, and the five divisions of teachings according to the Huayan School are: The Hinayana Teachings for Savakas, which interprets Nirvana as annihilation; the Primary Teachings of the initial stage of Mahayana, with two sections — the realistic and the idealistic; the Final Teachings of Mahayana in its last stage, teaching the universal Buddhahood; the Teachings for Immediate Comprehensive, applied in Mahayana as the key to immediate enlightenment by right concentration of thought, or faith; and the Complete Teachings of the Huayan sect, combining all the rest into one all-embracing vehicle. Du Shun also formulated five forms of meditation. After its decline and the disappearance of its literature at the end of the Tang Dynasty, the school still found some people devoted to the study and rejuvenation of Huayan Buddhism during the Yuan, Ming and Qing dynasties.

Founder: Fazang became a disciple of Zhiyan, the second patriarch of the Huayan School, when he was 17 and won his master's favor by excelling in his study of the *Garland Sutra*. In 670, Fazang passed an imperial examination and won the opportunity to be sworn into his monkhood in the imperial court. Empress Wu Zetian personally selected ten famous monks to preside over his ordination ceremony. For a while, Fazang was part of the celebrated monk Xuanzang's team of Buddhist translators, but he quit over some disagreements on translations. Together with Yijing, who had just returned from his studies in India, he joined Siksananda (652-710) in translating the 80-volume *Garland Sutra*. After the work was finished, he again participated in a translation workshop organized by Yijing (See Chapter 2). Fazang personally initiated two Tang emperors, Zhongzong (in reign 705-709) and Ruizong (in reign 710-712), into the Bodhisattva Sila (Bodhisattva Commandments). For this he was honored as "Imperial Tutor." With wide knowledge and high moral accomplishment, Fazang made great contributions to the development of Buddhism, including a wealth of works, most of which were findings on his research of the *Garland Sutra.*

Beliefs: The doctrines of the Huayan School cover all the Five Divisions of Buddhism and the Ten Schools of Buddhist thought, the Six Characteristics (whole and parts, unity and diversity, entirety and its fractions) and the Ten Metaphysical Gates of Thought: 1) All phenomena exist simultaneously and correlate with each other; 2) The relationship between them is like the endless Indra Net; 3) The visible phenomena exist within one unit; 4) Even the smallest particles retain their own nature while mutually penetrating. 5) Dharmas in ten epochs are manifest without separation; 6) Dharmas in all traditions have virtues whether pure or impure; 7) Each thing and all other things intermingle, but do not lose their own character; 8) Various dharmas exhibit phenomenal identity, free from resistance; 9) All dharmas exist as the reflection of the Tathagata's mind; 10) Profound theory can be illustrated and perceived with things. The Huayan School holds that the universe is all-inclusive. All the things in it, be it *samskrta* (active being) or *asamskrta* (non-active being), have their origin in *pratityasamutpada* (conditional causations), interact with one another in harmony, and form what looks like a multileveled and unending network. From the perspective of the nature of the various doctrines, one is all, and all is one, and the relationship between all things is one of harmony and mutual incorporation, with no distinction made between them. Such a relationship is not only one of interdependence between the phenomenal and the noumenal, but also interdependence among the phenomenal. That is why the Huayan School is called a school of perfect harmony without impediment.

Ancestral Hall: The Huayan Temple — as its name suggests — is considered the cradle of the Huayan School of Chinese Buddhism. Built in 803 during the Tang Dynasty, the temple at one time commanded a vantage point on a plateau in Chang'an County, Shaanxi Province, about 9 miles or 15 km from Xi'an. During the Qianlong reign (1736-1795) in the Qing Dynasty, the foundation of the temple collapsed, destroying all the halls and chambers and pavilions. Only two pagodas survived. One is dedicated to Du Shun, the father of the Huayan School. Popularly known as Huayan Pagoda, it is a square structure in seven stories, with two Chinese characters that mean "Patriarch of the Huayan School" inscribed on the top layer, and six Chinese characters meaning "Dust-free Precious Pagoda of Pure Light" on the third layer. The other is a five-story hexagonal structure, dedicated to Chengguan, the 4th-generation patriarch of the Huayan School. There are also some stone inscriptions that offer information on the monks and deeds of this school.

4. Ci'en School 慈恩宗 (Cí'ēn Zōng)

In Brief: The Ci'en School, or Dharma Laksana or Vijnanavada School, was founded by Xuanzang (600-664), the celebrated Tang Dynasty monk and translator (See 3. The Scripture Translators, Chapter 1), and his disciple Kuiji (632-682). The school holds that all things in universe are converted into reality through the perception of the mind, and its analyses of conception are so meticulous that they are akin to modern psychology. The canon of the Ci'en School, the *Vijnaptimatratasiddhi-sastra* by Xuanzang, is a compulsory course for students today at the Chinese Buddhist Seminary. The ancestral hall is Ci'en Temple in Yanta Village, southern suburbs of Xi'an, where Xuanzang lived and translated Buddhist classics. Another early example of a Ci'en School temple is Xingjiao Temple about 24 miles south of Xi'an that has a pagoda built to hold the remains of Xuanzang.

Background: At the heart of the Ci'en School is the philosophy of idealism that had its origin in the teachings of Maitreya, Asanga and Vasubandhu, who lived during the 4th and 5th centuries in India. Vasubandhu was the author of *Vijnaptimatrasiddhi-trimsaikakarika-sastra (Idealism in Thirty Lines),* which was later studied and enunciated by ten masters. Xuanzang studied Vijnanavada under the great Indian scholar Silabhdra while in India. After Xuanzang's return to China, his study focused on the theories of Dharmapala (c. mid-6th century) on Vasubandhu's work. Incorporating the theories of the other nine masters, he compiled the *Vijnaptimatratasiddhi-sastra*, which became the canon of the Ci'en School. That the Ci'en School has been a subject of academic study since its founding during the Tang Dynasty perhaps

Xuanzang, the founder of the Ci'en School
of Han Buddhism

has something to do with the prestige of Xuanzang. However, this did not prevent it from suffering the destructive blow of Emperor Wuzong's crackdown on Buddhism. Its literature fell into oblivion, and some of it was not retrieved from Japan until the modern times. During the interregnum between the Qing Dynasty and the Republic, there was an upsurge in the study of the *Vignanamatrasiddhi-sastra.*

Founders: Xuanzang (See also 1. Han Buddhism, Chapter 2) in his childhood lived in a monastery with his older brother, Changjie, who was a monk. At 13 Xuanzang also became a monk. In 622 during the Tang Dynasty, he was ordained and began traveling to call on established Buddhist masters. Puzzled by the contradictions and discrepancies in the Buddhist instructions available in this country, Xuanzang decided to go study in India and in 629 began his pilgrimage west. In 633, he arrived at central India's Nalanda Monastery, the Buddhist and cultural center then, and started studying the philosophy of Yogacara under Silabhdra (c. 6th-7th century), a famous Buddhist scholar who happened to be the abbot of the monastery. During his stay in India, Xuanzang was able to travel widely. For his superb accomplishments in his studies, Indian Buddhist scholars honored him as Mahayanadeva, or the Deity of Mahayana. In 645, he returned to China with a full load of scriptures and treatises in Sanskrit. With the support of the Tang imperial court, he put together a translation workshop, and personally translated 75 scriptures in 1,335 volumes. One of his translations is the *Vijnanamatrasiddhi-sastra* (*Treatise on the Establishment of the Doctrine on Consciousness*) by Vasubandhu, which Xuanzang had studied under Silabhdra in India and which became the foundation of the Ci'en School.

However, it was through the efforts of his disciple Kuiji that the Ci'en School finally stood on its own. Kuiji, son of a noble Chang'an family, began reading Confucian classics and writing when a child. His talent was not lost on Xuanzang, who offered to accept him as a disciple in 648. It was said Kuiji's parents were happy about the offer but their son thought otherwise. Kuiji raised three conditions for accepting the offer: First, he would never abstain from worldly desires and feelings; second, he should be allowed to eat meat; and third, he should be allowed to eat in the afternoon. All these three conditions violated Buddhist taboos.

Xuanzang consented, expecting to be able to educate the boy after he became a monk. Kuiji did become a famed scholar and Xuanzang's most trusted student. In Chinese Buddhist history, he was the "Master Interpreter of a Hundred Scriptures." His efforts enabled the Ci'en School to emerge as a major Buddhist sect in China.

Beliefs: The school holds that the "three realms originate from the mind and the cornucopia of laws are geared to realism." That is to say, all things in universe are converted into reality through the mind's perception. There are eight major perceptions, of which *alaya-vijnana* (storage consciousness), whose store of seeds spawn all the things in universe, is the most important. The Ci'en School's doctrine boils down to the five dharmas or laws (*pancadharma*) that govern phenomena; the three aspects of the nature of things (*trisvabhavata*): the illusory (*parikalpita*), the dependent (*paratantra*) and the perfected (*parinispanna*); eight kinds of consciousness (*parijnana*) that include the five senses as well as intellect or the mental sense (*mano-vijnana*), the discriminating and constructive sense (*klista-mano-vijnana*) as well as the source of all "seeds" of consciousness (*alaya-vijnana*); and two categories of *anatman* (no-ego): 1) There is no permanent human ego, or soul; and 2) There is no permanent individuality or independence in things. In this school the Buddha's teachings fall into three periods of time: Bhava Canon (the teaching of reality of ego and things), Sunya Canon (the teaching of unreality of ego and things), and Madhyama Canon (the teaching of the mean, that mind or spirit is real, while things are unreal).

Ancestral Hall: Ci'en Temple, the cradle of the Ci'en (Vinnanavada) School. In the Tang Dynasty, Xuanzang was the abbot and translated Buddhist scriptures in this temple, which was the largest of its kind in Chang'an at the time with a dozen or so courtyards. The Wild Goose Pagoda — built in Ci'en Temple to store the Sanskrit versions of Buddhist scriptures brought back to China from India by Xuanzang — is among the few Tang structures to have survived in present-day Xi'an. A symbol of Xi'an itself, the pagoda underwent major repairs during the Ming Dynasty. After Xuanzang died, his disciple Kuiji became the abbot. More than 1,000 years later today, the size of the temple has shrunk considerably, with less than one-tenth of its original buildings remaining. [Part of the skull of Xuanzang was enshrined prior to 1956 in a memorial hall dedicated to him at the Dabei Temple in Tianjin. See 9. Major Han Buddhist Temples, Chapter 4]

5. Chan (Zen) School 禅宗 (Chán Zōng)

In Brief: The Chan School of Buddhism is known to the Western world as Zen, the Japanese pronunciation of Chan from the Chinese character 禅, which is derived from the Sanskrit word, *dhyana*, meaning meditation. The Chan School holds that Buddhahood can be achieved by discovering one's own innate Buddha nature through meditation, without recourse to the written word. Its founder was Huineng (638-713), a highly accomplished monk of the Tang Dynasty, and its first patriarch was the legendary Bodhidharma (c. 520), who is recognized as bringing the Chan School philosophy from India as the 28th-generation disciple of Kasyapa, one of Sakyamuni's ten disciples. Huineng was the 6th Chan patriarch, having inherited his ideas from a line of monks in China starting with Bodhidharma and followed by Huike (487-593); Sengcan (?-606); Daoxin (580-651); and Hongren (602-675). Before Huineng, Chan was more of a discipline of learning than a school, with roots obscured in mythology. [The above line of heritage was composed by Qisong (1007-1072), a preeminent monk of the Song Dynasty]. Through his interpretations of Chan thinking and his work disseminating Chan doctrines in the south of China with a large team of disciples, Huineng established the Chan School that spread widely in China and to other countries and regions, especially Korea, Japan, and in modern times, the West. Both the martial arts and the tea ceremony — arts that today have a worldwide following — acknowledge roots in Chan Buddhist practice and philosophy, as well as in Daoism. The ancestral hall of the Chan School is Nanhua Temple in Qujiang County, Guangdong Province. Other notable Chan temples include Yufo Temple on Anyuan Street in Shanghai, known for its two valuable jade Buddha statues; Tanzhe Temple in Beijing; and Zhenjue Temple, one of the earliest temples of the Chan School, north of the city of Jiujiang in Hubei Province. The Longmen Grottoes also includes in its cave

Huineng, the sixth patriarch of the Chan (Zen) School of Han Buddhism complex the Kanjing Temple that is a sanctuary of the Chan School of Chinese Buddhism. A widely read classic today in China is *Analects of the Sixth Chan Patriarch Huineng,* based on a lecture delivered by Huineng as recorded by his disciple, Fahai.

Background: Since the Chan School chose to dispense with the written word, the school suffered no loss of scripture during the persecution of Buddhism under the reign of Emperor Wuzong at the later stage of the Tang Dynasty. During the long period that followed from the Five Dynasties to the Song (907-1279), the Chan School was able to continue to the height of its development through five branches and seven sub-sects, each of which flourished during different periods. Three of the five branches of the Chan School — Caodong (Soto-shu School in Japan), Yunmen and Fayan — trace back to Huineng's disciple Xingsi, who returned after initiation to his native Luling to settle in the Qingju Temple in the Qingyuan Mountain. The other two branches came from Huineng's disciple Huarang who settled in Mount Hengshan, the Southern Mountain Sanctuary, and whose disciple, Daoyi (709-788) a native of Shifang, Hanzhou (present-day Shifang, Sichuan Province), inherited his teacher's way to emerge as the patriarch of the Weiyang and Linji branches of the Chan School of Buddhism. The first major monastery in China was built by a disciple of Daoyi , the famed Chan master Huaihai (720-814) of the Tang Dynasty, when Huaihai carried out his master's directions to build a monastery to receive and provide lodgings for monks at the Baizhang Mountain in present-day Jiangxi Province. Huineng during his lifetime had many disciples, the most influential being Xingsi (?-740) a native of Luling in present-day Ji'an, Jiangxi Province; Huairang (677-744), a native of Ankang in present-day Shaanxi Province; and Shenhui (686-760). Shenhui, aside from providing information on Huineng's life (see below) in the *Platform Sutra,* was important in challenging the version of Chan that developed in the north of China under Shenxiu, another disciple of Hongren, who after his master's death exerted great influence on the religious life in north China, especially among the monks in the eastern capital of Luoyang and the western capital of Xi'an. As a disciple of Huineng in the south of China, Shenhui arrived in the north to challenge what was happening in the Chan School there. Shenhui called for a

Buddhist assembly at the Dayun Temple of Huatai (present-day Huaxian County, Henan Province). The assembly concluded that the southern branch, with its belief in instant enlightenment, should be designated the "instantaneous sub-sect of Chan," while the northern branch, with its belief in gradual enlightenment, should be called "progressive sub-sect of Chan." Thus the Chan School was divided into northern and southern branches. However, with the "instantaneous sub-sect" spreading northward, Shenxiu's northern sub-sect went on a decline and gradually disappeared. In all this Shenhui played a major role. (However, Shenhui's southern sub-sect also met its demise by the 6th generation. At the same time, another southern branch of Chan headed by Huairang gradually spread to the north.) Chan monks from China traveled abroad and monks from other countries came to China to study. Some stayed, most notably the Korean Gim Kyokak who arrived in China during the mid-Tang and settled down at Mount Jiuhua in present-day Qingyang County, Anhui Province, where he won the respect of local Buddhists. It is said that three years after his death at age 99 in 803, his remains in a stone sarcophagus in a sitting posture were found in perfect condition, leading local Buddhists to believe Gim Kyokak to be the reincarnate of Ksitigarbha, a bodhisattva belonging to Mahayana Buddhism. Thus Mount Jiuhua became one of the four major mountain sanctuaries of Chinese Buddhism and the mecca for tens of thousands of pilgrims from all over the world. In the Southern Song Dynasty, the Japanese monk Eisai trained in the meditation practice of Chan Buddhism under the Chan monk Huaichan of the Linji branch of Chan. In 1191 Eisai returned to Japan to establish the Rinzai School of Zen Buddhism. Eisai's disciple, Dogen, come to China in 1223 in the Southern Song and returned to Japan in 1227 from studies of the meditation practice of the Caodong branch under the tutelage of Rujing at the Tiantong Temple in Ningbo, Zhejiang Province. Dogen devoted himself to disseminating Zen Buddhism and established the Soto-shu Sect (Japan's version of the Caodong school) at the Eiheiji Temple. After the Song Dynasty, exchanges between Chan monks of China and Zen monks of Japan continued to grow unabated and continues to this day. The tradition of Chan as having nothing to do with written language is challenged by the emergence of quite a few books of quotations of Chan masters after the Song Dynasty. The quotation of Chan masters have themselves left to posterity a literature that has become a major component of the cultural heritage of Chinese Buddhism. In modern times, the celebrated Buddhist scholar Taixu maintained that the "Chan Tripitaka" — a collection of quotations of Chan masters — should be added to the *Tripitaka* of Chinese Buddhism.

Founder: A native of Fanyang (present-day Zhuoxian, Hebei Province), Huineng was the son of an official who was demoted to Xinzhou (present-day Xinxing County, Guangdong) in southern China. Much of what is known about Huineng's life comes from the Platform Sutra written by his disciple, Shenhui. It is said that after Huineng's father died when he was young, Huineng had to sell firewood to provide for his mother. One day, he overheard someone recite *Diamond Sutra*. Impressed by its meaning, Huineng discovered the reciter had learned it from Master Hongren (602-675). He then asked his mother's permission to travel to see the monk Hongren in a place known as Huangmei. When he arrived in Huangmei, Huineng was asked by Hongren where he had come from and the purpose of his visit. Huineng answered that he came from south of the Five Ridges (in present-day Guangdong and Guangxi) and wanted to become a monk. Hongren replied that men from south of the Five Ridges had no makings for Buddhahood.

"Men may came from south or north, but the capacity to comprehend Buddhism knows no geographical distinction," Huineng replied.

Hongren realized through this reply that he was facing a man who could be taught and amount to something, and he arranged for him as a start to work in a rice-husking workshop.

Eight months later Hongren decided to choose someone who could inherit his mantle from his disciples by asking each of them to compose a poem on their understanding of the Buddhist doctrines. Shenxiu, his top disciple, came up with the following:

The body is the Bodhi tree,
The heart a mirror on a stand.
I clean them from time to time,
To keep them free from dust.

Hearing this read aloud, Huineng composed a response. Not knowing how to read and write, Huineng asked a fellow monk to write down his composition right beside Shenxiu's:

There is no Bodhi tree,
There is no mirror on a stand.
Since the nature of Buddha means being empty and void,
What is there for dust to cling to?

When Hongren read the two pieces, he realized that Huineng had the better understanding of the nature of Buddha than did Shenxiu, who later became a prominent monk in northern China. That night, Hongren invited Huineng to his quarters and passed onto him the most secret part of his instructions, and gave him a monastic costume as a token of his trust. The same night, Huineng returned home in the south where he followed Hongren's instructions by consigning himself to an anonymous life among a team of hunters for 15 years. While the hunters ate meat, he kept to a vegetarian's diet by picking out the vegetables mixed in meat dishes. During a visit to the Faxing Monastery (present-day Guangxiao Monastery of Guangzhou) as a lay Buddhist, he attended Monk Yinzong's lecture on the *Mahaparinirvana-sutra.* In the audience, he witnessed two monks arguing about whether a streamer moved because of the wind or of itself. As the two of them were all worked up in the argument, Huineng chipped in:

"Why don't you stop arguing? The streamer moves not because of the wind nor of itself — it is because both of your hearts are moving."

Yinzong the lecturer was taken aback when he overheard the remarks.

"I have long heard of the arrival of a master from Huangmei," he said, coming down from his podium. "Are you that distinguished guest?"

Yinzong arranged for Huineng to settle down in the Faxing Monastery and ordained him as a monk. Huineng later in 677 moved to what is present-day Nanhua Monastery in Shaozhou and spent the next three decades there devoted to disseminating Chan Buddhism. In 705 Tang Dynasty Emperor Zhongzong (r. 705-710) sent a messenger to Nanhua to summon Huineng to the capital city of Luoyang. Huineng turned down the invitation, saying he was a long forgotten hermit, in old age and poor health. A sympathetic Zhongzong bestowed on him a kasaya, a quilted outer vestment, and large quantities of daily supplies. Following the death of Huineng in 713 at Nanhua Temple, his remains were mummified and are on view at the temple today.

Beliefs: Legend has it that once Sakyamuni brandished a bouquet of flowers at the audience at the Nirvana Assembly. Most in the audience were bewildered by the gesture, but Kasyapa, one of Sakyamuni's ten disciples, smiled in tacit understanding of the Buddha's intentions. That transmission of the Buddha's holy words by the mind was inherited by followers — including Bodhidharma, who brought this method to China. It is the belief of the Chan School that the mind is pure and clean to start with, but such purity fails to manifest itself because it has been obliterated by worldly worries. Once the mind obtains the straightforward guidance of knowledge of benevolence, it can see its true nature and achieve Buddhahood. Some in the Chan School believe that enlightenment comes through a sudden flash of insight. Others say it comes gradually through a long process of self-discipline, meditation, and instruction.

Ancestral Hall: The awesome scale and architectural grandeur of Nanhua Temple in Guangdong Province surrounded by towering ancient trees, creates an appropriate setting for the foremost establishment of the Chan School of Buddhism. Among the temple's host of valuable artifacts is the physical body of Huineng himself, mummified in a seated pose. Originally built in 504 as the Baolin Temple in the Liang Dynasty, the temple was renamed during the Tang Dynasty, "Zhongxing Temple," and later, "Faquan Temple." It assumed the name it has today of Nanhua in the early Song Dynasty. The original buildings of the temple are no more. The buildings as people see them today were built during the 1930s under the supervision of Monk Xuyun (1840-1959), the Dharma successor of all five Chan schools and a main reformer in Chinese Buddhism in the modern era. Arranged on its axial line are the Hall of the Heavenly Kings, the Mahavira Hall, the Tripitaka Pavilion, the Lingxing Pagoda, the Hall of Six Patriarchs, and the Abbot's Mansion.

6. Vinaya School 律宗 (Lǜ Zōng)

In Brief: The Vinaya (Disciplinary) School is also called the "Vinaya School of the South Mountain" because its founder, the prominent Tang Dynasty monk Daoxuan (596-667), lived in the Zhongnan Mountain to the south of Chang'an. The *vinaya* is the code of conduct or commandments for Buddhists. Daoxuan founded his school on the basis of the *Dharmagupta Vinaya* emphasizing the following of commandments so as to do good and not do evil. Like other religious schools in Chinese history, Vinaya flourished when someone was advocating and disseminating it. At other times, it went into decline. By the Yuan-Ming dynasty interregnum the Vinaya School of the South Mountain sank to an all-time low, and it did not show signs of a revival until the early Qing. In the 20th century Hongyi (1880-1942), born into a rich Tianjin family whose ancestral home was in Zhejiang, devoted himself to Vinaya studies after he became a monk in 1918. Held in high esteem both in China and abroad, Hongyi was the author of *A Record of Forms of Bhiksu Rules in the Four-division Vinaya,* and *Some Important Contents of the Southern Mountain Vinaya Prepared for Reading at Home.* The ancestral hall is Longchang Temple on Baohua Mountain north of Jurong County and about 50 miles east of the city of Nanjing in Jiangsu Province. Other notable Vinaya School temples are Daming Temple about 3 miles northwest of the city of Yangzhou in Jiangsu Province; and Jingye Temple about 20 miles south of the city of Xi'an on Zhongnan Mountain where the mountain itself is a favorite Chinese cultural, recreational and scenic area.

Background: The *Dharmagupta Vinaya* was compiled by Dharmagupta some 100 years after Sakyamuni went into nirvana by his putting together passages from the canons of Theravada that Dharmagupta thought matched his own viewpoints. His compilation comes in four parts: commandments for mendicants, commandments for nuns, the code for peaceful life, and the code for houses and miscellaneous situations. Chinese Buddhists began to turn attention to the commandments in the third century during the Three Kingdoms period of the Kingdom of Wei when the Indian monk, Dharmakala translated *The Heart of Sanghika-vinaya* and started training Chinese monks in the commandments.

Daoxuan, the founder of the Vinaya School
of Han Buddhism

For lay Buddhists there are the Pancasila (Five Commandments) and the Eight Commandments. There are the Sikasapada (Ten Prohibitions) for sramaneras (novices), 250 commandments for bhiksus (mendicants) and 500 commandments for bhiksunis (nuns). During the Southern and Northern Dynasties (420-589), studying the vinaya became popular among Chinese Buddhists. The *Dharmagupta Vinaya* was translated into Chinese by Sramana Buddhayasa from Kubha and Zhufonian, a Chinese monk translator. Famous figures that made names for themselves in the study of the *Dharmagupta Vinaya* prior to Daoxuan were Facong and Huiguang during the reign of Emperor Xiaowen of the Northern Wei (471-499). During the Tang, joining Daoxuan in preaching the *Dharmagupta Vinaya* were Fali (569-635) of the Riguang Temple of Xiangzhou and Huaisu (625-698) of the Dongta Temple of the West Taiyuan Monastery. These three masters had all written works on the creed, though they held different opinions on the embodiment of commandments. By "embodiment of commandments" is meant the function forestall erroneous thoughts and prevent evil a Buddhist acquires in his heart when he is ordained with the commandments. According to Fali, the embodiment of commandments is neither *rupadharma* (physical phenomenon) nor mental dharmas. Daoxuan, under the influence of Xuanzang's Yogacara theory, believed that the embodiment is a mental phenomenon. Huaisu, on his part, held that it is a physical phenomenon. Their depositions on the *Dharmagupta Vinaya* were known as the "Three Major Commentaries," which circulated in society at the same time. Only the Vinaya School of the South Mountain founded by Daoxuan has been able to survive to this day following its revival in the early Qing Dynasty when Jiguang — the abbot of the Longchang Temple on the Baohua Mountain and a disciple of Ruxin who was preaching the *Dharmagupta Vinaya* in the Linggu Temple of Jinling (present-day Nanjing) — converted his monastery into a major place for the preaching of the Vinaya School alone. The facility was later expanded continuously thanks to the efforts of Jiguang's disciples. Longchang Temple soon achieved a nationwide reputation as the uninterrupted venue of two major preaching ceremonies (one held in spring and the other in autumn) for the ordination of commandments every year.

Founder: Daoxuan came from Wuxing in present-day north Zhejiang. He began reading Confucian classics while a child and by nine was able to compose poetry and rhapsodies. At 16 he began his monastic life and at 20 was bestowed the Upasampanna (Complete Commandments). He then came under the tutelage of Zhishou, an erudite in the viyana (monastic rules) who taught him the commandments and the *Dharmagupta Vinaya*. After finishing one round of study of the vinaya, Daoxan decided to turn his studies to Chan Buddhism. His master did not agree but demanded that before starting Chan Buddhism lessons Daoxuan repeat his lesson on *Dharmagupta Vinaya* 20 times. In 624 at age 28, he arrived at the Zhongnan Mountain and settled down in the Baiquan Monastery. Shortly afterwards, he went on an itinerary to collect different theories on Buddhist commandments. On the basis of the *Dharmagupta Vinaya*, he drew on the strengths of different schools of Buddhism to come up with his own understanding of the vinaya thereby, creating the Vinaya School of the Southern Mountain.

Beliefs: Daoxuan preached that one must follow strictly the code of ethics to free oneself from the ocean of misery and prepare oneself for Buddhahood. The Vinaya School of the South Mountain divided the teachings of the Buddha into two categories: 1. The classics designed to educate the average person, such as *Agama Sutras,* and 2. *Pranna Sutras*, classics that provide a code of conduct for the average person.

Ancestral Hall: The Longchang Temple in Jurong County, Jiangsu Province, became the center of the Vinaya School beginning in the late Ming when Jiguang, a master in samathi (intense contemplation) had an altar built there to introduce the commandments. At that time, the temple's reputation rose to an all-time high. Jiguang's disciple, Jianyue (1602-1679), further expanded the temple and enforced strict discipline. Jianyue's *Standard Instructions on Commandments and Rules* spread all over China as a guide for all temples of the Vinaya School, thus turning the Longchang Temple into the *de facto* ancestral hall of the Viyana School. (The Fengde Temple in the Zhongnan Mountain, where the Vinaya School originated, is no more.) Predating the Longchang Temple on Baohua Mountain was the Public Baozhi Temple that dated back to 502 in the Liang Dynasty. During its heyday, the

Longchang Temple housed more than 300 monks. Its main buildings, including the Altar, the Dining Room, the Beamless Hall, the Bronze Hall, the Manjusri Hall (Institute of Wisdom), and the Cigu Chamber, nestle snugly against the contours of Baohua Mountain. The quadrangular courtyard containing the Mahavira Hall and the Mahakaruna (Great Mercy) Hall alone occupies an area of over 216,000 square feet or 72,000 square meters. Few Buddhist monasteries in south China can match the Longchang Temple in size.

7. Jingtu (Pure Land) School
净土宗 (Jìngtǔ Zōng)

In Brief: The Jingtu (Pure Land) School, also known in China as the Lotus School and in Sanskrit as the Sukhavativyuha School, has been thriving for the last more than 1,000 years and remains today the most influential school with the largest following among all the Buddhist schools in China. Its practice is simple: Chanting of the Amita Buddha's name. Shandao (613-681) is considered the founder for his popularizing the already existing Jingtu School. The ancestral hall is Xuanzhong Temple in the Shibi Mountain in Jiaocheng County, Shanxi Province. The Donglin Temple in Mount Lushan, Jiangxi Province, is also considered a cradle of the Pure Land School as it was the long-time home of Huiyan, one of the school's patriarchs. Other notable Pure Land temples include Lingyan Temple about six miles southwest of the city of Suzhou in Jiangsu Province.

Background: The beginning of the Pure Land School in China can be traced to Huiyuan (334-416), a native of Loufan (present-day Daixian County, Shanxi Province), who lived on Mount Lushan during the Eastern Jin Dynasty. Huiyuan was a disciple of the famed monk Dao'an (see Chapter 2). Having recruited a number of prominent followers, Huiyuan established the White Lotus Society that gathered to offer sacrifices to a statue of Amitabha and collectively chanted the Buddha's name with the hope of being reborn after death in the Pure Land. By the Southern and Northern Dynasties, another eminent monk to emerge in the Lotus School was Tanluan (476-542) who began

Shandao, the founder of the Jingtu (Pure Land) School of Han Buddhism his religious life as a Daoist intent on finding the pill of longevity. He once went all the way to the Maoshan Mountain in the south to seek instruction from Tao Hongjing, and returned to the north with ten volumes of Tao Hongjing's book *Classics on Immortality*. [Tao Hongjing (456-536), whose style name was Tongming, was a native of Molin in Danyang (in Jiangsu Province). A Daoist scholar and medical expert, he had been an official of Qi (479-502) in the Southern Dynasties. After the Northern Qi was toppled by the Liang Dynasty (502-557), he became a hermit on Maoshan Mountain, where he repeatedly turned down the offer of Emperor Wu of the Liang, to leave the mountain and serve him. The emperor, however, often consulted him on major issues. Hence Tao's nickname, "Prime Minister in the Mountains."] When Tanluan came across Bodhiruci (5th-6th century) during a visit to Luoyang, he asked the Indian monk if there was any book on longevity. Bodhiruci told him there was no such thing as immortality because every person in this world dies, but there are ways to prolong one's life. The monk give him a copy of *Amitayur-dhyana Sutra* (*Discourse Concerning Meditation on Amitayus*), telling him that this was the Buddhist book on long life, and asking him to practice self-cultivation accordingly. Tanluan, enlightened, burned the *Classic on Longevity* and concentrated on his study and practice of the Pure Land School. The ruler of the Northern Wei (386-534) called Tanluan the "Celestial Bird" for his devotion to the study of the Pure Land School.

Both Huiyuan and Tanluan chanted the name of Amitabha within, silently. It was not until Daochuo of the Sui and Tang time that Buddhists began chanting the name aloud. Daochuo (562-645), a native of Wenshui of Bingzhou Prefecture (present-day Wenshui, Shanxi Province), also began his religious life as a Daoist. During a visit to the Xuanzhong Temple on Shibi Mountain in 609 (5th year, Daye reign, Sui Dynasty), he read a stone tablet inscription on how Tanluan chanted the name of Amitabha and practiced the doctrines of the Pure Land School of Buddhism. He had an immediate conversion and made it a point ever after to chant the name of Amitabha 70,000 times a day. He would count the times of his incantation with beans or with a string of goldenrain nuts, thus becoming the first in China to use a rosary in religious meditation. With a charismatic personality, Daochuo acquired quite a following in and around Wenshui, and chanting the name of Amitabha aloud became a fashion. His disciple, Shandao, inherited the method and turned the name-chanting into a school of Chinese Buddhism, the Jingtu (Pure Land) School.

Founder: Through his studies of the classics, Shandao (613-681), a native of Linzi in present-day Zibo, Shandong Province, came to believe that the most convenient and easily mastered of all Buddhist commandments was the Dharma Door for Reciting the Buddha's Name, the principal belief of the Jingtu School. Following his conversion, he once traveled to Mount Lushan to explore the cultural heritage left by the Eastern Jin monk, Huiyuan. In 641 he settled in the Xuanzhong Temple in Bingzhou (present-day Taiyuan, Shanxi Province) to learn the creeds of the Jingtu School from Daochuo. After Daochuo died, in 645 Shandao went to Chang'an to disseminate the Dharma Door for the reciting of the Buddha's name. Practicing the most stringent type of austerities and meditation, he devoted all his time to chanting the name of the Buddha except when he was out begging for alms. It is said that Shandao copied 100,000 volumes of the *Amitayur-vyuha Sutra*, and drew some 300 pictures relating stories about the Jingtu School. He was also the author of five works on the dharmaparyaya (Dharma Door) to the Pure Land, all of which established him as the father of the Jingtu School in China.

Beliefs: The Jingtu (Pure Land) School's chief tenet is salvation by faith alone. The chant: "Namah Amitabha" is used constantly in liturgy, incantations, etc, as the formula of faith of the Jingtu School, representing the believing heart of all beings and Amitabha's power and will to save; repeated in the hour of death, it opens the entrance to the Pure Land. The school demands only that followers worship and pray to the Buddha by chanting the name of Amitabha, the Buddha of Boundless Light. All those who have faith in the Buddha and keep praying to the Buddha will be reborn after death in the Pure Land of the West Paradise. Worshipers need neither full understanding of the Buddhist scriptures nor the practice of long meditations. According to the *Amitayur-vyuha Sutra*, the Pure Land is the Paradise of the West, a place of sublime beauty where people live happily without knowing the meaning of pain. Access to the Pure Land comes through chanting the name of Amitabha as many times as possible. Chanting Amita the Buddha's name also calls for the union of the three behaviors: One should personally pay homage to Amitabha, always chant his name and always bear him in one's mind. Shandao developed a whole package of methods and set a series of requirements for his followers. According to him, those practicing the Dharma Door for the reciting of the Buddha's name should first set their minds at ease, something that requires sincerity, profundity, and *parinamana* (readiness for the transference of one's merits to somewhere). After one has focused his mind on these three aspects and begins self-cultivation, a believer is bound to arrive in the Pure Land so long as he or she persists in chanting the name of Amitabha. There are not many theories to speak of in this school of Chinese Buddhism, which advocates nothing but self-cultivation by chanting the name of Amitabha. Chanting the name of the Buddha is actually a way of self-cultivation, and self-cultivation is one of the *trisiksa* (three studies), which is a must for all schools of Buddhists despite any other differences. When chanting the name of the Buddha one is required to dispel all worldly thoughts and concentrate on a certain point — the Amita Buddha. To perform well in chanting the Buddha's name is *samadhi* (concentrating on Buddha). The Jingtu School is a simple and feasible practice.

Ancestral Hall: Xuanzhong Temple, nestled at the foot of Shibi Mountain in Jiaocheng County, Shanxi Province, was built in 472 in the Northern Wei Dynasty (386-534) and rebuilt and renamed "Shibi Yongning Temple" during the Zhenguan reign (627-649) of the Tang Dynasty. During the Northern Wei, the monk Tanluan lived in this temple, and during the Tang Dynasty, Monk Daochuo settled here. However, his disciple, Shandao, moved to Chang'an to preach the Pure Land doctrine as he became the *de facto* founder of the Jingtu (Pure Land) School of Chinese Buddhism. Its Hall of Ten Thousand Buddhas, Kusala (Mental Virtue) Hall, and east and west ancillary rooms were destroyed in a major fire during the Guangxu reign (1875-1908) of the Qing, and only the Pavilion of Thousand Buddhas survived. In 1956, the temple was rebuilt and restored to its old size. This is a temple of international influence. Both the Jodo Shinshu (True

Pure Land School) and the Jodo School of Japan also regard it as their ancestral hall and often send pilgrims to pay their respects to it.

8. Esoteric (Tantric) School 密宗 (Mì Zōng)

In Brief: The Esoteric (Tantric) School of Han Buddhism, known in China as Zhenyan (True Word) School, was founded during the Kaiyuan reign (713-741) of the Tang Dynasty by three Indian monks, Subhakarasimha (637-735), Vajrabodhi (669-741), and Amoghavajra (705-774). After the late-Tang suppression of Buddhism, this school gradually disappeared in China but continues to thrive in Japan. (The Esoteric School of Han Buddhism predates and should not be confused with the Tibetan Tantric Buddhism that was brought to Tibet from India in the 7th century. That Buddhism spread from Tibet to other parts of west China where it is still widely practiced. See section on Tibetan Buddhism.) In modern times, the monk Chisong (1894-1972) made two study trips to Japan with the intention to bringing the Esoteric School of Han Buddhism back to China, but was unsuccessful. One of the creators of the Dazu Grottoes was Zhao Zhifeng, a monk of the Esoteric School. The ancestral hall is Great Xingshan Temple in Xi'an, Shaanxi Province, one of the major Buddhist temples in the city.

Background: Chinese versions of the Esoteric mantra and classics had become available as early as the Three Kingdoms period (220-265), when some monks from Indian or the West Territory well-versed in the mantra were already spreading the practice in China. Among them were Fotucheng (232-348) and Bodhiruci (5th-6th century), who were masters of mantra. A legend about Bodhiruci's magic abilities has it that one day, when he went to fetch water from a well without bringing a pail, he found the water level in the well was so low that it was impossible to draw water from it. He tossed a tiny poplar tree twig into the well and recited the mantra for some time. Before long the water began to rise until it reached the brim of the well, allowing him to ladle water with his hands. The Chinese monks looked on and were surprised, and they called him a sage. Bodhiruci hastened to explain that he was no sage at all, and that things like this were not uncommon in India though they were unknown to the Chinese. He declined to pass on the secret to the Chinese for fear that odd things like this would have a pernicious influence on society. At the time Buddhism was still a novelty to the Chinese, the number of esoteric scriptures translated into Chinese were few and far between, and no monks were working to introduce this school of Buddhism. Esoteric beliefs or Tantrism failed to become a school in its own right during Bodhiruci's time. The situation changed during the Tianbao and Kaiyuan reigns (713-755) with the arrival of the three Esoteric masters — Subhakarasimha, Vajrabodhi, Amoghavajra. Thanks to the work of the trio, Esoteric Buddhism emerged as one of the schools of Chinese Buddhism. Quite a few Korean monks studied Esoteric Buddhism in China during the Kaiyuan reign, including Myonglang who in 635 returned home to become the father of the Tong-hae-shin-in School of Buddhism in Korea. The Esoteric School of Han Buddhism, like other Buddhist schools, was suppressed under Emperor Wuzong of the Tang Dynasty. The crackdown was followed by the war and turmoil of the Five Dynasties (907-960), and as a result the once prosperous Esoteric School gradually disappeared from the Chinese landscape.

Founders: Subhakarasimha (637-735), a scion of an Indian royal clan, became a military commander when he was 10, and ascended the throne when he was 13. After he quelled an armed rebellion launched by a younger brother, he abdicated from the throne and went on the road to pursue a religious life. He first studied Buddhism in a temple in a coastal area of south India, then he traveled to Magadha, where he entered the Nalanda Monastery to study Tantrism. In 716 (4th year, Kaiyuan reign) Subhakarasimha arrived in Chang'an, where he was given a courteous reception from Emperor Xuanzong. A year later he began translating Buddhist scriptures. Upon learning that the Huayan Monastery of Chang'an kept some Sanskrit versions of the Buddhist sutras brought back by Chinese monks back from India, he got the blessing of the emperor and went to the monastery with his disciples, and returned with a number of such books that were not translated into Chinese. In 724 (12th year, Kaiyuan reign), he followed the emperor to Luoyang, where he resumed his translation work in the Xianfu Temple. The four sutras he translated there were all Esoteric classics, one of which was the *Mahavairocana-sutra*, the fundamental canon of the Esoteric School.

Vajrabodhi (669-741), a south Indian born of the Brahman caste, was a child prodigy able to recite ten thousand words a day. He began his religious life as a student in the Nalanda Monastery. Later, he traveled to Saharatta, where he boarded a ship and arrived in Pulau Sumatera in present-day Indonesia. His journey eventually brought him to Guangzhou in 719. Emperor Xuanzong got the word about his arrival, and summoned him to Chang'an. A major esoteric master, he acquired many followers and presided over the *abhisekana* ritual (consecration ritual of Buddhism). The books he translated on esoteric ways and rituals laid a solid foundation for the introduction of Tantrism to China.

Amoghavajra (705-774), a northern Indian (another theory says he was from Saharatta) born of the Brahman caste who arrived in China as a young child with his uncle. He became a disciple of the Indian preacher Vajrabodhi at 13, took monkhood at 15, and was awarded the Mendicant Commandments at 20. For his high intelligence and photographic memory, he won the favor of his mentor, Vajrabodhi, who died in 741. A year later, Amoghavajra carried out his mentor's will by leading a 37-member Chinese delegation on a pilgrimage to Saharatta, where his studies covered both the open and Esoteric Schools of Buddhism. At the end of the journey, which also brought him to India, he returned to Chang'an and put together a workshop to translate large numbers of Sanskrit Buddhist scriptures and treatises into Chinese, most of which were Esoteric classics, thereby emerging as one of the four major translators in Chinese Buddhism history.

Beliefs: The Esoteric School in the Han-inhabited regions of China falls into two categories, the *vajradhatu* (diamond element) and the *garbhahatu* (womb treasury). Vajra, or diamond, means solidity, which is property to be utilized; while the womb denotes sustainability and concealment. The deeper meanings of both categories are complicated, requiring meticulous interpretations from esoteric masters. A salient feature of the Esoteric School is to establish an altar at which to practice austerities and recite the Honored One's mantra.

Amoghavajra, one of the founders of the Esoteric School of Han Buddhism

Ancestral Hall: Great Xingshan Temple in Xi'an, Shaanxi Province was built in 582 as a scripture translation workshop. In 720 the celebrated esoteric master Vajrabodhi (669-741) settled in the Great Xingshan Temple where he built an altar to preside over *abhiseka*, a ritual to consecrate novices. Through his work he laid down the foundation for the establishment of the Esoteric School in China. Vajrabodhi's disciple, Amoghavajra (705-774), followed his master's instruction and led a delegation to Sinhala to study the doctrines of Esoteric Buddhism, and returned to China to establish this school in Chinese Buddhism. The Great Xingshan Temple has had its ups and downs in the intervening years. In 1955, the government spent a huge sum of money to renovate the temple with imposing structures arranged in a methodical plan.

Chapter 4

Temples of Han Buddhism

1. Background

The Buddhist temple had its origin in the religious life of Sakyamuni's age in India. In Sakyamuni's lifetime and before, it was the custom in Indian society for *sramanas* (Sanskrit for monks and nuns) to settle in forests, often living in caves. Before Sakyamuni achieved Buddhahood under a bodhi tree, he practiced austerities in a mountain forest for six years, during which time he also lived in a cave. Even as his prestige mounted, he still preached in the forests. But as the ranks of his disciples grew, those disciples hoped for a more permanent residence. One of them, Bimbisara, king of Magadha and a devoted Buddhist, built the Veluvanaramaya or Bamboo Grove Monastery, in the city of Rajagrha for Sakyamuni and his disciples. Shortly afterwards, a rich merchant by the name of Sudatta built the Jetavanaramaya, or Jeta Grove Temple, in the city of Savatthi and dedicated it to Sakyamuni. The garden had been the private property of Prince Jeta who, impressed with Sudatta's devotion in buying the prince's garden so that it might serve as a monastery and temple for Sakyamuni, also donated funds to maintain the temple where Sakyamuni lived there for a long period of time and delivered many lectures. The Veluvanaramaya and the Jetavanaramaya are the two earliest temples in the history of Buddhism, known as "sangharama," meaning "residence shared by Buddhists and laymen."

The first Buddhist temple in China is considered the White Horse Temple, built in the city of Luoyang, the capital of the Eastern Han Dynasty, in the 1st century by Emperor Ming for the Indian monks Kasyapamatanga and Dharmaranya to translate Buddhist scriptures. At that time, the Chinese character for temple, *si*, stood for an official building that was used for distinguished foreign guests and ranked second only to the emperor's imperial palace. It indicates the respect Emperor Ming held for Buddhism that he designated the residence of the Indian monks a *si*, or temple, which ever after established the Chinese name for the Buddhist place of worship.

As Buddhism became more and more popular, more and more temples were built. According to Volume Three of *Apology for Buddhist Truth* by the eminent Tang monk Falin, in the cities of Luoyang and Chang'an, the two ancient Chinese capitals, there were 180 temples during the Western Jin Dynasty (265-316), with that number snowballing to an amazing 1,768 during the Eastern Jin (317-420) in just those two cities. In the ensuing Southern Dynasties the number continued to grow, reaching 1,913 during the Song (420-479); 2,015 during the Qi (479-502) and 2,954 during the Liang (502-557). The number might have been even greater during the Northern Dynasties. Nobody knows for sure the number of all the temples of every size and description that exist in all of China today, but the number can definitely be counted by tens of thousands. As for the major temples — that is, those with elaborate architecture and impressive buildings — these (including those of Han, Tibetan and Pali Buddhism) are estimated to number about 13,000, according to the latest government figures.

2. Layout and Design

In the earliest Han Buddhist temples, architecture and art also reflected the beliefs of the different schools. For instance, the temple built by Huaihai, the Tang Dynasty Chan master (720-814), was simple in structure. It had a chamber for the abbot, a hall for preaching the dharma, a sangha hall for meditation, and monks' dormitories. There was no hall of the Buddha out of the belief of the Chan School that one's own heart is the Buddha and that there is no need to worship an idol built of clay or wood. This conforms with the line in the *Vajracchedikaprajnaparamita-sutra*:

If by form one looks for the Buddha,
Or by the sound of the voice seeks me,
This person walks the wrong path,
And is unable to see the Buddha.

The absence of a Buddha shrine in the Chan temple built by Huaihai also is in accord with the practice of early Indian Buddhism — the sangharama (Sanskrit for "residence shared by Buddhists and laymen") also did not have a Buddha shrine but rather had a pagoda as the central structure. In the Dai-inhabited areas in Yunnan, as in other parts of South Asia where Hinayana Buddhism is practiced, major temples still follow this early Buddhist style with simple dormitories for the monks built around a pagoda. However, as Mahayana Buddhism became the dominant form in China, the Buddha Hall replaced the pagoda as the central structure. When pagodas were built, they were outside the temple.

On the other hand, the Ci'en Temple, the birthplace of the Ci'en School in the Tang Dynasty capital of Chang'an, served as a lively secular as well as religious center for the city. The temple was lavishly decorated with pearl, jade, gold and jadeite ornaments with more than ten courtyards, precious trees, fabulous gardens with peonies of every variety and a pagoda with murals painted by some of the great artists of the day. A major tourist attraction in its day, the temple even housed major theaters and was the principle center for the city's performing arts.

But with the merging of the various schools that integrated into a mainstream Buddhism after the Song Dynasty, Han Buddhist temples came to have more or less the same specifications. Temple architecture is traditionally Chinese, with wide columns and huge wooden beams. The walls are usually painted dark red or grey; the statues of Buddhas are usually of clay, gilded and painted. The temple complex generally faces south, and its buildings are arranged inside a high-walled compound along three lines: The central line and two side lines separated by courtyards planted with tall trees, mainly pine. Along the center north-south axial line are the main buildings — the front Gatehall ("Shanmen" in Chinese) followed by the Hall of Heavenly Kings, the Mahavira Hall, the Avalokitesvara Hall, and the Vairocana Hall (or Bhaisajyaguru Hall). To the east and west of this center line are

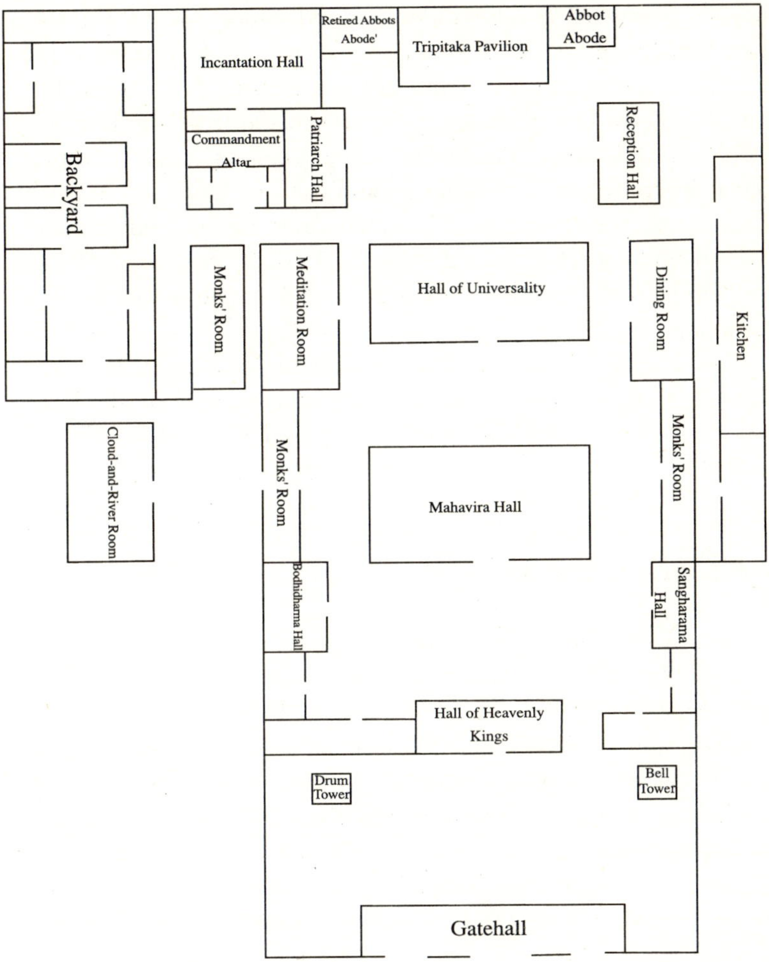

The Layout of the Guangji Temple in Beijing

arranged secondary buildings such as a reception hall, dining room, warehouse, abbot's chamber, preaching hall, meditation hall, and ancestral hall. If more such service buildings are needed, they can be built behind the eastern and western sides, or another courtyard can be added beyond either one of the two lines. Some monasteries have a pond in front and a square inside the front gateway, with bell and drum towers on both sides. The Tripitaka Pavilion is usually on the second floor of the last hall. (In Tibet and other Tibetan-inhabited regions, major temples follow an entirely different design and can be complexes of such colossal size that they look like small cities. On the other hand, in Pali Buddhist temples in the south, generally only one hall can be found on the premises dedicated to a single statue of the Buddha.)

The Guangji Temple of Beijing, now the headquarters of the Chinese Buddhist Association, gives a good example of the basic layout — minus the pond — of a temple of Chinese Buddhism. (see p.73)

3. Entering the Temple

Mountain Gate: On entering a temple, visitors first pass through Gatehall (or "Mountain Gate") where sometimes stand two ferocious warriors, General Heng and General Ha, actually guardian spirits in Buddhism. Those who are believers may be carrying sacrificial objects such as flowers, water, incense, food, and candles. These traditional offerings represent the six *paramitas*, the six things that ferry one beyond the sea of mortality to nirvana: 1) *Dana*, charity, or giving, including the bestowing of the truth on others; 2) *sila*, keeping the commandments; 3) *ksanti*, patience under insult; 4) *virya*, zeal and progress; 5) *dhyana*, meditation or contemplation; and 6) *prajna*, wisdom, the power to discern reality or truth. Following Mountain Gate is a forecourt with drum and bell towers on each side.

Hall of Heavenly Kings: A statue of Bodhisattva Maitreya, the Buddha of the Future who is known to the west as the "Laughing Buddha" for his smile and ample belly, greets visitors as they enter the Hall of Heavenly Kings. Maitreya was a native of south India and a disciple of Sakyamuni who once told Maitreya that he would become a Buddha but would continue to be known as Maitreya. However, the popular image of Maitreya as a plump monk with a smiling face holding a bag is based on a monk by the name of Qici who lived in present-day Fenghua in Zhejiang Province during the Five Dynasties (907-960). He was held in high esteem by the local people. Just before his death, Qici was heard saying, "The Maitreya is indeed who he is. With his identity split into hundreds of millions of bodies, his presence is ubiquitous so that he can teach people whenever it is necessary, but it is only natural that people in the mundane world do not know who he is."

From these lines people regarded Qici as the reincarnation of Maitreya, and statues of him were thus erected everywhere. Legend has it that prior to the Ming Dynasty (1368-1644), temples in China were not in the habit of enshrining a statue of Maitreya. Later, when Zhu Yuanzhang rose in an armed rebellion against the Yuan Dynasty, he expanded his forces by using the influence of the Maitreya cult. When he established the Ming and became Emperor Taizu, he showed his gratitude to Maitreya by having his statues erected in monasteries throughout the country. Whether this legend tallies with history has not been confirmed.

In front of this central figure is a simple table with five ritualistic objects on it: Two vases, two candlesticks, and an incense burner — placed there for Buddhists to offer flowers, light candles or burn incense. On the eastern and western sides of the hall are statues of the four Heavenly Kings, representing an early east Indian belief that four Deva-Kings ruled the four continents that lay around the insurmountable Mt. Sumeru in an ocean that made up the whole world. The kings are Dhrtarastra, the Deva King of the East, who protects his territory and people by holding a *pipa* or lute in his hand and is called the God of Music; Virudhaka, the Deva King of the South, who helps people do good and accumulate merits, holding a sword; Virupaksa, the Deva King of the West, who observes the world with his eyes peeled, holding a dragon that coils in his hand; and Dhanada, the Deva King of the North, who can safeguard people's wealth, holding an umbrella.

Mahavira Hall: The next courtyard usually has the biggest and the largest hall, the Mahavira Hall that houses the statue of the main Buddha, Sakyamuni, and his attendants. Made of wood, molded clay, or stone, the statues of Buddha are customarily gilt, to represent his golden body. A large incense burner cast in bronze or iron stands on a platform in front of the hall for worshippers to burn incense. As the central hall, the Mahavira has more ornamentation, such as streamers, flags and canopies, as well as percussion instruments used by monks in chanting the scriptures such as bells, drums, hollow wooden blocks — all designed to accentuate the solemnity of the religious aura in the temple. Because Chinese Buddhism belongs to the Mahayana branch whose pantheon includes more than one Buddha, some temples are obliged to put statues of other Buddhas together with that of Sakyamuni in the Mahavira Hall. Sakyamuni may be standing or sitting. The one and only standing posture of Sakyamuni in Buddhist sculpture has him hanging his left hand down in what is known as the "Posture of Willing to Grant," or extending right hand upward in the so-called "Posture of Vaisaradya (Self-Confidence)." In either posture the Buddha is trying to dispel his followers' misgivings by promising them that he is capable of satisfying all the desires of the multitude and delivering them from their miseries. If sitting, the Buddha can assume several postures. If he sits cross-legged with the palms of his hands coupled in front of his chest, this is known as the "Image of Meditation." If he places his left hand in front of him while hanging his right hand below his knees and pointing at the ground, it is known as the "Posture of Touching the Earth" or the "Image of Attaining Enlightenment." Another kind of statue has the Buddha sit on his throne with his legs crossed and the soles of his feet turning upward, while his left hand is placed horizontally at his left front side and his right hand extends upwards with the index finger forming a ring in what is known as the "Posture of Preaching the Dharma," or "Image of Preaching the Dharma." The old man standing by the left side of the statue of Sakyamuni is Mahakassapa, and to his right is a young man, Ananda. Both are the Buddha's most favored disciples who made invaluable contributions to the dissemination of Buddhism. The Mahavira Hall in many temples is enshrined with the trikaya (threefold body) of the Buddha as well as the Buddhas of the past, present and future. The former refers to the Dharmakaya (embodiment of Truth and the Law) of Vairocana, the Sambhogakaya (reward body) of Losana, and the Nirmanakaya (incarnation) of Sakyamuni. The latter include the Buddhas of the Three Vertical Forms, that is, Kasyapa, Sakyamuni, and Maitreya, and the Buddhas of the Three Horizontal Lands, that is, Bhaisajyaraja-vaidurya-prabhasa (Buddha of Medicine) of the Land of the Bhaisajyaraja, Amitabha of the Sukhavati Western Paradise, and Sakyamuni of the Saha Endurance Land. In a few monasteries, the Mahavira Hall is enshrined only with the Dharmakaya of Vairocana. In the Pure Land Sect, it is the domain of Sakyamuni or the Three Amita Saints of the West — Amitabha, Avalokitesvara, and Mahasthamaprapta. Amitabha is portrayed as holding a tiny lotus throne on the palm of his hand in a posture to greet those bound for the Western Paradise. The Buddha in the Mahavira Hall is also flanked by 16 arhats (saints), who are disciples of the Buddha, sometimes with the addition of two more later arrivals. Legend has it that when the Buddha was achieving nirvana, he instructed his disciples to preside over the dharma and not to enter nirvana until the birth of Amitabha, the Buddha of the future. It is said that in Sinhala in ancient times there lived a monk known as Nandimitra, who wrote the book *Nanadimitra on the Continuity of Dharma*, in which he recorded the deeds of the 16 arhats disseminating the law of Buddhism, which was translated into Chinese by Xuanzang, the celebrated Tang monk. In honor of both the author and the translator, Buddhists in China erected statues for them and placed them among the 16 arhats. Thus the ranks of arhats swelled to 18. In the rear of the Mahavira Hall, standing behind the Buddhist sages are the trinity of Manjusri riding on the back of a lion, Samantabhadra mounted on an elephant and Avalokitesvara riding a mythological animal known as "*hou*." In some cases the position is occupied by a statue of Avalokitesvara standing on an island in ocean in the company of Sudhana, a virtuous boy referred to in the *Buddhavatamsaka-mahavaipulya-sutra* (*Garland Sutra*), and Nagakanya, a virtuous girl mentioned in the *Saddharmapundarika-sutra* (*Lotus Sutra*).

Avalokitesvara Hall: Also known as the Hall of Mahakaruna (Great Mercy) or Hall of Universality, the Avalokitesvara Hall is reserved exclusively for a statue of the Bodhisattva Avalokitesvara, who assumes the image in Han Buddhism of the Goddess of Mercy (Guanyin), the most popular Buddhist deity in China. However, Avalokitesvara can assume other forms as well since the god is capable of taking on whatever identity necessary to answer the call of a person who is to be delivered from his misery. Avalokitesvara's body is also seen in these following forms:

- Arya-avalokite'svara (Sacred Avalokitesvara) — a person with one head on two shoulders, sitting on crossed legs and holding a lotus flower in his hand, with a figurine of Amitabha imbedded in the center of his crown.
- Pandaravasini (Avalokitesvara in a White Robe) — a beauty holding a holy-water vase and a poplar twig in her hands.
- Avalokitesvara with a Free Mind — a lady sitting on one leg, with the other leg extended in a posture of leisure and repose.
- Ekadasa-mukh-avolokitesvara (Eleven-faced Avalokitesvara) — a creature with 11 faces, three of which stare down on the evil ones, three with benign-looking faces that educate good people, and three with quiet faces providing guidance for those belong to super natural realms. As each of the three categories of people belong to the Trilokya or Three Realms， so altogether nine faces are needed. Above these nine faces is the face of solemnity and smile, meaning that only with awe and a ready willingness can education of the multitude of people become effective. Atop all these are the Buddha face, which gives expression to both good and evil, and quiet and composure.
- Sahasrabhuja-sahasranetra-avalokitesvara (Thousand-Armand Thousand-Eye Avalokistevara). In this form, Avalokistevara puts the multitude under the protection of her 1,000 hands while keeping the mundane world under 1,000 watchful eyes. Both the hands and the eyes are manifestations of Avalokistevara's great magnanimity and mercy. One eye grows in the palm of each hand.
- Forty-eight-arm Avalokistevara. Each arm has a special connotation, and all of the arms are designed for the good of the multitude.

Hall of Ksitigarbha: Visitors will find the Hall of Ksitigarbha of a Buddhist temple generally of a small size, with a sitting or standing statue of Ksitigarbha, one of the eight celestial Bodhisattvas with power over the hells who is devoted to saving all creatures between the nirvana of Sakyamuni and the advent of Maitreya, the Buddha of the Future. In his right hand, Ksitigarbha holds a staff as a symbol of his love of the people, and in his left hand is pearl, indicating he is able to meet all the desires of the people. However, the image of Ksitigarbha in various parts of China is often mixed up with the image of what is actually the likeness of the Korean monk, Gim Kyokak who is described in the section on the Chan (Zen) School.

The Hall of Samgharama: It is a memorial hall dedicated to those who have rendered meritorious deeds for Buddhism. In this hall, a statue of Prasenajit, a contemporary of Sakyamuni who converted to Buddhism, is flanked by Siddhartha (the name given Sakyamuni at his birth) to the left and Prince Jeta, also a contemporary of Sakyamuni who donated his lavish garden to Buddha and his disciples, to the right.

The Hall of Patriarchs: Also known as the "ancestral hall," this hall generally honors the patriarchs associated with the school to which the temple belongs. For example, a Chan School ancestral hall always houses images of Bodhidharma (?-293), Huineng (638-713) and Huaihai (720-814).

Hall of 500 Arhats: Some temples have a hall to honor the arhats, or saints. The first Hall of 500 Arhats probably appeared during the Five Dynasties (907-960), built by the king of Wuyue at the Fangguang Temple in the Tiantai Mountain. In 954 in Later Zhou, the Chan priest Daoqian began erecting statues of the 500 arhats at the Jingci Temple of Hangzhou. The idea may have originated in the fact that after the Buddha achieved nirvana, 500 of his disciples gathered in Rajagrha.

During the tour of a temple, a visitor may hear the tolling of the temple bell. The tolling of the bell in a Buddhist monastery may vary in rhythm and tonality, but the number of the tolls is the same at 108. The Buddhist interpretation of it is that there are 108 misgivings in the mundane world, and the 108 bell tolls may help dispel them.

Courtesies in Temples

The common way of greeting in Buddhist temples is to put your two palms together, with fingers aligned, in front of your chest, and slightly lower your head, for a few seconds. Normally you do not shake hands with monks, or have any other physical contact. When there is a religious ceremony going on in the temple, you may stand there quietly and watch. Loud talking or laughing is considered blasphemy against the gods. You may address ordinary monks respectfully as "shifu" (master). Chief monks, you may call "Zhanglao" (elder), "Zhuchi" (abbot) or "Fangzhang" (abbot). And senior monks of great attainments, you may cal "Fashi" (master of the law). The monks in a lamasery, you may call "lama" which means "senior master."

4. Everyday Life in a Han Buddhist Temple

Generally speaking, life in a temple is marked by serenity and regularity. Free from the worries of a layperson and the traffic and noise and cares of the mundane world, monks are resigned to the leisure, peace and quietness of the monastic life — sometimes to the great envy of those who have had their fill of worldly trepidations. For the monks who make their home in the residential areas of a temple, life is both physical and spiritual. In the physical aspect, a monk needs to be fed and clothed. In the spiritual aspect, they practice austerities in search for Buddhist truth, attends sutra-chanting sessions in the halls and studies the creeds. The daily monastic follows an invariable routine of chanting, prayerful meals, meditation and self-cultivation, and making sure the temple and its grounds are spotlessly clean.

Under normal conditions, a monk gets up at 5 a.m. After he has finished tidying up and puts on his habit, he lines up with fellow monks, and then the *karmadana* (deacon) leads them into the Mahavira Hall, where the monks who live in the meditation rooms stand along the eastern wall and those who live in other dormitories stand along the western wall. With the deacon taking the lead, they sing hymns and chant. All the while bells, drums, wooden-fish and chimes are struck to mark the beats of the hymns and the rhythm of the chanting. Among these concussion instruments, the wooden fish has a special function to play: It serves to admonish those who have renounced the mundane world to follow the example of the fish, which never sleeps, and be assiduous in seeking self-cultivation through meditation. The morning session in the Mahavira Hall last about one hour. The afternoon session, which begins at four, is the same as the morning session in duration and rituals, but the chants are different.

After the morning session, the monks who live in the meditation rooms are the first to leave the Mahavira Hall and return to their rooms. When the bell is tolled, they file into the dining room to be seated in a prescribed order. The dining room is furnished with long tables and benches. Those whose task it is to dispense the meals lay out the bowls and chopsticks and fill the bowls with food. After everybody is ready, the monks together say a prayer before setting chopsticks to bowl. The meal is supposed to be eaten in silence. After the meal is over, the monks chant a meal-ending invocation, file out of the dining room and return to their dormitories. The lunchtime ritual is more or less the same, but the food served is better. No rituals are held for supper. This practice has something to do with the commandment that monks should not eat anything after noontime, and because supper is not offered, there is no need for such rituals. However, in China most monks are followers of Mahayana Buddhism. So, generally they do not observe this commandment and, there being no such taboo, it is therefore customary for them to have supper.

But why the commandment forbids monks from eating supper? Monks are asked to give up supper as one way to keep greed from rising in the heart. Thus the saying, "Monks most of the time should look 30 percent sick." The commandment against eating after noontime is carried out strictly in Buddhist countries in Southeast Asia, where a monk is considered in disgrace if he is found eating in the afternoon or at night.

In the Chan School, monks meditate while in the Pure Land they chant the Buddha's name. The meditation room where Chan monks attend such sessions includes a Buddhist shrine around which the monks turn clockwise. During the process, the monks' steps gradually accelerate until they find themselves running. Incense sticks are burned to mark the time needed for the procession. While the monks are rotating the shrine, they are spurred on by a head monk who stands by holding a wooden stick in his hand. After a while the run slows down to a walk, and then the monks stop and sit down on crossed legs to begin the next part of the session: Meditation. In each meditation session the monks are asked to mull over a single question, such as "What was I like before my parents were born?" The supervisor continues to patrol with his stick, tapping back of anyone who might doze off. After sitting and meditating for some time, the monks are asked to relax and flex their muscles. The self-cultivation session is repeated three times a day in a temple where order is strictly maintained.

In the Pure Land School, self-cultivation takes the form of chanting the Buddha's name, but the rituals and time arrangement is more or less the same as in the Chan School. The monks are also required to turn around the Buddha's shrine in the hall in a clockwise fashion while chanting "Namah Amitabha." After chanting the Buddha's name for some time, the monks sit down on crossed legs to meditate and ask themselves the question, "Who is the one who chants the Buddha's name?" This ritual, which came in vogue with the merger of different schools of Han Buddhism after the Song Dynasty, is known as "self-cultivation by meditation in the fashion of Chan and chanting the name of the Buddha in the fashion of the Pure Land." But in some temples of the Pure Land School the monks only chant the Buddha's name and do not sit down to meditate.

Monks are fastidious about environmental sanitation and personal hygiene. As a temple covers a wide area, the workload to keep it clean and tidy is so heavy that it calls for the coordinated efforts of all the monks. The sanitation work in a temple is routine, nobody does it out of someone else's pressure. Apart from these aspects of daily life in the temples, monks also arrange their own self-cultivation and study. In rural areas, they are required to till the land.

Ritual performances beyond the daily routine for monks include the Water-and-Land Service, the ritual to offer alms to fire-spitting hungry ghosts, the Forty-nine-day Period of Self-Cultivation, Liturgy for Confession, *Ullambana*, the Festival in Memory of Ancestry, Home service to recite sutras and worship, and worshipping services.

The Water-and-Land Service (水陆法会) is a large-scale alms-giving activity in Buddhism, an elaborate and grand occasion that takes place on the internal altar and the external altars in a temple. But most of the rituals are performed on the internal altar, which is therefore more solemnly decorated for this purpose. Altogether there are six external altars: the Primary Altar, manned by 24 monks to recite the *Confession of the Emperors of the Liang*; the Sutra-recitation Altar, where seven monks read aloud all kinds of Buddhist scriptures; the Fahua Altar, where seven monks chant the *Saddharmapundarika-sutra* (*Lotus Sutra*); and the Yogacara Altar, manned by a team of monks whose task is to appease the fire-spitting hungry ghosts once a night. The entire Water-and-Land Service lasts for seven days and nights, and is generally funded by moneyed patrons. Today, it has evolved into Water-Land-Air Service to ward off disaster during air travel. The Water-and-Land Service is attributed to a legend about Emperor Wu (502-548) of the Liang during the Southern and Northern Dynasties. It is said that he dreamed of a celestial monk who spoke to him about the six cycles of transmigrations and the four forms of birth. (See Appendices V: Buddhist Terms) The celestial monk said to him: "To go through the Six Cycles of Transmigrations and the Four Forms of Birth involves untold sufferings. Why don't you perform the water-and-land service to deliver the souls of the dead from misery?"

Emperor Wu consulted Baozhi, a famous monk of the day, who suggested that he consult the sutras for the answer. After three years of intensive reading of the Buddhist scriptures, Emperor Wudi composed the "Water-and-Land Rhapsody," had an altar built in the Jinshan Temple in Runzhou (present-day Zhenjiang, Jiangsu Province), and invited monks of the temple to perform the Water-and-Land Service to redeem the souls inhabiting the waters and the land. This religious ritual was rather simple in the beginning. During the Xianheng reign (670-672) of the Tang, it was combined with the esoteric Buddhist services to offer sacrifices to ghosts, and became very fashionable during the Song. Xiao Yan's (Emperor Wu of Liang) "Water-and-Land Rhapsody" has been repeatedly revised and added to become the version that is performed today.

The ritual to offer alms to fire-spitting hungry ghosts (焰口) is a service to redeem the souls of the deceased closely associated with Tantrism, the school of Han Buddhism that all but disappeared towards the end of the Tang. However, its ritual to appease the hungry spirits by offering them alms has survived, from a scripture translated into Chinese by Amoghavajra, the founder of the Esoteric School. According to this scripture, once when Ananda was meditating, the king of fire-spitting hungry ghosts said to him, "You'll die and find yourself living among hungry ghosts in three days. If you do not want to suffer, you'd better give me a serving of food today and tomorrow."

Ananda reported this to the Buddha, who gave him incantations to chant when handing out alms. These incantations became part of a Buddhist's daily meditation ritual. After the Song Dynasty, different versions of alms-giving incantations appeared, and only in the recent past was a unified version adopted to be routinely performed at the end of any major religious ceremony.

Forty-nine-day Period of Self-Cultivation (打七) is divided into seven seven-day phases in which a monk is required to intensify his meditation or chanting. It is said that some monks have achieved enlightenment through intensive self-cultivation during these seven seven-day phases. During this period, a monk is supposed to meditate or chant continuously except when he is eating or sleeping. There is no leave of absence, no going outdoors, and no contact whatsoever with the outside world.

Liturgy for Confession (礼忏) is yet another form of self-cultivation. A number of texts are to be chanted for this ritual, including the *Thousand-Buddha Confession*, *Ten Thousand-Buddha Confession*, *Confessions of Emperors of the Liang* , *Confession of Great Mercy*, and the *Water Confession*. These rituals vary in length, and are selected to meet specific requirements. Each confession consists of a text to be read aloud, as well as the names and titles of the Buddhas and bodhisattvas, which are to be worshipped during the ritual. Through the Liturgy for Confession, a monk hopes to own up to his misdeeds, repent for them, and ask the Buddha and bodhisattvas for forgiveness.

***Ullambana*, the Festival in Memory of Ancestry (盂兰盆会)** is a routine ceremony held on the 15th of the 7th lunar month every year in a temple to redeem the souls of ancestors. According to the *Ullambana Sutra*, Mahamaudgalyayana, one of the ten major disciples of Sakyamuni, acquired *divyacaksus* (instantaneous view of anything anywhere) and found that his deceased mother was among the hungry ghosts and suffering. Wanting to come to his mother's rescue, he asked the Buddha for instruction. The Buddha told him to perform the Ullambana Service on the 15th of the 7th lunar month, at which he was supposed to offer generous delicacies to fete the hungry ghosts. By this virtuous deed he could deliver his mother from the misery. "Ullam" is a Sanskrit term that means "hung something upside down," and "bana" denotes utensils for holding alms. Using the "bana" to offer alms can immediately deliver the hungry ghosts from the pain of being hanging upside down. The Ullambana Service is performed in Chinese Buddhist monasteries for monks to show compassion for those in misery.

Home service to recite sutras and worship (应赴经忏) involves monks of a monastery going to a lay follower's home to chant sutras or confessional texts for him or her. It is rather popular in southern China and is a major source of income for many monasteries. Whenever someone has died in the family, the lay Buddhist is obliged to send for monks to perform religious rituals to redeem the soul of the deceased. By paying a certain amount of money, a patron has the right to decide how many monks to be hired, for how long the ritual should last, what sutras or confessional text to be chanted, and where should this ritual be performed. After a monastery has received such an assignment, it goes out of its way to meet the patron's demands. Every monastery has set prices for this service, and the monks assigned the job are also paid. However, many temples refuse to offer this service in the belief that offering this service is tantamount to selling the Law of the Buddha for money and therefore blasphemes the good name of Buddhism.

Finally, monks of a monastery are often asked by lay people to chant sutras and make confessions on their behalf as a way of helping to redeem the souls of the deceased but also to ward off disasters and prolong life in regard to themselves. A patron may request that a monastery hold a special service for him or her. A patron may also ask the monastery to chant and pray for him in passing during a routine session in the Sutra Chanting Hall. In the process, the patron is obliged to hand out red envelopes containing a certain amount of cash among the monks as a donation. This service is offered even in temples that refuse to offer compensated home services.

5. Festivals

Han Buddhist festival dates are marked by the Chinese lunar calendar, which like the Western one is a yearly calendar, but with the start of each lunar year based on the cycles of the moon. Because of this cyclical dating, the beginning of the year can fall anywhere between late-January and mid-February, so lunar dates vary each year in their coordination with the Western calendar. The three foremost festivals for Buddhists worldwide mark the occasions of Sakyamuni's birthday, his achievement of enlightenment and his entry into nirvana. Han Buddhists observe Sakyamuni's birthday on the 8th of the 4th lunar month with a "Bathing-the-Buddha" ceremony held in pomp and pageantry for laity as well as monks. During the ceremony, a basin filled with sandalwood-soaked water is placed in front of the statue of Sakyamuni in the Mahavira Hall. Placed in state in the basin is a figurine of Sakyamuni several inches in height as a newborn infant, the little Prince Siddhartha, pointing one hand upward at the sky and the other hand downward at the ground. Circling the basin, a monk leads the crowd in singing hymns and chanting as the gathered take turns to bathe the baby prince by using a prepared tiny ladle to pour water on him. The Birthday of the Buddha is an occasion of joy, and is so celebrated.

Sakyamuni's enlightenment falls on the 8th of the 12th lunar month and Sakyamuni's entry into nirvana falls on the 15th of the 2nd lunar month. In Han Buddhist temples in China, no special ceremony is observed on either occasion. However, on the 8th day of the 12th lunar month, Han Buddhist temples are in the habit of dispensing a porridge prepared of cereals, beans, nuts and dried fruit among patrons to mark Sakyamuni's achievement of enlightenment.

For followers of Theravada Buddhism in Southeastern Asian countries, these three Buddhist festivals fall on the same day, the 15th of the 4th lunar month (the day of the full moon in May). The margin of error in dating the Buddha's birthday may be the result of different understandings of the concept "fortnight." As a month contains 30 days, the period from the 1st to the 15th is a fortnight; whereas it takes exactly a fortnight for the full moon to appear. Thus Buddhists of Southeast Asia count the Buddha's birthday by the number of days in a fortnight, while Chinese Buddhists calculate the date by the fortnight cycle of the full moon. In the 1950s, the World Federation of Buddhists (WFB) passed a resolution to designate the day of the full moon in May, that is, the 15th of the 4th lunar month, as the birthday of the Buddha. Buddhists of various countries, however, stick to the their traditional ways.

Festivals honoring the other deities in the pantheon of Mahayana Buddhism are generally observed with simple ceremonies in Han Buddhist monasteries. But among them the most popular festivals are those associated with Avalokitesvara, that is, the Goddess of Mercy (Guanyin). The major festivals celebrate:

Birthday of Maitreya, the Buddha of the Future: 1st day of 1st lunar month.

Birthday of Guanyin (Avalokitesvara) or the Goddess of Mercy: 19th day of 2nd lunar month.

Birthday of Samantabhadra, the Bodhisattva of Universal Benevolence: 21st day of 2nd lunar month.

Birthday of Manjusri, the Bodhisattva of Wisdom: 4th day of 4th lunar month.

Festival of Avalokitesvara's achievement of enlightenment: 19th day of 6th lunar month.

Birthday of Mahasthamaprapta, the bodhisattva representing the Buddha-wisdom of Amitabha: 13th day of 7th lunar month.

Birthday of Ksitigarbha, the bodhisattva who protects children and travelers and intervenes in Hell for those suffering there: 30th day of 7th lunar month.

Anniversary of the tonsuring of Avalokitesvara as a monk: 19th day of 9th lunar month.

Birthday of Bhaisajyaraja, the Buddha of Healing and Medicine:

30th day of 9th lunar month.

Birthday of Amitabha, the Buddha of Immeasurable Splendor: 17th day of 12th lunar month.

Who was the Goddess of Mercy (Guanyin)?

The statue of Guanyin can be seen everywhere in Buddhist temples. Its name is Avalokitesvara in Sanskrit. It usually stays at the side of Amitabha, sometimes it is housed in side halls or stays together with other bodhisattvas. It has 33 incarnations according to *Saddharmapundarika-sutra* (*Lotus Sutra*), and in almost all cases, Guanyin is female in appearance, though it is in fact a male god in India. It is believed to be able to save the lives of the people from misery, and also treated as a goddess who will give sons to barren women. This is why Guanyin was widely worshipped in China.

6. Temple Rules, Management and Sources of Income

The Buddhist term *sangha* means the assembly of at least three monks, one of whom is the leader empowered to hear confession, grant absolution, and ordain. The principles for the *sangha* are known as the "Six Points of Reverent Harmony" that demand strict observation and tolerate no violation. The Six Points of Reverent Harmony were laid down for the s*angh*a during the time of Sakyamuni some 2,500 years ago, and they have been in force since Buddhism spread to China during the Han Dynasty. These six points are:

1) Harmony in the form of worship, without fighting;

2) Harmony in word, in chanting, and in refraining from quarrels;

3) Harmony in mind, in faith, and the sharing of happiness;

4) Harmony in morality, in observing the commandments

and self-cultivation;

5) Harmony in doctrine, in views and explanations;

6) Harmony in economy, in community of goods, deeds, studies, or charity.

For a time different schools of Buddhism had different organizational systems, but after the Song Dynasty the influence of the Chan school became so dominant that its management system was copied by the other schools.

The abbot is the master of a Chinese temple. Under him are four supervisors and eight executives who preside over the practice of self-cultivation and conduct of the monks and take care of daily life according to a division of labor. The four supervisors are the *sthavira* (the superintendent), the supervisor of the western chamber, the supervisor of the rear chamber, and the supervisor at large, and their task is to provide leadership over the search for Buddhist truth and the chanting of incantations in the prayer hall. These four positions are filled by veterans with high accomplishment and appointed by the abbot.

The eight executives are professional managers of various affairs in the temple. They are:

1) Jianyuan: Popularly known as the "homemaker," who handles general affairs, and controls the financial affairs in particular;

2) Zhike: In charge of the reception room and receiving visiting monks and laity.

3) Sengzhi: Supervises the enforcement of monastic rules and regulations, and the deportment of monks.

4) Weina: Supervises the meditation hall and provides leadership over daily religious rituals.

5) Dianzuo: Manages the kitchen and canteen and takes care of meals for the entire monastic order.

6) Liaoyuan: Takes care of the Hall for Roaming Monks and receives the vagrant monks who stay in the temple.

7) Yibo: Takes care of the abbot's mansion, assists the abbot in running the mansion and handling personnel affairs.

8) Shuji: The secretary in charge of drafting and writing document concerning public relations.

These eight executives are appointed by the abbot for a term of one year. Where and when necessary, assistants are appointed to serve as the accountant, warehouse manager, alms collector, doorman, vegetable garden manager, water-fetching foreman, bell-tolling manager, drum-beater, man who burns incense sticks and light lamps, manager of vagrant monks, meal dispenser, etc. Thus life in the monastery goes on smoothly with the coordination of supervisors and executives and their assistants. In some temples there is also the position of a general executive, but this is actually an honorary title, and the holder of it actually is not required to do anything.

7. Commandments and Prohibitions

The commandments were prescribed by the Buddha, and followers are required to obey unconditionally. According to history books, no such commandments existed in the first 12 years after Sakyamuni achieved Buddhahood. But with some members of the *sangha* following no rules of conduct led to improper conduct unbecoming to their status. To safeguard the honor of the *sangha*, the Buddha began to formulate the commandments. But he completed this task not all at once but rather laid down a commandment whenever a misdeed was committed. The commandments accumulated in this fashion until they formed a complete body. The reasons behind each command are given in detail in the "complete collection of monastic rules" in the *Tripitaka*.

The commandments fall into two categories: Commandments for those who have renounced the world and those who have not. Lay Buddhists are required to abide by either the Five Commandments or the Eight Commandments. The Five Commandments, or *Pancasila* in Sanskrit, are: Buddhists must not kill, steal, commit adultery, tell lies, or drink alcohol. The Eight Commandments also include not to indulge in cosmetics; personal adornments, dancing or music; sleeping in fine beds; and eating outside of mealtimes. For those who have renounced the world, a monk is required to observe 250 commandments and a nun, 500 commandments.

The commandments are the rule of conduct governing the body, language and will of a Buddhist. Accordingly, monks in a temple are required to congregate on the 15th and 30th of each lunar month to chant the commandments. Such gatherings serve two purposes. One is to remind the monks of these commandments; and the other is that it gives an opportunity for malfeasants to make confessions. A monk who refuses to confess is held guilty, and if his misconduct has been exposed, he will be given a good talking to or, if the case is serious, expelled. The fortnightly recitation of the commandments is known as *upavasatha* (retreat for spiritual refreshment). Today, *upavasatha* is not held in the temples of most schools, but remains a compulsory formality in the Vinaya School.

Commandments hold an important position in Buddhism. They are the foremost of the *trisiksa* or three studies: Learning by the commandments, or prohibitions, so as to guard against error by words, deed, or thought; by *dhyana*, or meditation; and by philosophy, i.e., study of principles and solving of questions. The Buddha's purpose in laying down the commandments was to prevent misconduct and ward off evil, and promote the accumulation of morality.

Apart from the commandments laid down by Sakyamuni, monks in China are also subjected to a series of prohibitions the eminent monk Huaihai of the Tang Dynasty set forth in light of Chinese customs and habits following the some 800-year practice of Buddhism in China after its arrival during the Han Dynasty.

Huaihai (720-814) created the first temple for monks of the Chan School. Monks of the Chan School previously did not have fixed residences — most of them were put up in temples of the Vinaya School. Huaihai created the *Rules of Conduct for the Chan School,* known to posterity as "Monastic Prohibitions," after the population of his temple grew to a considerable size, giving rise to the need to enforce certain rules and regulations. The original version of "Monastic Prohibitions" is not extant, but judging from an introduction in Volume Six of the *Quotations of Buddhists in Jingde Reign of the Dynasty* by Daoyuan, they were rather simple rules and regulations.

Huaihai was a native of Changle in present-day Fuzhou. Surnamed Wang, he was tonsured and became a disciple of Huaizhao at the Xishan Temple in Chaoyang and was ordained with the commandments by the monk Falang in Mount Hengshan.

A similar book like Huaihai's *Rules of Conduct for the Chan School* appeared in the Song Dynasty, which caused some confusion about which was correct. In 1335 the court of Emperor Shun of Yuan Dynasty ordered Dehui, the abbot of a monastery on Baizhang Mountain in Jiangxi, to compile a new version. The book thus compiled was the *Imperial-Mandated Monastic Prohibitions of Baizhang Monastery*, which was distributed among monks nationwide and has been in use ever since. The new version was far more comprehensive than Huaihai's original, but its spirit remained the same, that is, how to run the *sangha* and the monasteries well.

The emergence of the "Monastic Prohibitions" was, to a certain extent, a transformation of the commandments that was necessary to prevent the *sangha* from being detached from a society that provides the lifeblood for the existence of monasteries.

8. Sources of Income

A monk is not supposed to have his private possessions other than his *tricivara*, that is, his regulation garments, begging bowl and his cloth used for bedding or a cushion for meditating. The monastery, however, is allowed to own property to be shared by all the monks. "Egalitarianism in property and interests" is an organizational principle for the *sangha.*

In the past, land was a major source of revenue for Buddhist temples across China. A temple lent its land to local farmers in return for an annual rent to be used as upkeep and to provide for the monks. With Land Reform following the founding of the People's Republic of China in 1949, the temples lost the land in their possession. A monk in rural areas was allotted the same amount of land as a local farmer. As a matter fact, for monks to till their own land goes back a long way. As early as the Tang Dynasty, when the famed Chan monk Huaihai built the first temple of the Chan School, he attached as much importance to farming and as to Chan meditation, and his "Monastic Prohibitions" contained clearly set rules for monks to participate in farm labor. The rules, known as "Rules for

Collective Labor," required monks to share all the chores in a temple. In his old age, Huaihai insisted on taking part in collective labor. One day, the monk in charge of collective labor, wanting Huaihai to take a rest on account of his advanced age, concealed his tool. Huaihai could not find his tool, but he refused to take a rest. "I am an immoral man if I shift my end of physical labor onto other people," he said, adding that he would refuse to eat if he was not allowed to work. This story later evolved into the famed adage: "I'll eat nothing the day I have done no work."

The financial sources for a Buddhist temple in China today are mainly as follows:

(1) Visitor tickets. Buddhsit temples or monasteries, no matter where they are, are always regarded as cultural facilities, and tickets are sold to visitors to earn the upkeep. As a matter of fact, tickets have become a major source of revenue for the temples and monasteries. The earnings can be very impressive if a temple is a big one or situated in a famous mountain.

(2) Almsgiving (*dana*). Since the advent of Buddhism, monks who renounce the world have lived on alms contributed by lay followers. Even today, lay Buddhists are in the habit of contributing money and materials to Buddhist monasteries in the belief that this helps them accumulate virtue and attain the Buddha's blessings.

(3) Collection Box. In the Mahavira Hall of most temples there is a collection box, into which pilgrims and visitors toss whatever amount of money they like as a token of their faith. The box can yield a substantial amount of money every year. In some monasteries a collection box is fixed in every hall.

(4) Souvenir Shops. Though not big, the souvenir shops sell Buddhist scriptures, statues and other religious objects, and souvenirs as well. If run well, such a shop can collect a good income.

(5) Vegetarian restaurant. For the convenience of pilgrims, patrons and visitors, some temples run restaurants to serve vegetarian food. This also is potentially a good source of income.

(6) Religious services. The Chinese who believe in Buddhism are in the habit of sending for monks to recite scriptures to seek the Buddha's blessings. When someone has died in the family, monks are invited to come to a home to perform rituals to expiate

the sins of the dead. These services are another major source of income for a temple.

(7) Farming. In temples situated in rural areas, most monks earn a living by doing farm work. The monks of the Guoqing Temple in Mount Tiantai, for instance, till the land while cultivating themselves in search of enlightenment. They run their own farm so well that the crops yield a surplus on a yearly basis. Another source of income for this temple is the woods on its premises.

(8) Government subsidy. Temples with historical and cultural importance are duly protected by the government, which usually subsidizes the major repairs and expansion projects.

With the abovementioned sources of collective income, a Buddhist temple is able to offer allowances to its monks according to their responsibilities and contributions. Even those who do not shoulder any responsibilities are also entitled to an allowance.

9. Major Han Buddhist Temples

Despite their similarity in overall layout, major temples of Han Buddhism in China have their own particular histories, customs, attractions and surroundings — including the local vendors who gather near the entrance gates of Buddhist temples in China to hawk food and souvenirs much as they do in front of medieval churches in Europe. Visitors might plan a day's trip around a temple while taking in other nearby sightseeing activities. For instance, the first temple listed here, Fayuan Temple in Beijing, is located in the interesting *hutong* environment of old Beijing's lanes and alleys, within walking distance not only of the Niujie (Cattle Street) Mosque in the heart of Beijing's Muslim community, but of places like the Temple of Heaven, the Great Hall of the People and the Forbidden City. Other temples mentioned here are in places of fabled scenic beauty. Most temples with long histories have gone through name changes and renovations or entire reconstructions following wars, fires or other natural disasters. The following offers the most distinctive features of some of the major Buddhist temples that can be visited today in China.

MUNICIPALITIES

Beijing

Fayuan Temple 法源寺 (Fǎyuán Sì)

A horizontal board graces the entrance of Fayuan Temple inscribed in 1780 in the Qing Dynasty with four Chinese characters in Qing Emperor Qianlong's own handwriting: "Genuine Source of the Sea of Dharma." The original temple on the site where Fayuan Temple now stands was built in 645 in the Tang Dynasty, making this the oldest site of a Buddhist temple in the city of Beijing. Tang Emperor Taizong (Li Shimin) built the temple and named it "Temple to Mourn the Loyal War Dead" in memory of the generals and soldiers who died in an eastern expedition. In 1437 in the Ming Dynasty, the temple was repaired and renamed "Chongfu Temple." In the 1723-1735 period of the Qing Dynasty the temple was given its present name, "Fayuan Temple." In the first half of the 20th century, the temple again fell into disrepair. After the founding of the People's Republic of China, the temple was restored with the help of government funds and reopened in 1956 when it also became the home of the China National Buddhist Seminary. Like many Buddhist sites in China, the Fayuan Temple was shut down and vandalized during the "cultural revolution" (1966-1976). In 1979 it was once again restored to its present condition.

The Fayuan Temple hosts the Chinese Buddhist Books and Artifacts Museum with an impressive collection of precious artifacts and original versions of classical books that help tell the long story of Chinese Buddhism. Other treasures include a three-tiered Ming bronze sculpture of the Buddhas of Five Directions that rises to a height just below the ceiling of the hall. The bottom layer of this sculpture is in the shape of a huge lotus flower throne, with a Buddhist figurine standing on each of its 1,000 petals; sitting on the middle-layer are the Buddhas of Four Directions; and sitting in the center of the upper layer is a likeness of the Buddha Vairocana. The temple also has a large Ming-dynasty wood carving of the sleeping Buddha (5.4 meters long). All information signs in the temple are in Chinese, no English.

Serene and stately, the Fayuan Temple stands off the beaten

track in southern Beijing in the midst of a *hutong*, the small winding streets that make up old Beijing residential areas. To get there, take a taxi and be sure to have a bilingual map of the city to show the driver. The temple is also near the muslim section of Beijing, within walking distance of the Chinese Islamic Association as well as the Niujie (Cattle Street) Mosque, originally built in 996 during the Song Dynasty after Islam was first introduced into China, which is also open to the public.

Guangji Temple 广济寺 (Guǎngjì Sì)

The Guangji Temple, an old establishment of Buddhism in West Beijing, serves as headquarters for the Chinese Buddhist Association. The temple is known for its immense size, imposing buildings, and vast trove of treasures that include a copper structure of the four deva-kings, a richly engraved tripod, a stele inscribed with a poem of Emperor Qianlong of the Qing Dynasty, and a huge scroll of painting done with fingers rather than a brush. The original temple on the site was the Temple of West Liu Village built during the Jin (1115-1234) Dynasty, which at some point fell into ruins. In the Ming Dynasty, someone digging at the site unearthed Buddhist statues and other relics to reveal that a temple had once been on the site. A new temple was built and since then resident monks have kept expanding the temple. The Hall of Multiple Treasures offers a public display of the valuable gifts the Chinese Buddhist Association has received from various countries in the last few decades.

Yunju Temple 云居寺 (Yúnjū Sì)

The Yunju Temple, or the Temple of Cloud Dwelling, is found in the Zhuolu Mountain in Fangshan District about about 45 miles or 75 km from downtown Beijing. It is known not for its temple buildings but for its 14,278 stone slabs engraved with Buddhist scriptures dating back a thousand years to the Sui and Tang dynasties. The Sui Dynasty monk Jingwan started the monumental project of engraving the full texts of the voluminous *Tripitaka* on stone slabs. The temple once was an immense architectural phenomenon in itself, consisting of five compounds and six rows of major halls flanked by monks' dormitories and guest rooms. However, during the 1930s the Yunju Temple was razed to the ground temple by Japanese invaders. In 1956, to commemorate the 2,500th anniversary of the nirvana of Sakyamuni, the Chinese Buddhist Association spent three years producing rubbings from the inscriptions of all the stone slabs stored in the mountain. The stone scripture slabs are on display in an exhibition hall built in 1980 in the temple, which a few years ago underwent major reconstruction. The stone slabs were put in an underground hall specially built for them on September 9, 1999 for fear of further damage caused to them by weathering. Over 10,000 people from home and abroad took part in the ceremony.

Lingguang Temple 灵光寺 (Língguāng Sì)

The Lingguang (Divine Light) Temple in the Western Hills of Beijing is famous for its pagoda that houses what is said to be one of the teeth of Sakyamuni preserved after his cremation. The temple was known as Longquan (Dragon Spring) Temple when it was first built in the Tang Dynasty. By the side of the temple there used to be a Liao-dynasty pagoda of ten stories which was destroyed by the Allied Forces of Eight Powers invading Beijing in 1900. According to legend, Buddha's tooth ended up in Beijing in the following way: In the 5th century, the eminent Chinese monk Faxian paid a visit to Khotan, Xinjiang where one of the Buddha's teeth had found its way. (The other ended up in Sinhala.) Faxian brought the tooth with him back to the capital city of the Southern Qi (present-day Nanjing, Jiangsu Province). After the Sui unified China, the tooth somehow found its way to Chang'an, the national capital, and then ended up in present-day Beijing, then capital of the Liao Dynasty (907-1125). In 1071, the tooth was enshrined in the Zhaoxian Pagoda, according to the *History of the Liao Dynasty • Records of Emperor Daozong*, and never to be heard of again until the pagoda crumbled some 800 years later. When sorting out the debris of the foundation of the pagoda, the monks accidentally came across a sandalwood box containing the Buddha's tooth, an event that shook the entire Buddhist world. In 1964, the Chinese Buddhist Association had a new pagoda built at the old site to provide a permanent shrine for the tooth. The tooth has also played an important role in the relationship between Buddhists in China and Myanmar (formerly Burma). In 2001, a jade Buddha was presented by the Myanmar government to the Chinese Buddhist Association in appreciation for the relic's several visits to Myanmar. On a nine-inch pedestal, the 4-foot 6-inch tall jade Buddha is enshrined in the Jade Buddha Hall of Lingguang Temple.

Wofo Temple 卧佛寺 (Wòfó Sì)

The Wofo (Recumbent Buddha) Temple stretches up the slope of the Western Hills in Beijing inside the Beijing Botanical Gardens. Originally built in the Zhenguan reign period of Tang Dynasty (627-649), the temple was expanded in the Yuan Dynasty and in 1321 some 50 tons of copper were used to cast an enormous statue of a bare-footed, sleeping Buddha that has been in the temple ever since. The temple was renamed repeatedly before it got its present name following major reconstruction during the Ming Dynasty. The architecture of the temple is typical Han Buddhist structure with a mountain gate, Davaraja Hall, the Hall of the Buddhas of the Three Ages and the Hall of the Recumbent Buddha. The temple includes a pond, and one of its pavilions is now a teahouse. The grounds also feature rare and beautiful trees — cypress, sal trees from India, pines, locust, as well as wisteria, lilac and forsythia bushes.

Biyun Temple 碧云寺 (Bìyún Sì)

The Biyun Temple, or Temple of Azure Clouds, is a compound of six courtyards that cover a scenic area in the Fragrant Hills Park in Haidian District, where old pines and cypresses soar high to provide a scenic setting for the temple first built in 1289. A major Beijing tourist destination, the Biyuan Temple offers three particular attractions of cultural and historical interest: First, the Arhats' Hall that holds 508 gilded statues, including Statue No. 444, the Divine One Who Subdues Evils, which is an actual likeness of Emperor Qianlong made to the order of the emperor. Second, the Diamond Throne Pagoda, a square white-marble terrace built at the site of graves prepared by two Ming eunuchs, Yu Jing and Wei Zhongxian, for themselves. A taller pagoda stands in the center and is surrounded by four shorter ones on the four corners of the terrace. To the front of the Diamond Throne Pagoda is a pair of Tibetan-style pagodas, or dagobas. Third, the Sun Yat-sen Memorial Hall, where the coffin containing Sun's remains temporarily rested in state after his death in 1925. The hall has since been dedicated to the memory of the father of China's democratic revolution, and some of his clothes were buried under the Diamond Throne Pagoda.

Jietai Temple 戒台寺 (Jiètái Sì)

The Jietai Temple, or Ordination Altar Temple, lies at the Ma'an Hill in the suburban district of Mentougou and 21 miles or 35 km west of downtown Beijing. The Jietai Temple's history goes back to its days as the Huiju Temple, and it was built in 622 in the Tang as the hermitage of Zhizhou, a Chan master well-versed in the study and practice of Buddhist commandments. During the 11th century a monk named Fajun founded altar to the left of the temple for the ordination of priest, the source of the temple's present name. During the Yuan Dynasty, the temple came under the care of another eminent monk, Yuequan, who rebuilt the halls, but towards the end of that dynasty, war and turmoil reduced both the temple and the altar to debris. The temple was rebuilt in 1434 in the Ming Dynasty and renamed Wanshou Temple. More halls were added to the temple during the Qing Dynasty, but the temple gradually fell into oblivion during the Republican years. After the founding of the People's Republic of China, this thousand-year-old temple came into its own once again. The Jietai Temple stands facing east on a gentle mountain slope, and its halls are laid out along two parallel axial lines that run east and west. Between these two clusters of halls lies a Peony Garden, in the southern Chinese landscape style. The Jietai Temple is noted for its five ancient pine trees, one of which is called the "sensitive pine" that quivers if one of its branches is touched.

Tanzhe Temple 潭柘寺 (Tánzhé Sì)

The oldest of its kind in Beijing, the Tanzhe Temple on Tanzhe Mountain was first built during the Western Jin (265-316), founded by a Chan master, Huayan. The age of the temple is reflected in the saying, "The city of Beijing was nowhere before the Tanzhe Temple was built." For a long time, it was one of the most important temples in north China, flourishing in the Tang Dynasty (618-907). During the Five Dynasties (907-960), Congshi, another master of Chan Buddhism, arrived with more than 1,000 disciples. After the Jin Dynasty (1115-1234) unified north China and established its capital in Beijing, a monk by the name of Tongli expanded it and renamed it Great Wanshou Temple. The temple was destroyed towards the end of the Yuan Dynasty (1279-1368), was rebuilt during the Ming (1368-1644), and renamed "Youyun Temple" in 1692 in the Qing. The gigantic complex of the Tanzhe Temple is laid out along three lines on a typical Chan Buddhist temple plan. Among its cluster of old buildings is the Floating Winecup Kiosk, a marble structure with a double-eaved roof is paved with a mixture of tiles glazed green and gold. Its marble floor is carved with a water channel in the fashion of a gyrating dragon. The Tanzhe Temple is also known for its ordination altar, a three-terraced structure built entirely with white marble blocks engraved with elaborate ornamental patterns. The temple's other legacies include an ancient gingo tree.

Shanghai

Longhua Temple 龙华寺 (Lónghuá Sì)

The Longhua Temple, in Longhua Town in the southern suburbs of Shanghai, is a large Buddhist sanctuary with a long history. Its compounds cover a vast area, and with halls in an impressive architectural style. The Longhua Pagoda in front of the temple has been there for more than 1,700 years. It is a seven-story octagonal structure with a wooden stairway inside it providing access from the ground to the top floor. Legend has it that the pagoda was built in 274 in the Three Kingdoms period. As history books indicate, Empress Wu Zetian of the Tang was the first person to donate money to build a hall at this temple, but the hall was destroyed in a later time. In 977, or the 2nd year of the Taping Xingguo reign of the Northern Song, a temple and a pagoda of considerable size were built on the site with donations from Qian Shu, King Zhongyi of the Wuyue State, but these, too, were razed to the ground towards the end of the Yuan Dynasty. The buildings extant today were mostly built during the Guangxu reign (1875-1908) of the Qing. More buildings were added during the Republican years, but it did not become an influential temple until the 1930s. The Longhua Temple today is a major tourist attraction in Shanghai, respected for its time-honored history. A solemn atmosphere prevails over the buildings of the temple. Incense sticks burn everywhere in this temple, and a constant stream of pilgrims and visitors come and go on a daily basis.

Yufo Temple 玉佛寺 (Yùfó Sì)

The main halls of Yufo (Jade Buddha) Temple on Anyuan Road, Putuo District, are considered paragons of Chinese architecture. The foremost Buddhist establishment in Shanghai, the temple houses the Shanghai Buddhist Seminary, includes a collection of different versions of the *Tripitaka*, and features an exquisite Burmese clear jade statue of the Buddha brought to the temple in the Qing Dynasty. During Buddhist festivals and the Chinese Lunar New Year, tens of thousands of pilgrims arrive at Yufo Temple to burn incense sticks and pray. The temple also operates a restaurant that serves all sorts of vegetarian delicacies.

Tianjin

Dabei Temple 大悲禅院 (Dàbēi Chányuàn)

The Dabei (Mahakaruna) Temple on Tianwei Road in Hebei District is the only Buddhist temple of good size in Tianjin. It differs from its counterparts in that it is composed of two parts, the Old Temple and the New Temple, that are linked by a moon-shaped gate. Because Tianjin is a relatively young city, the Dabei Temple has a relatively short history. The Old Temple was built in 1661 in the Qing Dynasty and rebuilt in 1669. It went through major repairs in 1875 to assume its present form as a tripartite compound comprising the Gatehall, the Mahavira Hall and the Anterior Hall. The New Temple was built in the 1940s and is larger than the Old Temple. All the halls are linked with corridors. The major earthquake that hit Tangshan in 1976, and the 1966-1976 "cultural revolution" rendered great damage to the Dabei Temple. Renovated in the 1980s, the temple today operates two memorial halls, one of which is dedicated to the celebrated monk of the Tang Dynasty who founded the Ci'en School, Xuanzang, and part of his skull was enshrined here prior to 1956. The other is in memory of Hongyi, an eminent monk who happened to be a Tianjin native. The Tianjin Municipal Buddhist Association is also headquartered here.

Dule Temple 独乐寺 (Dúlè Sì)

The major attraction of the Dule Temple is clay statue of the Guanyin (Goddess of Mercy) built in 984 in the Liao Dynasty that stands 52 feet or 16 meters in height sheltered in a wood-framed pavilion under a roof with three-layered eaves. Its four walls are graced with murals that portray 16 arhats in lifelike images nearly six feet or two meters in height. These murals done during the Liao were later covered up with mortar, and it was not until 1971 that they were uncovered. Also known as "Temple of the Great Buddha," it is situated in the western gate of Jixian County, Tianjin Municipality. Most of the buildings of this temple were ruined during the 841-846 reign of Emperor Wuzong of the Tang. Some of the buildings were restored in 984 during the Liao Dynasty, and more buildings were added during the Ming and the Qing.

Chongqing

Luohan (Arhat) Temple 罗汉寺 (Luóhàn Sì)

Built during the Zhiping reign (1064-1066) of the Song Dynasty, the Luohan (Arhat) Temple at Minzu Road in the Central District, the temple is regarded by many pilgrims as an ancient Buddhist center although the elegant buildings of the temple that stands on the site today are a product of the last half century. Built and rebuilt several times before the Qing Dynasty, when it was quite an extensive complex, the temple was destroyed in an air raid by Japanese invaders in 1940. Only the compound of the Pavilion of Scripture Repository remains of the Qing complex. As its name suggests, the temple is the site of an arhats' cave and a hall of five hundred arhats.

Ciyun Temple 慈云寺 (Cíyún Sì)

The halls of Ciyuan (Cloud of Benevolence) Temple climb up the slopes of the Shizi (Lion) Mountain on the northern bank of the Yangtze River, where the Jialing River flows into it. Its predecessor was the tiny Guanyin Temple established during the Tang Dynasty. Rebuilt in 1757 in the Qing Dynasty, it was transformed in 1927 in a major construction project into a large temple and given its present name. The expansion project was done to accommodate the pilgrims who came and went by way of the harbor at the foot of the mountain on which the temple stood. Access to the Mahavira Hall behind the gatehall is up several flights of stone steps. Chinese architectural style is blended with a Western influence in this temple. Glazed-tile roofs with upturning eaves mingle with multi-floored chambers and terraces to create a formidable landmark that is set off nicely by the tumbling rivers. The man-made rockery behind the temple is built of numerous rocks of exotic shapes and images, and landscaped with a number of features, including a Pond of Eight Merits and a Lotus Pool, something that belongs only in the lore of Buddhism — an imitation of the pond in which nine dragons spit water to bathe the newborn baby who is to become Prince Siddhartha.

PROVINCES

Heilongjiang Province

Jile Temple 极乐寺 (Jílè Sì)

The Jile Temple is a major site of religious life for Harbin in northeast China and a popular tourist spot as well. The temple is a large affair founded in the 1920s by Tanxu (1875-1963), an important 20th century monk and a native of Ninghe County, Hebei Province, who was tonsured at the age of 43. During his lifetime he had a number of temples to his credit, and the Jile Temple was one of them. The architecture of Jile Temple is marked by an elegance that reveals no traces of ostentation. The pagoda outside the compound built in 1941 is dedicated to a number of bronze statues of the Buddha and bodhisattvas in stately images, and its walls are covered with murals. Four major halls form the centerpiece of the complex. In the Hall of Deva-kings is a 2.7-meter-high bronze statue of Maitreya; in the Mahavira Hall is a bronze sculpture of Sakyamuni, which is 3.34 meters high; in the Trinity Hall behind the Mahavira Hall are Maitreya, Guanyin and Mahasthamaprapta, also portrayed in bronze statues. Bringing up the rear of the complex is the Tripitaka Pavilion that houses a Qianlong edition of *Tripitaka* printed during the 1735-1738 period, an edition of *Tripitaka* engraved and printed in Qisha in present-day Wuxian County, Jiangsu Province in 1322, and the Kalavinka edition of *Tripitaka* of 1913.

Jilin Province

Banruo Temple 般若寺 (Bānruò Sì)

Built in the 1920s, the Banruo (Prajna) Temple in Changchun features massive bronze statues of Buddhas, bodhisattvas and the 18 arhats. It also features a likeness of Guanyin made of porcelain. The statue of Sakyamuni in the Mahavira Hall stands more than 9 feet or 3 meters tall, and the 18 arhats sitting beside him are about three feet or one meter tall. The ground floor of the two-story Tripitaka Pavilion is occupied by 1.51-meter-high statues of the Trinity of the West (Maitreya, Guanyin and Mahasthamaprapta), and against its side walls stand an array of cabinets that contain Buddhist scriptures; and the second floor is devoted to a four-foot or 1.5-meter-high silver stupa.

Liaoning Province

Ci'en Temple in Shenyang 沈阳慈恩寺 (Shěnyáng Cí'ēn Sì)

Situated in Shenhe District, Shenyang, the Ci'en Temple is a relatively old Buddhist establishment in northeast China. It is said to have been first built in the Tang Dynasty, rebuilt in 1628 the Ming, and repaired and expanded on a large scale in 1644 in the Qing. Then the temple fell into disrepair and was eventually deserted. It took eight years beginning from 1912 (the founding year of the Republic) to rebuild it. The temple boasts a 6,500-volume version of *Tripitaka,* as well as a host of cultural relics dating back to the years before the influence of the Manchus crossed the Shanhaiguan Pass and spread to north China. The Ci'en Temple today is the headquarters of the Shenyang Municipal Buddhist Association.

Hebei Province

Longxing Temple 隆兴寺 (Lóngxīng Sì)

Longxing Temple in Zhengding County is popularly known as the "Temple of the Great Buddha" for its giant Song-dynasty bronze statue of Guanyin with a thousand hands and a thousand eyes standing in its major architecture, the Moni (Mahavira) Hall. For its sheer size — some 65 feet or 22 meters in height — the bronze sculpture is a rarity in China. Established in 586 during the Sui Dynasty, the temple was expanded during the early Song Dynasty, and was expanded again and assumed its present name during the Qing. A horizontal board bearing the name "Emperor-Mandated Longxing Temple" in the handwriting of Emperor Kangxi of the Qing is hung on the lintel of the arched gate of the gatehall.

Bailin Temple 柏林寺 (Bǎilín Sì)

The Bailin Temple in Zhaoxian County was known as the "Convent of Guanyin" when it was first built during the Eastern Han Dynasty. Once it was the domain of Congnian, a Chan master who was revered as the "Venerable Buddha of Zhaozhou" for his accomplishments and prestige. Congnian was forced to live a hermit's life in the Culai Mountain when Buddhists were persecuted by Emperor Wuzong of the Tang during his 841-846 reign. He returned to the temple after Emperor Xuanzong took the throne and set about restoring Buddhism, and stayed there until he lived to a ripe old age of 120 years. The Bailin Temple was destroyed in war during the Five Dynasties (907-960), and was rebuilt during the early Song, but it was razed to the ground during the Republican years, leaving only a solitary pagoda standing. In recent years, under the auspices of the Hebei Provincial Buddhist Association, the temple has been gradually restored. It is emerging as a major Buddhist sanctuary in north China.

Henan Province

Baima Temple 白马寺 (Báimǎ Sì)

The Baima or White Horse Temple in Luoyang is considered the first temple in the history of Chinese Buddhism. Legend has it that in 64 AD, or the 7th year of the Yongping reign of the Han, Emperor Mingdi dreamed of seeing a golden man with light around his neck flying past his palace. The following day the emperor related what he saw in his dream to his court ministers and asked them to interpret what this was all about. One minister answered that what His Majesty had seen was actually the god of the West whose name was Buddha. The emperor immediately dispatched an 18-member mission headed by Cai Yin to travel to the west in search of the truth of the Buddha. In 67 AD , the Indian monks Kasyapamatanga and Dharmaranya arrived in China. While they settled down in the Temple of Grand Celebrations, the emperor had the White Horse Temple built for them as a studio to translate Buddhist scriptures into Chinese. The White Horse Temple was a center for scriptural translators during the period from the Han to the Three Kingdoms period, and reached its heyday during the Tang as its halls looked resplendent in pomp and pageantry and there was a big population of three thousand monks. The temple is a veritable treasure house of cultural relics and sites of historical interest that today probably retains its size and layout as constructed in the Ming Dynasty (1368-1644). Visitors will find a treasure-trove of relics at White Horse Temple.

Shaolin Temple 少林寺 (Shàolín Sì)

Shaolin Temple, located not far from Zhengzhou, the capital of Henan Province, and Luoyang, was built in 495 under the patronage of Emperor Xiaowen of the Northern Wei Dynasty to accommodate a visiting Indian monk. Like most early temples, the Shaolin Temple during its 1,500 years of history has gone through many ups and downs — at times a vast and thriving establishment at others in decline and abandonment. Tradition ascribes the beginnings of the Shaolin Temple to the Indian monk Bodhidharma who came to China and lived in the Shaolin Temple early in the 6th century. It is said that Bodhidharma developed a set of exercises for the monks to practice after their long periods of meditation, and that this formed the basis of modern-day China's Shaolin martial arts and Japanese karate. However, according to Li Tianji (1914-1996), the modern martial arts master, in his book *A Guide to Chinese Martial Arts*, published by the Foreign Languages Press, there is no evidence that Bodhidharma ever stayed in Shaolin Temple for any length of time or that he knew anything about martial arts. Nevertheless, historical material does suggest that almost immediately after its founding, self-defense or some other form of physical training became a part of life at the temple. And physical evidence of the monk's martial arts does still exist in the sunken areas of the stone floor of the temple where they stood for hours to practice. By the end of the Sui Dynasty (581-618), the outstanding combat skills of the Shaolin monks became well known after Li Shimin, prince of Qin who later became Emperor Taizong of Tang, called on Shaolin monks to help him defeat his military rival, Wang Shichong at Luoyang. This historical fact became the basis for the story told in the film, *Shaolin Temple*, produced in the early 1980s starring China's national *wushu* team headed by Li Lianjie who later became the film star known in the West as Jet Li. Thanks in part to the popularity of this film both in China and abroad, many martial arts schools have sprung up in recent years near the Shaolin Temple, making it once more a true center of martial arts practice. The Shaolin Temple also has 250 tomb pagodas of various sizes, making it the biggest pagoda forest — as groups of pagodas are known — in China. The pagodas, dating from 791 to 1803, all carry the exact year of construction and many carvings and inscriptions. A good time to visit the temple might be during Zhengzhou's annual International Martial Arts Conference and Competition that attracts participants from all over the world. [The martial arts also have strong links with Daoism. The *yin-yang* symbol frequently associated with martial arts as practiced in the West, for instance, is a Daoist *taiji* symbol.]

Xiangguo Temple 相国寺 (Xiàngguó Sì)

Most of the structures of this temple are a legacy of the Qing, the last feudal dynasty of China, although the site has a much earlier history. A temple was established here in 555 in the Northern Qi Dynasty (550-577), then destroyed in war. After it was rebuilt during the Tang, the famous Japanese monk Kukai (774-835) settled for a while in the Xiangguo Temple during a tour of China to study Buddhism. In the early Song Dynasty, the Xiangguo Temple was expanded to become a complex of eight courtyards. During the Chenghua reign (1465-1487) of the Ming, the temple was named "Chongfa", but soon afterwards was inundated along with the city of Kaifeng when the Yellow River overflowed its banks. The temple resumed its present name when it was rebuilt in 1661, but it again underwent major reconstruction during the Qianlong reign (1736-1795) of the Qing Dynasty. Outstanding among the Buddhist sculptures of this temple is one carved out of a huge gingko tree trunk in four images of Guanyin with a thousand hands and a thousand eyes that each face one of the four directions.

Hubei Province

Guiyuan Temple 归元寺 (Guīyuán Sì)

The Guiyuan Temple at Cuiwei Road in Hanyang District, Wuhan has a relatively short history. Built in the 17th century in the Qing Dynasty, it was destroyed when the Taiping Heavenly Kingdom troops attacked Wuchang in 1852. It was later restored only to be razed to the ground once again by the gunfire of the Qing army during the 1911 Revolution. After the war quieted down, it was repaired and restored once again. A main feature of the temple is its Hall of 500 Arhats in which the sculptures in their expressions are imbued with a lifelike quality. On display in this temple are a good assortment of precious cultural artifacts that have been collected in the last three centuries.

Baotong Temple 宝通寺 (Bǎotōng Sì)

The heyday of Baotong Temple, situated on the southern side of the Hongshan Mountain, came during the Yongzheng reign (1723-1735) of the Qing, when the temple had a total population of 1,500 monks with six major halls, some 100 other buildings, and 12 meditation chambers. But all this was destroyed in an attack of Wuchang in 1852 by the Taiping Heavenly Kingdom troops. Originally known as the "Eastern Rock Pavilion," the temple was built during the Zhenguan reign (627-649) of the Tang; expanded and renamed "Chongning Wanshou Temple" during the Song; reduced to a pile of ruins during the war in 1356 in the Yuan Dynasty; and rebuilt during the Ming (1368-1644) when it assumed its present name, Baotong Temple. The buildings on the premises today are a legacy of the Guangxu reign (1875-1908) of the Qing Dynasty. Standing on the mountain behind the temple is the Baotong Pagoda, a seven-story octagonal structure with a masonry interior and an exterior built of stone and brick. It was built in 1270 and rebuilt in 1332 during the Yuan Dynasty. Access to the top of the pagoda is by a staircase built inside, which commands an all-encapsulating view of Wuhan. The temple is the site of the Wuchang Buddhist Seminary.

Hunan Province

Kaifu Temple 开福寺 (Kāifú Sì)

The buildings of Kaifu Temple outside the northern city gate of Changsha were constructed in the 1920s, the latest in a long line of reincarnations for a temple that was first built in 927 in the Tang Dynasty. The temple was first rebuilt during the Jiayou reign (1059-1063) of the Song Dynasty, and rebuilt twice during the Ming, only to be destroyed in war towards the end of that Dynasty. Reconstruction was done twice (in 1660 and 1669), but the temple was burned down in a major fire and rebuilt again in 1772. Major repairs and restoration were done in 1887 but was burned down once again in 1920. The temple was restored thanks to the efforts of two monks, Huixiu and Baosheng. A stone archway rises in front of the gatehall, and along the axial line are the three major halls — the Maitreya Hall, the Mahavira Hall and the Vairocana Hall — which are flanked to the east by guest rooms, the dining hall, the monks' dormitories, and the abbot's residence, and to the west by the preaching hall, the meditation hall and the incantation chamber. The entire layout is neat and well conceived, with the courtyards linked with corridors and fronted with porticos. In front of the temple is a pond, known in old times as "Blue Wave Lake," into which captive aquatic animals are released to freedom.

Lushan Temple 麓山寺 (Lùshān Sì)

The Lushan Temple, which stands on the Yuelu Mountain on the western bank of the Xiangjiang River of Changsha, is popular destination for both pilgrims and tourists, located in an area with many scenes and sites associated with the Buddhist culture. Built in 268, in its early years, the temple covered a vast track of field, with its gatehall standing right by the river at the foot of the mountain, and its main buildings extending from the foot to the top of the mountain. This magnificent complex, however, was demolished during Tang Emperor Wuzong's crackdown on Buddhism. When it was rebuilt towards the end of the Tang, the temple lost much of its former size, and many of its old halls were never rebuilt again. The temple suffered repeated destruction during the Song, Yuan and Ming dynasties but was restored after each major destruction. In 1944, most of the buildings of the temple were destroyed during a Japanese air raid. In recent years the Changsha Municipal Buddhist Association pooled money to restore the temple to turn it into a new scenic attraction. Quite a few famous men are associated with 1,700-year history of Lushan Temple. One of them was the monk Dacheng, who successfully disseminated the doctrines of Chan Buddhism from south China to Tibet after he debated with the famed Indian monk Kamalasila (730-800) for three years, an event which came down in Buddhist history as the "Lhasa Debate on the Dharma."

Guangdong Province

Nanhua Temple 南华寺 (Nánhuá Sì)

Nanhua Temple in Qujiang County, Guangdong Province is known as the birthplace of the Chan School of Han Buddhism. [See 4. Chan (Zen) School, Chapter 3]

Guangxiao Temple 光孝寺 (Guāngxiào Sì)

The Guangxiao Temple on Hongshu Road North, Guangzhou, first built during the Three Kingdoms period (220-265), is where Huineng (499-569), the sixth patriarch of Chan Buddhism, became a novice and received his ordination. Starting in the Eastern Jin (317-420) Indian monks lived here and translated Buddhist scriptures, including the eminent Gunabhadra (394-468) and Paramartha (499-569). After the Southern Song (1127-1279), the temple was renamed repeatedly, until it finally assumed the name in 1151 that has remained to this day. Covering an area of over 30,000 square meters, the Guangxiao Temple once had 12 major halls, six chambers as well as the bell and drum towers and a Sleeping Buddha Pavilion. Some of these buildings, however, gradually crumbled and fell into disrepair with the passage of time. Only the Mahavira Hall, the Hall of the Sixth Patriarch, the Samgharama Hall, and the Hall of Deva-kings are still there today, which combine with a vast collection of cultural relics and quite a few sites of historical interest to justify the temple's fame as the oldest Buddhist sanctuary in Guangzhou. During holidays, the temple is always crowded with visitors.

Liurong Temple 六榕寺 (Liùróng Sì)

The Mahavira Hall in Liurong Temple houses three six-meter-high imposing bronze Buddhist statues of great cultural value. The temple also has bronze sculpture of Huineng, the sixth patriarch and founder of the Chan School of Han Buddhism. Although the halls of the Liurong Temple were built in recent years, the temple traces its history back 1,400 years ago during the Liang Dynasty (502-557). The original temple was burned down in the early years of the Northern Song and rebuilt in 989. In 1100, the celebrated Song Dynasty man of letters, Su Shi (also known as Su Dongpo), was delighted to see six banyan trees growing in the compound during a visit to the temple. He wrote in calligraphy the two Chinese characters, *liu rong,* meaning "Six Banyan Trees," and presented the inscription as a gift to the temple. The monks thus renamed their temple "Liurong Temple." In the center of the complex there used to be a pagoda built during the Liang Dynasty that was later destroyed. During the Song Dynasty, a 57-meter-high nine-story octagonal pagoda, named the Flower Pagoda, was built, which is still there today.

Shandong Province

Xingguo Temple 兴国禅寺 (Xīngguó Chánsì)

The Xingguo Temple that perches half way up the Qianfo Mountain in the southern part of Jinan is a favorite with tourists not only for the temple and its grottoes, but also for its pleasant scenery. Access to this temple is up a stone stairway of more than 300 steps. The southern wall of the temple is elevated on the top of a cliff, into which a beehive of caves have been hollowed out, with Buddhist statues enshrined in those caves at the foot of the cliff. This is none other than the well-known Thousand-Buddha Grottoes that has been there for more than 1,400 years. Many of the statues in these caves were crafted during the Zhenguan reign (627-649) of the Tang, and some 130 of them are still in good shape today, under protection as a site of foremost historical interest in Shandong province. When it was established during the Kaihuang reign (581-604) of the Sui, however, it was known by another name: Qianfo (Thousand-Buddha) Temple. Only after it was rebuilt during the Zhenguan reign of the Tang that it was given its present name. It was expanded during the Song (960-1279), only to be destroyed by war in the early Ming. Reconstruction of it took place in 1468 (4th year of Chenghua reign, Ming). After the Jiaqing reign (1796-1820) of the Qing, new halls were added, until the temple grew into an impressive affair with seven major halls and four courtyards. The layout is formal and the architecture imposing.

Zhanshan Temple 湛山寺 (Zhànshān Sì)

The Zhanshan Temple was built in modern times. Sitting on the southwest foot of the Zhanshan Mountain and facing the sea in the east of Qingdao, the temple itself is a popular tourist attraction. Its front gate is guarded by a pair of chiseled stone lions that once belonged to the mansion of the Prince of Qingzhou of the Ming. Its buildings, including the Hall of Deva-kings, the Mahavira Hall, the Trinity Hall, and the Tripitaka Pavilion on the axial line, copy Ming structures that form a mingled picture of architectural pomp and religious solemnity. The two-story Tripitaka Pavilion houses a Qianlong version of the *Tripitaka* on the ground floor and a Buddhist bone relic on the second floor. The brick pagoda outside the temple is a seven-floored octagonal structure, with a staircase conducting to three of these floors that offer a picturesque view of the seascape.

Jiangsu Province

Qixia Temple 栖霞寺 (Qīxiá Sì)

Qixia Temple in the Qixia Mountain in the suburbs of Nanjing, Jiangsu Province is known as the birthplace of the Sanlun School of Han Buddhism. (See 2. Sanlun School, Chapter 3)

Longchang Temple 隆昌寺 (Lóngchāng Sì)

Longchang Temple on Baohua Mountain north of Jurong County and about 50 miles east of Nanjing, known as the birthplace of the Vinaya School of Han Buddhism. (See 6. Vinaya School, Chapter 3)

Jiangtian Temple 江天寺 (Jiāngtiān Sì)

Popularly known as Jinshan Temple as it sits atop the Jinshan Hill in the suburbs of Zhenjiang, a city by the Yangtze River, the temple is cleverly tucked away along the contours of the hill in the depth of the woods so that its buildings cannot be seen from a distance, However, close at hand, they emerge as magnificent buildings while the hill itself recedes. The temple was first built as the Zexin Temple in 325, eight years after the founding of the Eastern Jin Dynasty, and its prestige is associated with its having been the domain of Foyin, a celebrated monk of the Song Dynasty. The temple was renamed "Longyou Temple" during the Tianxi reign (1017-1021) of the Song, and during one of his south China tours, Emperor Kangxi of the Qing changed it into the present name. The Jinshan Hill used to be a small island on the Yangtze River, but during the Qing Dynasty, the river course gradually silted up into a peninsula. The temple area is studded with scenic spots and sites of historical and cultural value. Among the major ones: 1) the Cishou Pagoda built during the Liang Dynasty (502-557), a seven-story structure poised atop the Jinshan Hill with staircases providing access to each of its seven floors; 2) the Fahai Cave, the dwelling of Fahai, the legendary monk who was endowed with divine power who once dug up gold from underneath the hill and used it to rebuild the temple; 3) the Miaogao Terrace, also known as the "Sutra Sunning Terrace," reportedly built by the famous Song monk Foyin; 4) the Lanka Terrace, also known as "Sujing Altar", which was built during the Qiandao reign (1165-1173) of the Southern Song; and 5) Liuyun Terrace, also called "Pavilion to See the River and the Sky at a Glance", which is perched on the northern corner of the hilltop to command a scenic overview of the surroundings.

Dinghui Temple 定慧寺 (Dìnghuì Sì)

The Dinghui Temple, located on the Jiaoshan Isle on the Yangtze River to the northeast of Zhenjiang, has retained its Ming-dynasty layout and architectural style in a place of picture-perfect landscape and pleasant climate. Whenever emperors Kangxi and Qianlong of the Qing Dynasty sailed down the Beijing-Hangzhou Grand Canal on a south China tour, they never fail to stop over at the Jiaoshan Hill. Originally built as the Puji Convent in 194 in the Eastern Han, the temple changed names and form various times over history, with the addition of a good number of halls. During the Ming Dynasty, the temple became a major Buddhist sanctuary south of the Yangtze.

Tianning Temple 天宁寺 (Tiānníng Sì)

The Tianning Temple in Changzhou, founded as "Guangfu Temple" in the Tang Dynasty and given its present name in 1111 in the Song Dynasty, was considered in its heyday the No. 1 temple in southeast China for its size — its halls, chambers and pavilions totaling more than 500 bays. The buildings at the site today were built during the Qing, including the Mahavira Hall, the Vajra Hall, the Samantabhadra Hall, the Manjusri Hall, the Guanyin Hall and the Arhats' Chamber. The 500 arhats of the temple are a rare example of high artistic attainment and lifelike images.

Zhejiang Province

Guoqing Temple 国庆寺 (Guóqìng Sì)

Guoqing Temple, about 100 miles south of Ningbo in Zhejiang Province, is known as the birthplace of the Tiantai School of Han Buddhism. (See 1. Tiantai School, Chapter 3)

Lingyin Temple 灵隐寺 (Língyǐn Sì)

One of the largest Buddhist temples in southeast China and a national cultural treasure, the 1,600-year-old Temple of the Soul's Retreat in Hangzhou, Zhejiang Province is nestled in the woods across from a hill with over 300 rock carvings dating from between the 10th and 14th centuries, important examples of sculptural art in south China. The original temple is said to have been built in 326 by the Indian monk, Huili, whose remains are contained in the some nine-meter-high, hexagonal seven-storied Monk Huili Pagoda, rebuilt in 1590, near the entrance to the temple grounds. Ruined and rebuilt many times over the centuries, Lingyin Temple went under large-scale construction in the 10th century when the ruler of the Wuyue State Kingdom in the Five Dynasties period was converted to Buddhism. At that time the temple boasted nine towers, 18 pavilions, over 72 halls and 1,300 rooms for 3,000 monks. The present temple structures, including its two main halls — the Hall of the Four Heavenly Kings in the front and behind it the main Mahavira Hall from the Qing Dynasty, were extensively restored in the early 1950s. The statue of Sakyamuni in the Mahavira Hall is some 56 feet or 19.6 meters high and carved from 24 blocks of camphor wood, constructed by folk artists and sculptors from the Zhejiang Fine Arts Institute. Based on a carving from the Tang Dynasty, it is twice as high as the original statue and towers over visitors in the hall. Behind this stature is a sculpture of the Guanyin Mountain, with a likeness of Guanyin sitting in a cave, Sudhana and the 53 wise ones mentioned in the *Huayin Sutra* occupying every rock on the mountain. Along the side walls of the Mahavira Hall are arrayed the sculptures of the 20 devas in lifelike images. During the "cultural revolution", some rock carvings suffered minor damage but the temple was spared serious destruction after Premier Zhou Enlai ordered the place closed and protected.

Jingci Temple 净慈寺 (Jìngcí Sì)

The Jingci (Pure Compassion) Temple, at the foot of the Nanping Mountain by the West Lake in Hangzhou, has been built and rebuilt several times, beginning in 954 in the Late Zhou of the Five Dynasties period. By the Southern Song (1127-1279) it had acquired a sizeable scale with 32 halls, chambers and pavilions and a population of more than 1,000 monks. What remain of the Jingci Temple today are three halls, among which the Mahavira Hall was rebuilt in recent years. To the west of the temple is the "Well for Timber Transportation." As legend has it, when Monk Daoji was rebuilding the temple during the Song, he had all the timber shipped in from below this well, and the last piece of it still remains inside it today.

Seven-Pagoda Temple 七塔寺 (Qī tǎ Sì)

The Seven-Pagoda Temple just east of downtown Ningbo is special in that its Mahavira Hall is the domain of Guanyin with a Thousand Hands, rather than Sakyamuni. Pilgrims often make it a point to stop by and pay homage to the Seven-Pagoda Temple before crossing the sea to visit the island, Mount Putuo, one of the four sacred Buddhist mountains. Founded in 858 in the Tang Dynasty, it has been built and rebuilt several times. The temple as it stands today was the result of reconstruction during the Guangxu reign of the Qing Dynasty, following its destruction in the Heavenly Kingdom Peasant Uprising. Its immense complex of lofty buildings include the Hall of Deva-kings, the Trinity Hall, the Mahavira Hall, the Jade Buddha Chamber, the Huayan Chamber, the Scripture Repository, and the Cloud-and-Water Hall.

Tiantong Temple 天童寺 (Tiāntóng Sì)

The Tiantong Temple at the foot of the Taibai Mountain in Yinxian County is known for its scenic beauty. This temple started out as a monk's thatched hermitage in the Tang Dynasty and in 1979, with the support of the People's Government, the temple underwent large-scale repairs, and emerged as a major Buddhist temple in southeast China. The buildings renovated were themselves the results of reconstruction during the Qing Dynasty. It boasts an impressive trove of cultural artifacts.

Anhui Province

Mingjiao Temple 明教寺 (Míngjiào Sì)

The Mingjiao Temple in downtown Hefei has a history dating back to the Tianjian reign (503-519) of the Liang Dynasty. But like other temples of such age, it has been ruined and rebuilt several times. Initially called Tiefo (Iron Buddha) Temple, it was renamed "Mingjiao Temple" during the Ming Dynasty. The temple crumbled in war and turmoil in 1853 but was later gradually restored. The Mahavira Hall and the Posterior Hall have retained their original forms dating back to 1886.

Yingjiang Temple 迎江寺 (Yíngjiāng Sì)

One of the famous Buddhist sanctuaries in Anhui Province, The Yingjiang (River-Greeting) Temple stands by the Yangtze River in the city of Anqing. First built in 974, it was rebuilt in 1892 to attain its present size with five main buildings (the Hall of

Deva-kings, Mahavira Hall, Zhenfeng Pagoda, Vairocana Hall, and Tripitaka Pavilion) that combine with the Yiyuan Garden, the Dashi Pavilion, the Ciyun Pavilion, the Riverside Chamber, and the Garden of Miniature Landscapes to form something that is both a solemn religious sanctuary and a scenic resort. The gatehall of the Yingjiang Temple is flanked by a pair of iron anchors weighing three tons apiece. The temple's seven-story Zhenfeng Pagoda, with a staircase installed inside it, is an 82-meter-high octagonal structure that commands a good view of the Yangtze and the city of Anqing.

Shanxi Province

Xuanzhong Temple 玄中寺 (Xuánzhōng Sì)

Xuanzhong Temple, nestled at the foot of Shibi Mountain in Jiaocheng County, Shanxi Province, known as the birthplace of the Pure Land School of Han Buddhism. (See 7. Pure Land School, Chapter 3)

Jiangxi Province

Youmin Temple 佑民寺 (Yòumín Sì)

The Youmin Temple has played a major role in the history of the Chan School of Chinese Buddhism. After the celebrated monk Mazu (709-788) achieved enlightenment as a disciple of the Chan master Huairang (677-744) in Mt. Hengshan, known as the "Sacred Mountain in the South" and arrived in Hongzhou in present-day Nanchang, he settled in the Youmin Temple (called "Kaiyuan Temple" in the Tang time) and devoted himself to preaching the Chan discipline. He eventually acquired a following of more than 130 disciples, who helped spread Huairang's theories in the Yangtze River valley to form a school of their own — the Hongzhou School of Chinese Buddhism with the Youmin Temple as its cradle. The predecessor of the Youmin Temple in Nanchang was the Dafo (Great Buddha) Temple founded in 547 in the Liang Dynasty. It burned down and was rebuilt during the Shunzhi reign (1644-1661) of the Qing Dynasty. It was not until the Republican years that it assumed its present name. Only a few buildings at Youmin Temple today are a Qing legacy, the others were built in recent years. The temple is situated in a place of fabulous scenic beauty, with the clear waters of the Nanhu Lake right beside it, a popular spot for tourists on weekends and during holidays. It is also the headquarters of the Jiangxi Provincial Buddhist Association.

Donglin Temple 东林寺 (Dōnglín Sì)

The Donglin Temple on Mount Lushan, Jiangxi Province, was founded more than 1,600 years ago by Huiyuan (334-416), a renowned monk of the Eastern Jin Dynasty. It had its heyday during the Tang Dynasty when it emerged as a colossal establishment with more than 300 halls and dormitories. The temple was ruined during the Shaoxing reign (1131-1162) of the Song Dynasty, and rebuilt once during the Ming Dynasty and twice during the Qing. Some of the buildings on the premises were built during the Ming and Qing dynasties, and the others were constructed in recent years. The Donglin Temple was converted into a cradle of the Pure Land School of Han Buddhism thanks to the efforts of Huiyuan, who gathered 123 disciples under him to form the White Lotus Society. For his high moral integrity, Huiyuan was highly esteemed and counted among his friends, including the famous poet Tao Yuanming (365-427) and the great man of letter Xie Lingyun (385-433). During Huiyuan's more than three decades of stay in Mount Lushan, it is said: "His person never moved out of the mountain, and his footprints were never found in the mundane world." He also never went beyond the Tiger Stream in front of the temple whenever he was sending off a guest — except once, an occasion celebrated in the story, "Three Laughs over the Tiger Stream." Once upon a time, Tao Yuanming and Lu Xiujing, another man of letters at the time, arrived at Mount Lushan and joined Huiyuan in a discussion about Buddhism, Confucianism, and Daoism. An entire day passed quickly. When Huiyuan was walking his two friends out of the temple and sending them off, they continued their discussion. In no time they had crossed the Tiger Stream, and it was not until the God of Tiger started howling that Huiyuan realized that he had violated his own taboo. He could not help laughing loudly.

Nengren Temple 能仁寺 (Néngrén Sì)

Nengren Temple in the east of Jiujiang hosts a number of historical and cultural sites, including a seven-story hexahedronal brick-and-masonry pagoda with a door built into each of its six sides (but three of them are merely ornamental), with a stone stairway inside to its top floor. Today's temple was preceded by a number of temples over the dynasties, starting with a temple named "Chengtian" that was established during the Liang Dynasty (502-557), rebuilt during the Dali reign (766-779) of the Tang Dynasty, destroyed by troops during the Yuan Dynasty, and rebuilt again in 1379 (12th year, Hongwu reign, Ming Dynasty). The temple assumed its present name in 1489. More buildings were erected during the Chongzhen reign (1628-1644) of the Ming, but it collapsed once again in war in 1853 in the Qing Dynasty. It was rebuilt in 1870 and has remained largely intact since. Along the axial line are three courtyards containing the Hall of Deva-kings, the Mahavira Hall and the Tripitaka Pavilion respectively, with the anterooms serving as the patriarch's hall, the preaching hall, the abbot's mansion, and the monks' residential quarters. The entire complex is laid out according to an impeccable plan.

Fujian Province

South Putuo Temple 南普陀寺 (Nánpǔtuó Sì)

The South Putuo Temple in Xiamen (Amoy) was originally the Puzhao Temple established during the Tang Dynasty. It was renamed "Sizhou Monastery" when it was reconstructed during the Five Dynasties (907-960), but was restored to its original name during the Song. It was destroyed during the Yuan. When it was rebuilt again during the Hongwu reign (1368-1398) of the Ming, an Avalokitesvara Hall was added to it, but all this was burned down towards the end of the Ming. Because the temple is situated south of Mount Putuo in Zhejiang Province, it was renamed "South Putuo Temple" after it was reconstructed during the Kangxi reign (1662-1722) of the Qing. The temple enjoyed its peak of popularity during the 1920s and the 1930s, when the Southern Fujian Buddhist Seminary headquartered in the temple turned out large numbers of monks. The seminary was forced to close down after Japan invaded China in 1937, and was not reopened until recent years. A good number of new structures have been added over the last few years, turning the South Putuo Temple into the foremost Buddhist sanctuary in Xiamen. On any given day the temple is crowded with visitors.

Yongquan Temple 涌泉寺 (Yǒngquán Sì)

The Yongquan (Gurgling Spring) Temple on the Gushan Mountain in the eastern suburbs of Fuzhou is another famous Buddhist establishment in Fujian Province. Significant expansions were made during the Qing Dynasty so that despite the temple's 1,000-year long history, the buildings remaining of it are mostly a Qing legacy. The temple is hailed as a fine example of classic Chinese architecture. All its main structure — the Hall of the Deva-kings, the Mahavira Hall and the Preaching Hall — as well as its ancillary halls and domiciles are integrated by a labyrinth of corridors to form a gigantic engineering complex that covers the entire length of a mountainside. Among the Yongquan Temple's collection of precious artifacts are three renowned treasures: a fireproof almsgiving table made of iron wiring and wood that dampens whenever it is raining; a 1,000-year-old *sago cycas* (*Cycas revolute*) that blossoms every year, and 657 volumes of Buddhist scriptures written in blood. The picturesque mountains around the temple are favorite tourist destinations. The name of the temple, which was founded during the Five Dynasties, is derived from a spring in front of it. In 999 during the Song Dynasty, Emperor Zhenzong bestowed a nameboard in his own handwriting on the temple, calling it "Gurgling Spring Temple on the White Peak of the Gushan Mountain." During the Ming Dynasty the name was abbreviated as "Yongquan (Gurgling Spring) Temple." During the period from 1408 to 1542 during the Ming, the temple caught fire twice, but on both occasions it was rebuilt.

Sichuan Province

Wenshu Monastery 文殊院 (Wénshū Yuàn)

The Wenshu (Manjusri) Monastery in Chengdu is a major Buddhist sanctuary in Sichuan, impressive for its careful layout and the classic forms of its 200-odd buildings, including main halls and monastic residential quarters, which are uniform carpentry-masonry structures. Its predecessor was the Xinxiang Temple founded during the Sui Dynasty, a temple that was expanded during the Song, only to crumble in war and turmoil towards the end of the Ming . When the temple was rebuilt in 1697 (36th year, Kangxi reign, Qing Dynasty), a horizontal nameboard was bestowed on it inscribed in Emperor Kangxi's personal calligraphy. A few years ago, a pagoda was erected there, the "Thousand-Buddha Pagoda of Peace," and 999 Buddhist figurines are carved into the stone walls of each of its 11 floors.

Baoguang Temple 宝光寺 (Bǎoguāng Sì)

Baoguang (Precious Light) Temple in Xindu County a few miles from downtown Chengdu as it stands today was rebuilt in 1670 in the Qing Dynasty, an impressive complex that contains a pagoda, five main halls and 16 compounds, covering a total area of 80,000 square meters. The centerpiece consists of the Hall of Deva-kings, the Sarira (Relic) Pagoda, the Seven-Buddha Hall, the Mahavira Hall and the Tripitaka Pavilion. All the side rooms and quadrangles are connected by corridors. The magnitude of the entire cluster is vastly enhanced by an ocean of roofs covered with green-glazed tiles and decorated with vermilion-painted eaves. Originally the temple was established during the Han Dynasty, and legend has it that Emperor Xizong of the late Tang Dynasty took refuge here when the capital city of Chang'an fell into the hands of peasant rebels led by Huang Chao. One night during his stay in the temple, the emperor espied light emitting from a Buddhist bone relic enshrined in one of its halls, and he issued the instruction to give the temple a new name: Baoguang Temple, meaning the "Temple of Precious Light." During the Song Dynasty, it was once renamed "Dajue (Great Enlightenment) Temple." Towards the end of the Ming Dynasty it was razed to the ground in war. On public display in the temple are a vast collection of precious scrolls of calligraphy, Chinese religious paintings, and other valuable artifacts.

Guizhou Province

Hongfu Temple 宏福寺 (Hóngfú Sì)

Hongfu Temple, on the Qianling Mountain just west of

downtown Guiyang, sits in the sequestered repose of towering trees that have been around for ages, and draws droves of pilgrims and travelers from all over the world on a yearly basis. Originally built in 1672 in the Qing Dynasty, the temple acquired its present size after repeated repairs and expansions. During the decade-long chaos of the "cultural revolution" (1966-1976), the Hongfu Temple fell victim to wonton vandalism. The temple as we see it today were restored to its former glory in 1978, with the support of the local government and the donations of Buddhists from all walks of life. In each of the halls a complete array of deities of the Buddhist pantheon are presented in finely crafted statues. A Qianlong edition of the *Tripitaka* is found in the collection of scriptures of the Tripitaka Pavilion. The vicinity of the temple has many sites of cultural interest, including the Unicorn Cave, the Old Buddha Cave, the Alms Bowl Washing Pool on the Qianling Mountain, and the "Holy Spring" behind the mountain.

Yunnan Province

Yuantong Temple 圆通寺 (Yuántōng Sì)

The Yuantong Temple in Kunming had its origin in the Butuoluo Temple founded during the Nanzhao period (738-902). During the period from Yuan Dynasty, the temple was reconstructed and given its present name, and a new Guanyin Hall was added to it. Repeated repairs were done during the Ming and Qing dynasties. According to historical records, the Yuantong Temple once was converted into a Daoist temple for a brief period, and as a result both Buddhist and Daoist influences are felt in some buildings, stele inscriptions, and religious statues. The topography of the Yuantong Temple is unusual; few temples in China are built the way it is with its front towering over its back down a mountain slope. In other words, one can peep through its front gate and get a panoramic view of the entire temple . As behooves Kunming — city where it is spring all the year round — the Yuantong Temple includes landscaping that turns the place into both a religious center and a botanical garden of blossoming flowers and green trees.

Huating Temple 华亭寺 (Huátíng Sì)

The Huating Temple, 15 kilometers to the southwest of Kunming, is tucked away in an ocean of bamboo groves in Kunming's Western Hill Scenic Resort, with its glazed-tile rooftops gleaming in an orderly way among cypresses and pines. The Huating Mountain rises in the background and the vast Dianchi Lake extends an arm right beyond the front gate. No one is sure when the temple was first established. It is known, however, that the first reconstruction dates back to 1320 in the Yuan Dynasty. The temple was rebuilt once again and renamed "Greater Yuantong Temple" during the Jingtai reign (1450-1456) of the Ming, only to succumb to a major fire towards the end of that dynasty. During the Qing Dynasty, it was rebuilt in 1687, destroyed in 1857, and restored again in 1883. In 1922, the temple received a major facelift when its old halls were refurbished and more halls built, and for a time it was called "Yunqi Monastery for the Stabilization of the Country."

Shaanxi Province

Huayan Temple 华严寺 (Huáyán Sì)

Huayan Temple in Chang'an County near the city of Xi'an, (See 3. Huayan School, Chapter 3)

Ci'en Temple 慈恩寺 (Cí'ēn Sì)

Ci'en Temple in the city of Xi'an, known as the birthplace of the Ci'en (Vinnanavada) school. (See 4. Ci'en School, Chapter 3)

Great Xingshan Temple 大兴善寺 (Dàxīngshàn Sì)

Great Xingshan Temple in the city of Xi'an, known as the birthplace of the Esoteric School of Han Buddhism. (See 8. Esoteric School, Chapter 3)

Wolong Temple 卧龙寺 (Wòlóng Sì)

The Wolong Temple in Xi'an, which dates back to the Han Dynasty, was the Fuying Chan Monastery during the Sui Dynasty and the Guanyin Temple during the Tang. In the founding year of the Song Dynasty in 960, it became the Wolong Temple, named after Wuiguo, the abbot and celebrated monk who styled himself as "Wolong (Sleeping-Dragon) Monk." In the past the Wolong Temple was an enormous complex rebuilt during the Ming Dynasty. By the Qing Dynasty, it had emerged as the leading Buddhist sanctuary of Xi'an. During the Republican years it suffered major destruction until it was rebuilt in 1931. The Wolong Temple as it is today is a compound of dignified halls with a methodical layout.

Xingjiao Temple 兴教寺 (Xīngjiào Sì)

The Xingjiao Temple, or Temple for Promoting Buddhism, was founded in 669 in Shaoling Tableland on the outskirts of Xi'an when Emperor Gaozong of the Tang Dynasty had the tomb of the monk Xuanzang moved there and a temple and a pagoda built in memory of this great Buddhist master (See 4. Ci'en School, Chapter 3). The emperor named it "Great Tang Temple for Protecting the Country and Promoting Buddhism." However, the temple fell into disrepair later until it was restored in 828. It again fell into dilapidation during the war-torn Tongzhi reign (1862-1874) of the Qing Dynasty, and was rebuilt in 1922. After the founding of the People's Republic of China, the People's Government had the temple repaired on two occasions, enabling it to emerge as one of the major Buddhist sanctuaries in China. Xingjiao Temple is also noted for a Burmese jade statue of the Buddha. The temple boasts more than 10,000 volumes of Buddhist canons, and many other precious cultural artifacts. A series of stone tablets in it are inscribed with the full text of the *Diamond Sutra*. Standing in front of it are three pagodas. The Xuanzang Pagoda in the center of the cluster is a five-floor structure with a statue of Xuanzang enshrined on the ground floor. The two flanking pagodas are dedicated to Xuanzang's two famous disciples, Kuiji and Yuance.

Caotang Temple 草堂寺 (Cǎotáng Sì)

Caotang Temple in Huxian County southwest of Xi'an City, houses a Tang-dynasty pagoda said to have been built for the remains of Kumarajiva (344-413), the noted translator of Buddhist classics and eminent monk of the Later Qin Dynasty. The pagoda has a special structure. Although a pavilion-style pagoda, it has a base in the shape of mountains and waves and its pedestal is carved with designs of waves. Its lower base, in the shape of a lotus flower carved with designs of waves, supports the octagonal pavilion-style main body. A door and windows with straight lattices are sculptured on its sides. The roof is formed by four square sections, and under the eaves are engraved, vivid images of flying Apsaras. The pagoda's steeple also has its own unique style. The plain base is carved into huge petals of lotus-like flowers for supporting a huge oblate bead. The whole structure of the pagoda and its carvings are vigorous and graceful. The pagoda's main body is carved from jade of eight colors — white, greenish, black, bright yellow, reddish, light blue, purple and dark gray — hence it is known as the Eight-Color Jade Pagoda.

Chapter 5

Major Buddhist Grottoes

Introduction

The most extensive examples of early Chinese Buddhist images that survive in China are in the grottoes — the cave temple sites that stretch from Dunhuang in the west of China into the heart of the country. Three of them are World Cultural Heritage sites:

— Dazu Stone Carvings near Chongqing. The earliest sculpture dates from the late Tang Dynasty, an example of China's grotto art of the later period.

— Longmen Grottoes near Luoyang, Henan Province. Work here began in the Northern Wei Dynasty and continued over 400 years leaving some 1,345 caves and niches, 3,600 inscribed tablets, over 50 pagodas and more than 100,000 statues.

— Yungang Grottoes, southern foot of Mount Wuzhou, west of Datong, Shanxi Province. They are the oldest, most intact and largest-scale group of grottoes in China. The Gandhara and Quetta artistic styles originating in Indian Buddhism can be seen in the carvings here.

But Buddhist grottoes in China can be found in Kuqa and Qoco in Xinjiang Autonomous Region; Dunhuang, Tianshui and Yongqing in Gansu Province; Yungang in Datong, Shanxi Province; the Tianlong Mountain in Taiyuan, Shanxi Province; the 10,000-Buddha Chamber in Yixian County; Longmen in Luoyang, Henan Province; the Southern and Northern Xiangtang Mountain in Handan, Hebei Province; the Qianfo (Thousand-Buddha) Mountain in Jinan, Shandong Province; the Qixia Mountain in Nanjing, Jiangsu Province; Feilaifeng in Hangzhou, Zhejiang Province; Guangyuan, Sichuan Province; Dazu in Chongqing Municipality, and Jianchuan in Yunnan Province. Construction of grottoes began in China during the Han Dynasty with the introduction of Buddhism, especially along the "Silk Road" — the route of travel and communication that linked China to the rest of the world. The speed at which grottoes were constructed in China is as amazing as their colossal sizes and wide geographical distribution.

In the earliest days of Buddhism, grottoes, small or large, were abodes for monks. The Buddha himself lived in such a cave while practicing austerities in a mountain. A year after his death, some 500 disciples headed by Mahakasyapa (Kasyapa) gathered to recall and summarize the sermons he had preached and the commandments he had set for his followers. That this large Buddhist gathering took place in a cave in the suburbs of Rajagrha is testimony to the size of Saptaparna (Seven-Leaf Tree) Cave. Today, quite a few grottoes can still be seen in the southwest of India. The Ajanta Caves, built during the period from 1st century BC to 5th century AD, has walls and ceilings carved with pictorials about the life of the Buddha, the Eight Aspects of Buddha's Life, and so on. These grottoes started as simple cave dwellings for monks, but they gradually grew in size, and their carvings and murals became more and more exquisitely done. Eventually they emerged as veritable treasure houses of art. The murals in them reflect the styles of art of different historical periods and their themes were closely associated with the life and society of the time. The Mahayana branch of Buddhism that spread to China encouraged the fashioning of images of Buddhas, Bodhisattvas and Pure Lands for the dual purposes of worship and attaining merit. As in India, the grottoes in China gradually evolved into projects for art's sake to become favorite destinations for travelers. There are so many of them in China that a comprehensive introduction is out of the question for this book. The following is a brief introduction to a few of them.

Mogao Caves at Dunhuang
敦煌莫高窟 (Dūnhuáng Mògāo Kū)

The Mogao Caves, seated on a cliff at the eastern foot of the Mingsha Mountain in the Gobi Desert southeast of the Dunhuang City, Gansu Province, are a treasure of Buddhist culture with wall paintings and statues created in some 500 grottoes cut over

Mogao Caves at Dunhuang in Gansu Province

hundreds of years. Construction of the Mogao Caves is believed to have started with one monk's dwelling somewhere in the 3rd — 4th centuries, but the huge complex of caves that developed did not come to completion until more than a 1,000 years later, a period which saw the rise and fall of the Sixteen Kingdoms, the Northern Dynasties, the Sui and the Tang dynasties, the Five Dynasties, the Song Dynasty, the Western Xia, and the Yuan Dynasty.

The Mogao Caves are a collection of cave architecture, painted sculpture and wall paintings. The sculptures in all ranges of sizes include Buddhas, bodhisattvas, Lokapala (heavenly kings, the four guardians of the world and of the Buddhist faith), patrons and attendants. The murals are mostly Jataka stories on the life of the Buddha and the Eight Aspects of Buddha's Life, with a rich variety of ornamental patterns in such designs as Apsaras. Based on the different styles of art housed in these caves, the following list was devised by Chinese archaeologists on the some 480 caves that still exist:

Time of Construction	Number of Caves Built
Western Jin, Sixteen Kingdoms, and Northern Dynasties	32
Sui	100
Tang	232
Five Dynasties	40
Song and Western Xia	59
Yuan	9
Time unknown	8

These statistics indicate that no more caves were built at Dunhuang during a period of about 270 years that covered the Eastern Jin Dynasty and the Southern dynasties. The reason is simple: both the Eastern Jin and the Southern dynasties were situated south of the Yangtze River, whereas Dunhuang is located in the northwest. Construction resumed after the Sui Dynasty unified China, and this is shown clearly in the above table.

The murals that dominate the Mogao Caves are of the highest artistic level. They give an extensive and detailed account of the Buddhist sutras and beliefs of the times. They also offer a wide range of subjects: the Buddha in various manifestations; a biographical series on Sakyamuni the Buddha and the legends of his enduring humility and sacrifice to rescue souls; traditional folk tales of the major Chinese ethnic groups as well as historical events related to the Buddha, and eminent monks in disseminating Buddhism. In the paintings are also portrayals of human figures, flying birds, pavilions, and descriptions of grotto builders and their families, including how they dressed.

A salient feature of the Dunhuang Grottoes is that the soft and loose texture of the rocks of the Mingsha Mountain made it possible for people to hollow out caves in the first place, and also made stone carving impossible. Artists had to sculpt clay statues inside the grottoes and mortar the walls before painting them. Apart from a wealth of sculptures and murals, more than 20,000 Buddhist sutras were found in Cave No. 17. Most of them were hand-copied volumes, but early woodblock printed versions were found as well. During the Guangxu reign (1875-1908) of the Qing Dynasty, Cave No. 17 came under the care of a Daoist priest Wang Yuan who sold to European "explorers" more than 10,000 sutras, priceless objects now in museums in Britain and France.

Maijishan Grottoes
麦积山石窟 (Màijīshān Shíkū)

Maijishan Mountain stands in the midst of a jumble of mountains and 30 kilometers to the southeast of Tianshui City, Gansu Province. With a pagoda perched on its top, from a distance it looks like a haystack with an oversized top. But what makes Maijishan famous is the beehive of grottoes dug around its middle, where row-upon-row of cave-shrines, with murals on their walls, provide shelters for some 6,200 stone and clay figures. This cave complex forms a major gallery of Chinese art second only to the Mogao Caves at Dunhuang.

Construction of the Maijishan Grottoes began during the reign of the Western Qin (384-431), slightly later than the Mogao Caves. The number of caves kept growing in the ensuing years — the Northern Wei, Western Wei, Northern Zhou, Sui, Tang, Northern Song, Yuan, Ming and Qing. During this course of some

Maijishan Grottoes, Gansu Province

1,500 years, Maijishan enjoyed its heyday during the Western Wei, Northern Zhou and Sui , but construction of new caves slowed down considerably after the Tang. Today, some 174 cave-temples are still there. Archaeologists' work to number, date and classify them has resulted in the following table:

Time of Construction	Number of Caves Built
Western Qin — Northern Dynasties, the first stage	15
Northern Dynasties, the second stage	17
Northern Dynasties, the third stage	51
Northern Zhou — Sui	47
Tang	5
Song	9
Ming	4
Qing	1
Dates unknown	25

The place had fallen into oblivion for more than a century after the last cave-temple was dug there. It was rediscovered during an archaeological survey organized by the country's cultural authorities in 1953. A research institute was established to put the grottoes under protection and refurbishment.

Repeated earthquakes over the years caused the Maijishan Grottoes to split in two sections — eastern and western. Access to both sections were provided by plank ways built into the cliffs.

The major grottoes in the eastern section are:

(1) Nirvana Cave (Cave No. 1). Built in the late Wei Dynasty in about the 6th century, with six stone pillars standing in front of it. The sculptures inside it were repaired during the Ming, but their original style of the Wei is clearly visible.

(2) Thousand-Buddha Corridor (Cave No. 3). Another product of the Wei Dynasty, this is actually a 32.74-meter-long corridor of two floors crowded with a total of 258 clay figures of rough stone cast.

(3) Seven-Buddha Tower atop the Sanhua Pavilion (Cave No. 4). This is the largest group of caves of the Maijishan Grottoes, where eight pillars divide a huge cave into seven bays. The murals on the ceiling are probably works of the Western Wei or Northern Zhou. The partitioning walls between the shrines are also covered with murals depicting celestial beings playing Chinese musical instruments, burning incense sticks or tossing flowers. There are a total of 75 sculptures inside, some of them works of a later age.

(4) Buffalo Chamber. This cave-temple is named after its sculpture of a buffalo being trampled under the heels of a heavenly king. Four pillars divide it into three shrines, and each shrine used to be occupied by a set of sculptures. Today, only the heavenly king and the buffalo are still there.

The three major grottoes of western section are:

(1) Ten-Thousand-Buddha Chamber (Cave No. 133). Also known as "Stele Cave," it is 4 meters high, 14.91 meters wide and 11.58 meters deep. A legion of Buddhist figurines are carved into all its walls. On its lintel stand the likenesses of many patrons against a relief landscape. Inside the cave stands a statue of the Receptionist Buddha — Amitabha, 3.50 meters in height. Built probably during the Tang but repaired during the Song, this work is notable for its high artistic attainment. The ceiling was

painted with murals of flying Apsaras, but most of them have peeled away. A number of stone steles carved with portraits are found inside the cave, which are treasured for the valuable historical information contained in the portraits and inscriptions.

(2) Tiantang (Paradise) Cave. Paintings of soldiers at war, their colors fading and some of them already peeling off, are found on the walls of this cave. In its center stands a statue of the Buddha flanked on either side by the representation of a bodhisattva. The trio is believed to be made during the Northern Wei Dynasty.

(3) Cave No. 127. The central part of this cave is occupied by a Buddhist statue made during the Western Wei Dynasty. The nimbus behind the statue is surrounded by the likenesses of ten deva-dancers each holding a musical instrument in hand. Despite weathering, the murals on the ceiling and walls of this cave are still of a highly ornamental value.

All the caves of the Maijishan Grottoes were dug high on the vertical cliff of a mountain. This begs the question: How did the ancients do this? Historical information indicates that they did it the hard way. They stacked up firewood at the foot of the cliff to a height that allowed them to tunnel, sculpt and paint. Obviously, the plank ways that provide access to the cave-temples were built in the same fashion.

At the foot of the cliff stands the Ruiying Temple, now property of the local archaeological department.

Yungang Grottoes 云冈石窟 (Yúngǎng Shíkū)

The third leading groups of grottoes behind Dunhuang and Maijishan, the Yungang Grottoes complex is found in a mountain just west of Datong in Shanxi Province. The Yungang Grottoes extend east and west in a row along the side of a mountain known as Wuzhou in ancient times, which assumed its present name, Yungang, during the Ming. Fifty-three caves remain today, housing some 51,000 statues.

Construction of Yungang Grottoes began in 453 during the Northern Wei Dynasty under the supervision of a monk named Tanyao and with the approval of Emperor Wencheng. These five major grottoes are known as "Tanyao's Five Cave-temples." Legend

A Buddhist statue at Yungang Grottoes in Datong, Shanxi Province has it that the Buddhist statues enshrined in these grottoes are images of the five emperors of the Northern Wei — Daowu, Mingyuan, Taiwu, Jingmu and Wencheng. However, since strict Buddhist requirements on the sculpture of deities would have made it impossible for a Buddhist statue to assume the looks of an emperor, perhaps it is more appropriate to say these Buddhist statues were erected in honor of the five emperors. In each of Tanyao's Five Cave-temples — that is, Caves 16-20, is a major statue surrounded by tiny niches of Buddhist figurines. The front of Cave No. 20 has collapsed so that its statue of the Buddha looks as if sitting in state in the open, an image that has becomes the symbol of the entire Yungang Grottoes.

The second-stage construction of the Yungang Grottoes began probably during the period from 465, the year Emperor Wencheng died, to 493, when Emperor Xiaowen moved the capital of the Northern Wei to Luoyang. More grottoes were dug during this stage than during the previous stage to form the major body of the entire Yungang Grottoes. There are 12 of them, that is, in a numerical order, Cave Nos. 1-3 and 5-13. The sculptures in them feature richly varied images. Apart from different likenesses of the Buddha, there are also bodhisattvas, dvarapalas (guardian deities) and patrons, as well as pagodas and pillars. Some of the murals are depictions of flying devatas (Apsaras), and some Jataka stories about the life of the Buddha and events in Buddhist history. At a height of some 56 feet or 17 meters, the statue of the Buddha in Cave No. 5 is the largest of all the stone Buddhas of Yungang.

In the third-stage construction that began after Emperor Xiaowen moved the Northern Wei capital to Luoyang, mostly small grottoes and shrines were built, scattered at both ends of the original row and in the vicinity, but the forms and themes were even more diversified.

Northern Wei later split into the Eastern Wei (534-550) and the Western Wei (535-557), and then after the downfall of both, construction of the Yungang Grottoes came to a standstill. During its heyday, in front of the Yungang Grottoes were ten temples, with a monastic population of several thousand, and for a time making it the Buddhist center of north China. The Yungang Grottoes underwent repeated refurbishments and major repairs during the periods after the Sui and the Tang, and restoration work reached its climax during the Liao and Jin dynasties.

The Yungang Grottoes were built in a way different from its counterparts. At Dunhuang and Maijishan, builders had to dig the caves first, and then erect the statues. At Yungang, the tunneling of the caves and the chiseling of Buddhist statues took place at the same time.

Longmen Grottoes 龙门石窟 (Lóngmén Shíkū)

For sheer numbers, Longmen stands out as the largest of all the grottoes in China. The Longmen Grottoes is named after a mountain just 13 kilometers to the south of Luoyang, Henan Province. Two lofty peaks stand facing each other, and in the ravine down below, the Yishui River tumbles by away. The vertical

Longmen Grottoes in Luoyang, Henan Province

cliffs on both banks of the river have been converted into beehives of grottoes that are divided into five zones — four on the eastern bank and one on the western bank. A total of 1,021 of the cave-temples have been identified and numbered by the local archaeological department: Zone One includes 61 caves; Zone Two includes 97 caves; Zone Three includes 386 caves, Zone Four includes 399 caves and Zone Five includes 78 caves. These numbered caves do not include those caves that are too far gone in dilapidation, empty, too small, or contain nothing valuable.

Construction of the Longmen Grottoes began during the Northern Wei, when local bureaucrats opened a number of small grottoes or Buddhist shrines up in the Longmen Mountain. In the year 493, Emperor Xiaowen moved the capital from Pingcheng (present-day Datong), Shanxi Province to Luoyang. In 500, Emperor Xuanwu followed the example of the Yungang Grottoes in the Wuzhou Mountain near Pingcheng, and had three grottoes tunneled into the Longmen Mountain. This ushered in a period of large-scale construction. According to historical records, construction of the Longmen Grottoes reached its peak during the 500-528 period, which encompassed the Xuanwu and Xiaoming reigns of the Northern Wei. But it then came to a stop because of war and turmoil arising from brutal infighting within the ruling class. Construction continued on and off during the period that saw the rise and fall of the Northern Qi, the Sui, the Tang, and the Northern Song, but none of these dynasties equaled the Tang in the number of grottoes built and the scale of construction at the site.

Signature inscriptions on stone sculptures indicate monks and nuns joined the ruling class in building Longmen Grottoes. A salient feature of Longmen is that all the Buddhist statues were carved into the rocks at the same time as their cave shrines were being chiseled into the mountainsides. Even the ornamental patterns are fine examples of Chinese religious stone carving. Not a single mural, however, has been found in them. The following is a brief introduction to some of the representative works of Longmen.

(1) Guyang Cave. One of the earliest caves built at Longmen, Guyang Cave was completed around the time the Northern Wei

capital was moved to Luoyang. Inside the cave is a rich collection of Buddhist images arranged in three rows of Buddhist shrines. The Buddhist deities were all graced with elegant and exquisitely crafted nimbuses and their drapery comes in a rich variety as well. The images of patrons look so real they seem ready to step out at a visitor's beckoning. The inscriptions are fine examples of Chinese calligraphy in unadorned simplistic elegance, and furnish valuable material for the study of classical Chinese calligraphy.

(2) Binyang Cave is actually a trio of caves. Construction of the cave in the middle began in 500, but it took 802,366 workdays in a 24-year span to bring it to completion. Sitting in the center of this cave is the statue of Sakyamuni with his chief disciples Kasyapa and Ananda in attendance. The sharp touches of the chisel are still highly visible in the rich lines of these three images, as befitting the artistic style of Northern Wei sculpture. The southern and northern walls of this cave are each carved with statues of the Buddha and two bodhisattvas. The ceiling is embellished with a lotus flower and deva-dancers and musicians. The walls are also covered with large relief sculptures of Jataka stories about the life of Sakyamuni. Construction of the two side caves also began during the Northern Wei, but the sculptural work inside them did not come to a finish until the early Tang.

(3) Lotus Cave, also known as Yique Cave. Construction of this cave also began during the late Northern Wei. The statue of Sakyamuni inside it stands some 18 feet or 6.1 meters high, but, alas, damage of different degrees has been inflicted on the Buddha's face and hands. The statue of Kasyapa standing by the Buddha holds a Buddhist staff in his hand. The figurines in the many shrines come in quite a variety of forms. Oversized lotus flowers are carved in the center of the ceiling and surrounded by flying devatas (Apsaras).

(4) Yaofang (Prescriptions) Cave. This cave came under construction during the late Northern Wei, and interior sculpture was finished more than 200 years later during the reign period of Empress Wu Zetian of the Tang (684-704). This is the only cave at Longmen in which works of the Northern Qi (550-577) mingle with Northern Wei and Tang creations. The walls at the entrance of the cave are inscribed with some 140 medical prescriptions for various diseases. Hence the name of the cave: Prescriptions Cave.

(5) Qianxi Temple. This is an immense cave-temple that came under construction during the early Tang. It is dedicated to Maitreya, the Buddha of Future, who sits in the company of his two disciples, two bodhisattvas, and two lokapalas (heavenly kings). All the figures inside the Qianxi Temple have full faces in a style representative of Tang-dynasty sculpture.

(6) Wanfo (Ten-Thousand-Buddha) Cave. Construction of this cave started in 680, or the first year of the Yonglong reign of the Tang. In the center of it is a statue of Amitabha sitting on his lotus throne. The wall behind him is carved with 54 lotus flowers, with the representation of a bodhisattva or patron sitting on each of them, a design not seen elsewhere in the Longmen Grottoes. Fifteen thousand Buddhist statues are hewn into the southern and northern walls, hence the name: Wanfo (Ten-Thousand-Buddha) Cave. At the foot of this awesome array of Buddhist statues are deva-musicians and dancing gods in graphic images and figures. Standing outside the cave is a rendition of Guanyin, holding a duster in her right hand and a holy-water vase in her left hand. Unfortunately, the Guanyin's face has been marred by vandalism.

(7) Fengxian Temple. Built in 672, this is the largest Buddhist shrine among all the grottoes of Longmen, considering that the statue inside it, a likeness of Vairocana (the first of the Dhyani or Celestial Buddhas, the essence of wisdom or bodhi and absolute purity), is some 50 feet or 17.14 meters in height and that there are also ten huge sculptures of disciples, bodhisattvas, heavenly kings and guardians. Vairocana assumes the image of a man with a full face and long and narrow eyes under slender brows, and the corner of his mouth slightly tilting upward. The other sculptures inside the cave are also works of impeccable craftsmanship. Legend has it that Empress Wu Zetian donated 20,000 strings of coin for the construction of this cave-temple. When the temple was completed, she personally attended the consecration ceremony.

(8) Kanjing (Sutra-reading) Temple, built during the reign of Empress Wu Zetian (684-704). The caisson ceiling of this cave-temple is ornamented with lotus flower carvings flanked by chubby-faced Apsaras dancing in the heavens. The temple is dedicated to 29 arhats — the legendary patriarchs of the Western Heaven for 29 generations — evidence that it is a sanctuary of the Chan School of Chinese Buddhism. For the elaborate beauty of

their sculptured detail, these renditions of arhats are lauded as masterpieces of Chinese sculpture.

Dazu Grottoes 大足石窟 (Dàzú Shíkū)

The Dazu Grottoes in Chongqing can be considered latecomers in the Chinese history of Buddhism: Although some grottoes were built here in the Tang Dynasty, large-scale development started in the Song Dynasty (960-1279). One of the major creators of the Dazu Grottoes was Zhao Zhifeng, a monk of the Esoteric School. The grotto art of Dazu County incorporates elements of the three major religions of Confucianism, Buddhism and Daoism that happened to be developing at the time, but Buddhist elements dominate.

(1) Shimenshan (Stone Gate Mountain) Grottoes. This is a group of a dozen cave-shrines that provide shelter to more than 1,000 large and small statues belonging to Confucianism, Buddhism and Daoism. These include the Emperor Wuxian (a god in Chinese folklore) and Prince Bingling (the God of Fire in Daoism). In the center of Cave No. 6 is a statue of Amitayus, the Buddha of Boundless Life, flanked on either side by a statue of Avalokitesvara in a different image. The two side rock walls of the cave are carved with five Buddhist deities holding ritual objects in their hands. According to their signature inscriptions, these statues date back to the Southern Song (1127-1279).

(2) Shizhuanshan Grottoes. Confucianism, Buddhism, and Daoism coexist in the Zimu Hall and the Qianfo (Thousand-Buddha) Cliff that combine to form the Shizhuanshan Grottoes. The nine shrines in the Zimu Hall contain a mixture of Vairocana, Manjusri, Samantabhadra and Ksitigarbha of Buddhism; Confucius, the father of Confucianism, and other Confucian scholars; and Laozi, the founder of Daoism, and the Queen Mother of the West. All these sculptures renditions date back to the Northern Song (960-1127) and are of high artistic value. The Qianfo (Thousand-Buddha) Cliff is a domain of Buddhist statues done during the Ming Dynasty (1368-1644).

(3) Northern Mountain Buddhist Sculpture. Northern Mountain, known in ancient times as Longgang Mountain, is where the first

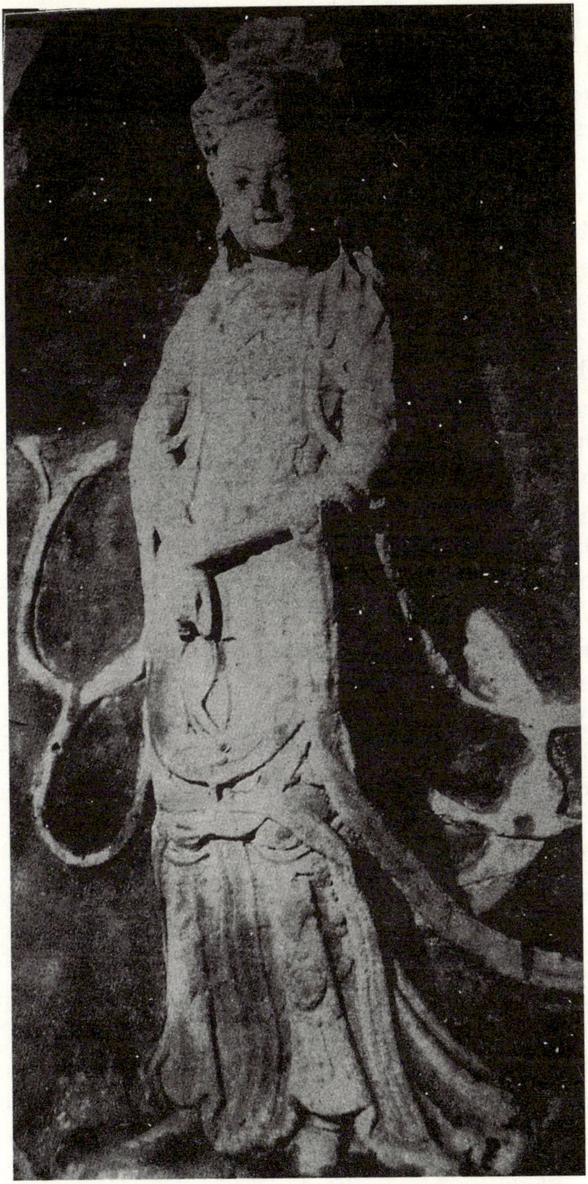

A statue of Guanyin, the Goddess of Mercy, in the Dazu Grottoes,Chongqing group of Buddhist statues appeared in 892 in the Tang Dynasty. Dubbed the "Bay of the Buddha," here some 264 cave-shrines are tunneled into the wide surface of a seven-meter-high and 500-meter-wide cliff. The statues inside them belong to both the Five Dynasties (907-960) and the Song Dynasty. Apart from stone sculptures, the place also abounds in stone inscriptions, and boasts an ancient pagoda.

(4) Baodingshan Grottoes. Baodingshan is known for its awesome collection of over 10,000 Buddhist sculptures and cliff carvings in three sections:

— Shengshou Temple. First built during the Song Dynasty, the halls as they are today are legacies of the Ming and the Qing. The main structures are the Hall of Heavenly Kings, the Hall of the Jade Emperor, the Mahavira Hall, the Incantation Hall, the Hall of Dipamkara and the Hall of Vimalakirti. Among the major statues is one of Vimalakirti (said to have been a contemporary of Sakyamuni, and to have visited China). Hollowed into the sides of the platform of this temple are 77 shrines each housing a Buddhist figurine. True to the Chinese religious tradition that a group of grottoes invariably contains a temple, the Shengshou Temple is an essential part of the Baodingshan grottoes and cliff carvings.

— The Lesser Bay of the Buddha. Also known as Dabao Chamber, this is right by the Shengshou Temple. It is said that this was where Zhao Zhifeng conducted experiments before he began large-scale construction of grottoes and cliff carvings at Baodingshan. The Lesser Bay of Buddha used to cover a wide area, but only 600 or so statues and four sculptures carved into the cliff walls exist today. There is also a three-tiered square stone pagoda with walls engraved with Buddhist portraits and titles of Buddhist scriptures.

— The Greater Bay of the Buddha. The largest cluster of the Baodingshan Grottoes and Cliff Carvings are found here in rock walls of a deep ravine carved with Jataka stories of Buddhism and texts of scriptures. A rendition of the Thousand-Hand Guanyin covered some 262 square feet or 88 square meters of the eastern wall of the bay. The statue portrays the Guanyin (Goddess of Mercy) as a study of serenity as she sits on her lotus throne, wearing a crown and cupping the palms of one pair of her hands together before her chest. Her other 10,00 hands are chiseled into the cliff wall behind her, and arrayed in neat lines in the shape of a fan that is evocative of a peacock fanning out its tail. Each exquisitely carved hand holds a different ritual object in it. The Greater Bay of Buddha also boasts a sleeping Buddha whose reclining body extends for some 90 feet or 31 meters, with part of his legs extending into the depth of the cliff. He is not alone there, as he has the company of his ten major disciples, all carved in busts. The entire group of sculpture is a superb piece of Chinese religious art.

(5) The Yuanjue (Perfect Enlightenment) Cave. Sitting in this cave are three statues of the Buddha with a number of disciples bowing in front of him, and 12 other disciples sitting beside him on lotus thrones. This group of stone carvings is regarded as quintessential art of the Greater Bay of Buddha.

Chapter 6

The Four Sacred Mountains of Buddhism

Introduction

China has many sacred mountains. The best-known sacred mountains of Buddhism are Mount Wutai of Shanxi Province, Mount Putuo of Zhejiang Province, Mount Jiuhua of Anhui Province, and Mount Emei of Sichuan Province — known collectively as the "Four Sacred Mountains of Buddhism." Besides being home to many temples and pagodas, these mountains feature beautiful landscape that may earlier have served as refuges for Daoist monks. (The Five Sacred Mountains of Daoism in China are Taishan, the Daoist mountain of the east, Shandong Province; Hengshan (Bei), the Daoist mountain of the north, Shanxi Province; Huashan, the Daoist mountain of the west, Shaanxi Province; Hengshan (Nan), the Daoist mountain of the south, Hunan Province; and Songshan, the Daoist mountain of the center, Henan Province.) However, over the centuries following the introduction of Buddhism to China, Mount Wutai, Mount Putuo, Mount Jiuhua and Mount Emei became known as sanctuaries of Buddhism, each associated with a venerated Bodhisattva. Mount Wutai is the domain of Manjusri, or the Universal Great Wisdom Bodhisattva; Mount Putuo is the domain of Avalokitesvara or Guanyin (Goddess of Mercy); Mount Jiuhua is the domain of Ksitigarbha (Guardian of the Earth); and Mount Emei is the domain of Samantabhadra, or Bodhisattva of Universal Benevolence (Universal Worthy Great Conduct Bodhisattva).

Mount Wutai was the earliest to open to Buddhism, and in the Yuan Dynasty (1368-1644) the mountain also became a sanctuary of Tibetan Buddhism; Mount Putuo, a beautiful small island offshore from Ningbo in Zhejiang Province has for centuries been a mecca of Buddhism for its scenery and its association with the popular Goddess of Mercy; Mount Jiuhua, a rugged range of mountains that snake through Anhui Province became a Buddhist mountain thanks to a Korean monk whose secular name was Gim Kyokak who lived here and became regarded as the reincarnation of Bodhisattva Ksitigarbha; and as for Mount Emei, its rugged topography has earned it the name: "No place under heaven is as beautiful as Mount Emei."

Mount Wutai 五台山 (Wǔtái Shān)

The five peaks that make up Mount Wutai in Shanxi Province shelter the town Taihuai, the center of the some 40 Buddhist temples in this mountain range in northeast Shanxi Province that are considered paragons of Chinese culture for their architecture, paintings and sculptures.

According to the *Gazetteer of Qingliang Mountain,*edited in the Ming Dynasty, Buddhist temples were established on Mount Wutai as early as the Eastern Han (25-220). This, however, may be hearsay because after Buddhism spread to China during the Han Dynasty, the establishment banned Chinese from abandoning the world to become monks. Since there were no monks at all, what was the use of temples? A plausible theory dates construction of Buddhist temples on Mount Wutai back to the Northern Wei (385-534) of the Northern and Southern Dynasties. Today, some 40 temples from that era remain on the mountain.

Mount Wutai's reputation as a Buddhist sanctuary probably stemmed from mention of the mountain in association with Bodhisattva Manjusri in the *Garland Sutra* translated into Chinese by the eminent Indian monk Buddhabhadra (359-429) during the East Jin Dynasty (317-420). The mountain referred to in the *Garland Sutra* may actually be another mountain of the same name, but it is an established fact that the mountain long has been considered the domain of Manjusri.

Following are descriptions of some of the temples.

(1) Xiantong Temple. This is the largest, most venerated, and foremost Buddhist establishment on Mount Wutai, noted for the magnificence of the architecture and the elaborate beauty of

detail in its sculptures. When it was first built during the 471-499 reign of Emperor Xiaowen of the Northern Wei, it was known variously as Great Futu (Buddha-stupa) Temple and Garden Temple. When Wu Zetian of the Tang Dynasty ruled the nation from 684 to 704, it was renamed Great Huayan Monastery. When it was reconstructed during the Ming Dynasty (1368-1644), the founding emperor Zhu Yuanzhang gave it a horizontal board inscribed with the name, "Great Xiantong Monastery," which is still there today. Reconstruction conducted during the Qing Dynasty expanded the temple to its present size that includes some 400 or so halls, chambers and pavilions laid out in an area of some 80,000 square meters. The seven main halls, arranged along the axial line, assume a different design each, and their flank buildings are of a uniform style. Adding luster to the entire assemblage is a three-bay finely cast bronze hall.

(2) Tayuan Temple. It was once a courtyard of the Xiantong Temple and the site of an imposing stupa that is an emblem of Mount Wutai. When the stupa was rebuilt during the Ming Dynasty, the courtyard became an independent temple. The archway rising before the front gate is also a product of the Ming Dynasty. The stupa forms the center of the temple, sandwiched between the Mahavira Hall in the front and the Tripitaka Pavilion in the rear. Its eastern side is lined with a row of auxiliary halls. The Tripitaka Pavilion differs from its counterparts in that it features a 20-tiered wooden wheel with various scriptures placed on it for the followers to worship or read. The stupa is a white affair about 150 feet or 50 meters in height. A total of 252 bells hanging on it sway gently in the wind to send out a pleasant tinkling sound.

(3) Shuxiang (Statue of Manjusri) Temple. Another major Buddhist sanctuary just south of Taihuai Town, it was built during the Tang, rebuilt during the Yuan, only to be burned down shortly afterwards, and built once again in 1487 during the Ming Dynasty. Sitting behind the front gateway and the Hall of Heavenly Kings is the Hall of Manjusri, behind which is the abbot's residence and the meditation hall. Both sides of the temple are lined with minor halls and corridors. The Hall of Manjusri is a dignified structure five bays in width, and looks unique under a roof that has double-tiered eaves and is graced with colorfully glazed fringes and

elaborated painted corbel brackets. In the hall the image of Manjusri sitting on the back of a lion is cast in a statue about 27 feet or nine meters in height. Behind him are the statues of the Buddhas of the Three Realms, that is, Bhaisajyaraja, Sakyamuni and Amitabha. Suspended on the sidewalls of the hall are sculptures of 500 arhats in graphic imagery and superb craftsmanship.

(4) Pusading Temple. Also known as Zhenrong Temple or Manjusri Temple, it was first built during the Northern Wei and repeatedly repaired and expanded in the succeeding dynasties. After the Ming Dynasty the place became a settlement of lamas from Mongolia and Tibet. Both emperors Kangxi and Qianlong of the Qing Dynasty stayed here during their repeated visits to Mount Wutai, and because of this link with the emperors, the temple had the unusual attention of the imperial court. Some of its buildings were constructed in a palatial style, and no other temple is in the possession of as many horizontal boards and stone tablets inscribed in the handwriting of various emperors as the Pusading Temple. The temple perches on the crest of a mountain, and access to the stone archway in front of it is by a 108-step trapezoidal stairway.

(5) Luohou Temple. Situated to the east of the Xiantong Temple, it is a Tibetan Buddhist Temple of considerable size and one of Mount Wutai's best-preserved temples. Construction of it began during the Tang, and it was rebuilt in 1492 in the Ming Dynasty. The Qing emperors Kangxi, Qianlong and Yongzheng rarely missed a chance to visit this temple during their repeated tours of Mount Wutai. On the 14th of the 6th lunar month, the lamas in this temple masquerade themselves as ghosts and celebrate the legendary birthday of Manjusri by mounting an entire day of sorcerers' dance, which never fails to attract a large crowd of onlookers. One of the halls houses a strange gadget, a round altar engraved with water-wave patterns and the portraits of 18 arhats. In the center of the altar stands a wood-carved lotus flower, which is fixed on a central axis dovetailed to a cogwheel. Pull the string attached to the cogwheel, and the petals will open and close repeatedly, now revealing a figurine of the Buddha in the center of the flower, now concealing it.

(6) Longquan (Dragon Spring) Temple. Also known as Jiulonggang Temple, it stands by the White Dragon Spring south

of Taihuai Town. Construction of it began during the Song, but it was rebuilt on three occasions during the Ming, the late Qing and the Republican years. A monumental brick carving of Manjusri riding his trademark lion, inlaid in the screen wall of the temple, is considered a masterpiece of sculpture for its ingenious and impeccable chisel work. A 108-step stone stairway leads to a stone archway that gives access to the temple's row of three courtyard that are interlinked yet independent of each other. The anterooms of the eastern courtyard, which is a combination of two smaller yards, are known for their colorful paintings. Two pagodas stand in the central and western courtyards which are skirted by zigzagging corridors. The Longquan Temple has a different layout than most Buddhist temples probably for topographical reasons.

(7) Jinge (Golden Pavilion) Temple. Nine miles or 15 kilometers from Taihuai Town, it is another renowned Buddhist establishment of Mount Wutai dating back to the Tang. Jinge Temple has all the major elements a Buddhist temple should have, such as the Hall of Vairocana, the Hall of Amitabha, the Hall of Avalokistevara, and the Hall of Ksitigarbha. But what's unique about this temple is that it is in the possession of a golden pavilion built to receive envoys sent by Emperor Daizong (reigned 762-779) of the Tang to perform ritual deeds for him there. The pavilion looks golden because its bronze tiles are gilded with gold powder. Enshrined in it is a 17-meter-high bronze statue of Guanyin sitting in the company of the 24 Buddhist patriarchs in Mahayana Buddhism.

(8) Nanshan Temple. Less than two miles or three kilometers to the south of Taihuai Town, it originally belonged to three temples — Youguo, Jile and Shande — when they were first built in 1296, the 2nd year of the Yuanzhen reign of the Yuan, and rebuilt during the Jiajing reign (1522-1566) of the Ming. By the Qing Dynasty more buildings were added, and the entire cluster was combined to form the Nanshan Temple. In an expansion project conducted during the Republican years, the interiors of the three main buildings were linked. The temple today is a colossal congregate of halls, towers, pavilions and chambers, totaling 300 bays, arranged in distinct rows along the contours of the mountain slope. Access to the front gateway is by a stone stairway of 108 steps. The brick engravings of the temple's

screen wall are renowned for their fastidious craftsmanship. The buildings come in a variety of architectural styles. The main hall is enshrined with the statues of Sakyamuni, Kasyapa, Ananda, the attendant bodhisattvas, and the 18 arhats, which are a legacy of the Ming. It is believed that the sculpture of the Nanshan Temple leads the entire Mount Wutai in artistic attainment.

(9) Guangjimaopeng Temple. Situated just to the northeast of Taihuai Town, the Guangjimaopeng Temple is said to have been built during the Northern Wei (386-534). This is a temple known for its beautiful carvings. In its front courtyard are the Hall of Heavenly Kings, the Bell and Drum Towers, the Hall of Vairocana, an altar, and eastern and western flank rooms. The backyard, higher in elevation than the front courtyard, features a floral-pendant gate, the Tripitaka Pavilion, meditation rooms and monastic dormitories.

(10) Foguang Temple. About 15 miles or 25 km to the northeast of the seat of Wutai County, it was built during the 471-499 in the Northern Wei Dynasty, but was demolished during the crackdown on Buddhism launched by Emperor Wuzong who reigned the Tang Dynasty in 841-846. It was not rebuilt until 857, after Emperor Xuanzong ascended the throne and resurrected Buddhism. The pagoda of the Foguang Temple of today is a Northern Wei legacy, while the Eastern Hall was built during the Tang. The temple is in the possession of a collection of Tang-dynasty sculpture, murals, stone pillars inscribed with incantations, stupas with remains of monks buried underneath, and marble sculptures. The main hall is a rare and extremely precious example of Tang-dynasty wood structure.

(11) Yuanzhao Temple. North of Taihuai Town, it was built during the Yongle reign (1403-1424) of the Ming Dynasty. It is said that at the time, the Indian monk Patra Lisha arrived in China and the imperial court honored him as State Tutor and bestowed a gold seal on him. He later settled in Mount Wutai, and the Xiantong Temple was his residence, where he died during the Xuande reign (1426-1435) of the Ming. After his remains were cremated, part of his remains were sent to Beijing to be enshrined in the Zhenjue (Five-Pagoda) Temple built specially for this purpose, and part of them were retained for the construction of the Yuanzhao Temple. The front gateway to the temple is guarded

by a pair of stone lions, and the Hall of Heavenly Kings, the Hall of the Great Buddha, the courtyard containing a pagoda, and the Tripitaka Pavilion, are all arrayed along the axial line. The statue of the Buddha in the Hall of the Great Buddha looks distinctive with his tall stature and calm composure. Behind the temple is a cluster of five pagodas elevated on a square base. With a small pagoda standing on each corner, and a large one in the center, the layout looks like a copy of Beijing's Five-Pagoda Temple.

(12) Zhenhai Temple. Half way up a mountain just south of Taihuai Town, it means "temple to subdue the son of the Dragon King." The spring running by the front of the temple, known as "Ocean Bottom Spring," is the legendary "eye of the sea." It is where the ninth son of the Dragon King fell in love with civilian girls and was creating havoc. When word about this reached Manjusri, the bodhisattva subdued him by holding him under a cauldron. The temple was built during the Qing. Containing the Hall of Heavenly Kings, the Hall of the Great Buddha, the Hall for Propagating Buddhism, and left and right ancillary room, it once was the residence of Lcan-Skya, a living Buddha of Tibetan Buddhism.

Mount Putuo 普陀山 (Pŭtuó Shān)

Mount Putuo is a beautiful island covering some 7 square miles or 12 square km of the Zhoushan Islands on the East China Sea, off the shore of Ningbo, Zhejiang Province. As a Buddhist sanctuary, Mount Putuo exerts a great influence on Chinese religious life because of its association with Avalokitesvara, also known as Guanyin, or the Goddess of Mercy, who is regarded by Chinese as perhaps the most endearing of all the celestial beings in the Buddhist pantheon.

Legend has it that in 858 during the Tang Dynasty, a Japanese monk by the name of Hui'e was shipping a statue of Guanyin he had acquired during a pilgrimage to Mount Wutai to Japan. Shortly after he began his sea voyage at present-day Ningbo, Zhejiang Province, a windstorm rose, and his boat was stranded among the reefs off an islet. Those on board panicked, and Hui'e prayed, "If the time is not ripe yet for this venerable statue to settle down on the eastern side of the sea, please allow me to leave it in this mountain." His prayer was hardly finished when the boat stirred and began moving towards Mount Putuo. The statue was thus move ashore. The experience deeply saddened the Japanese monk. Giving up his homecoming plan, he built a thatched hut on the island and stayed behind to take care of the statue. A different version of the story dates the event back to 916 in the Later Liang Dynasty and asserts that after the statue was moved ashore, a man surnamed Zhang evacuated his home to enshrine it, and named it "Temple of Guanyin Who Is Reluctant to Leave."

For centuries, Mount Putuo has been a mecca for pilgrims and visitors from at home and abroad all year round, especially during the three festivals in celebration of Guanyin's birthday (19th of the 2nd lunar month), achievement of enlightenment (19th of the 6th lunar month), and entry of nirvana (19th of the 9th lunar month). This has earned Mount Putuo the nickname, "Buddhist Kingdom on the Sea." Prior to 1949, incomplete statistics show that there were 218 temples and nunneries and more than 2,000 monks and nuns on the mountain, which helps explain an old saying that on Mount Putuo, "Whoever you see is a monk and whatever house comes in sight is a temple."

The following is a brief introduction to the three major temples and scenic spots with Buddhist associations of Mount Putuo:

(1) Puji Monastery. Also known as the Frontal Temple, this is the largest monastery of Mount Putuo. Perched south of the crest of the Baihua Peak, it was the Baotuo Guanyin Temple when it was first built in 1080 in the Northern Song Dynasty. The monastery has had its ups and downs through the years, and it was not until its main hall was reconstructed in 1699 that it assumed its present name by taking the hue from Emperor Kangxi's four-character inscription "puji qunling," meaning: "For the universal relief of souls." The size of the temple continued to grow in the intervening years, and by the time another round of major construction was finished in 1731 (9th year of Yongzheng reign, Qing Dynasty), it had more than 200 halls, chambers, pavilions and towers, covering a total area of 14,000 square meters. Arranged in a majestic fashion along the temple's axial line are the Hall of Heavenly Kings, the Avalokitesvara Hall, the Tripitaka

Pavilion, and the abbot's residence. In front of the temple is the Haiyin Pond, into which captive fish are set free, and in which lotus plants grow. Straightly facing the front gate are an octagonal pavilion and kiosk which provides a roof for a stone stele inscribed in the emperor's own handwriting.

(2) Fayu Temple. Situated to the left of the crest of the Baihua Peak is the Fayu Temple, or Posterior Temple, whose predecessor was the "Haichao Convent" built in 1580 in the Ming Dynasty. It was renamed Haichao Temple in 1594, but was destroyed in war shortly after it was renamed Huguo Zhenhai Temple (Temple for Protecting the Country and Guarding the Territorial Sea) in 1606. When it was rebuilt in 1699 during the Qing Dynasty, it was renamed Fayu (Rain of the Law) Temple, according to Emperor Kangxi's inscription "tianhua fayu," meaning, "heavenly flower and rain of the law," on a lacquered horizontal board bestowed to the temple. More halls were erected during the reigns of emperors Tongzhi and Guangxu that covered the 1862-1909 period. The main buildings on the temple's axial line are the Hall of Heavenly Kings, the Bell and Drum Towers, the Hall of Jade Buddha, the Guanyin Hall, the Yupai Hall, the Mahavira Hall, the Tripitaka Pavilion and the abbot's residence. The Guanyin Hall, known for its "Dome of Nine Coiling Dragons," is also called "Hall of Nine Dragons." The nine vertical rafters suspended from the ceiling of the hall's dome are each carved with a coiling dragon that rears its head in a scramble for a large ball hanging down from the center of the ceiling.

(3) Huiji Temple. Also known as Fodingshansi (Temple atop the Buddha's Mountain), this temple once was the site of a stone pavilion enshrined with a statue of the Buddha. During the Ming (1368-1644), the Huiji Convent was built, which was expanded and became a temple in 1793. In 1907, the temple acquired a complete collection of the *Tripitaka.* On the premises are four halls, seven palaces, and six towers, which are marked for their breathtaking architecture and impeccable craftsmanship. The scenic surroundings are embellished with age-old trees and exotic flowers.

(4) Luojia Mountain is part of Mount Putuo but stands opposite it across a narrow strip of sea, forming an islet a little over a mile or 2 km in circumference on the Lianhua (Lotus

Flower) Ocean. It is home to a convent. The top of the mountain offers an overview of the sea extending into the distance until it merges with heaven. At the foot of the mountain is the "Crystal Palace," a mountain cave that can accommodate visitors when the tide is out. During the time of the year when spring gives way to summer, the islet and the sea around it are wrapped in mist, which magically thickens and thins to conjure up one exotic scene after another.

(5) Purple Bamboo Grove. Legend has it that after the Japanese monk Hui'e had the statue of Guanyin moved ashore, he had the "Temple of Guanyin Who Is Reluctant to Leave" built in the Purple Bamboo Grove. Scattered on the floor of this grove are fragments of broken purplish slates with traces of bamboo leaves visible underneath their surfaces. They are fossils resulting from the movement of the earth's crust. A convent is tucked away in the heart of the purple bamboo grove, which was planted by local residents in relatively recent years.

(6) Chaoyin (Thundering Wave) Cave. It is in a deep recess in the mountain close by the Purple Bamboo Grove. When the sea surges, water tumbles into the cave and crashes into the rocks inside with a thunderous roar. Hence the name of the cave, "Cave of Thundering Waves." A wall in the cave is inscribed with three Chinese characters, meaning "Where Bodhisattva Avalokitesvara Was Seen." Towering over the Chaoyin Cave and overlooking the sea is an overhanging cliff called "Suicidal Crag," because — before barriers were set up — quite a few people committed suicide by jumping off it and plunging into the sea below.

(7) Southern Heaven Gateway. This turns out to be a mammoth monolith that soars into the sky and extends a solitary arm into the ocean, and is separated from the main island by a narrow strip of water. A stone slab is put astride the water to serve as a bridge. The area around the Southern Heaven Gateway is clustered with rocks, whose grotesque forms add a somewhat outlandish touch to the scene. In the neighborhood are a number of tourist attractions, including cliff carvings and the Dragon-eye Well.

(8) One-Thousand-Step Beach. The beach lies on the eastern rim of Mount Putuo. The best bathing ground one can hope for, it is covered with a layer of fine sand feeling so soft to the feet

that walking on it was like walking on a golden carpet.

(9) Western Heaven Gate. Arranged through the invisible hands of nature, two rocks facing each other soar into the sky, with a third one, inscribed with the wording "World of Law of the West Heaven," balanced horizontally atop them to form the lintel of the "gate." A footpath leads beyond the stone gate and reaches the summit of the Damo (Darma) Peak. North of the "gate" there are a string of tourist attractions, including the Meifu Convent, the Pantuo Rock, the Rock of Two Turtles Listening to the Preaching of Law, and the Guanyin Cave. Situated in the sequestered repose of verdant trees to the west of the Puji Monastery, it is also a site of a camphor tree (*Cinnamomum camphora*) that has been around for at least eight centuries.

With its caves enshrouded in religious mystery, its rocks assuming forms ranging from the fabulous to the grotesque, its peaks cocooned under luxuriant woods, and its ethereal maritime scenery seemingly changing all the time, Mount Putuo is at once a nice summer resort and a paradise for nature lovers.

Mount Jiuhua 九华山 (Jiŭhuá Shān)

Mount Jiuhua rose in fame as the domain of Ksitigarbha thanks to the Korean monk Gim Kyokak who chose this mountain range of striking natural beauty as his home in the Tang Dynasty. It is said that three years after Gim died in 794 at the age of 99 his remains, placed in a sitting position in a stone sarcophagus, were found intact three years after his burial. This struck awe into the hearts of the local people, who regarded Kim as the reincarnation of Bodhisattva Ksitigarbha. Large numbers of pilgrims from around the country all the year round began to visit the mountain, a range that snakes its way for some 56 miles or 90 km west of Mount Huangshan. Its nine peaks are a topographical turmoil of cliffs that overlap and overhang to create many scenic wonders.

Statuesque forms of mountains and a graceful landscape have earned Mount Jiuhua the reputation as the "No. 1 Mountain in Southeast China." Originally, the mountain was called Mount Jiuzi until Li Bai, the celebrated Tang-dynasty poet, composed a poem to eulogize the mountain's nine lotus flower-like peaks. The poem goes like this:

Sailing down the Jiujiang River the other day
I espied nine fabulous peaks in the distance.
Looking as if they were nine lotus flowers
Embroidered by the Heavenly River using its emerald water as thread.

Legend has it that in 741 Gim Kyokak, whose religious name was Ksitigarbha Kim, left Silla, a kingdom in present-day Korea for Mount Jiuhua to practice Buddhism. One day, he was stung by a poisonous insect, but he kept his composure and went on with his meditation session as if nothing had happened. In no time a beautiful young woman materialized, bowing to him and offering him a dose of medicine.

"This stupid child (the insect) is ignorant of who you are, and I'll atone for his misconduct by offering you a spring," she said, and disappeared without a trace. Presently clear water gushed out of a stone crevice, saving Kim the trouble of having to fetching water from a nearby ravine. People of later generations dubbed the woman "Goddess of Mount Jiuzi," and the spring "Spring of the Dragon King's Daughter."

When Kim was cultivating himself through religious austerities, he had the fortune of being provided for by a man named Min Ranhe (also known as "Old Man Min.") The man's son later became Jim's disciple and assumed the monastic name "Daoming." Later, Min himself was converted to Buddhism and came under Kim's tutelage.

History books show that by 1911, the year that saw the fall of the Qing, Mount Jiuhua was home to 150 or so Buddhist temples (another version puts the number at more than 300). However, during the Republican years, many of them were ruined as a result of long years of war and disrepair. A little more than 70 of such temples remain now. The major ones are as follows:

(1) Huacheng Temple. Situated in the center of Mount Jiuhua, with the Lianhua (Lotus Flower) Peak to the south, the East Cliff to the east, the Shenguang (Devine Light) Peak to the west, and the Baiyun (White Cloud) Mountain to the north, the Huacheng Temple looks very much like a town rimmed by mountains. Its

buildings, arranged in four courtyards that ascend a mountainside one atop another, are simple and compact in style, and methodical in layout. With a history of more than 1,400 years, it is the oldest temple of Mount Jiuhua. Legend has it that during a tour of the mountain, Zhuge Jie and some other squires from Qingyang County were able to see Gim Kyokak, who lived a Spartan life in a cave abode, and ate nothing but a mixture of millet and white clay. The sight of the monk's hard lot generated feelings of self-reproach in the visiting gentry for not having done their bit to provide for him. They immediately pooled money to build the Huacheng Temple, and moved Kim into it with pomp and ceremony. At the request of Zhang Yan, governor of Chizhou (present-day Guichi, Anhui Province), Emperor Dezong (ruled 780-805) gave the temple a horizontal board inscribed with its two-character name "Huacheng" in his own handwriting. More Ming and Qing monarchs followed suit. The imperial favor bestowed on the temple, however, failed to save it from repeated destructions in the intervening years. Among the buildings remaining on the premises, only the Tripitaka Pavilion is a Ming legacy. The others were all rebuilt during the Qing. Among the temple's collection of artifacts are a Ming-dynasty version of the *Tripitaka* and edicts issued by some emperors.

(2) Precious Hall of the Holy Body. Popularly known as Roushen (meaning "physical body," referring to one who becomes a bodhisattva in the physical body while still in the present world) Pagoda, the hall is poised on the Shenguang Peak of Mount Jiuhua, a grandiose architectural phenomenon whose double-eaved Chinese hip-and-gable roof is covered with cast-iron tiles and supported by elaborate corbel brackets. A stone balustrade runs around the hall, which looks resplendent with carved rafters and lacquered pillars. Access to the front of the hall is by a stone stairway with 81 steps (another version puts it at 84), its iron-chain railing offering a sense of security for those climbing up the steep mountain. Placed in state in the hall is a 17-meter-high wooden pagoda with eight niches for figurines of Ksitigarbha on each of its seven layers. Inside the pagoda, the Guardian of the Earth whose mission is to deliver the suffering beings from the torments of hell, gazes down at the world from a portrait that is flanked by the standing statue of the ten kings

presiding over the ten departments of purgatory (The ten kings presiding over the ten departments of purgatory are known popularly as "ten kings of hell," and Yama, the King of Hell, is actually the name of the 5th of these kings.) Inscribed in gold on the walls of the pagoda is the full text of the *Ksitigarbha-sutra*. Underneath the pagoda is the chamber where the physical body of Gim Kyokak is preserved. On a platform behind the hall, incense sticks keep burning all day long in an iron tripod. The hall and its pagoda were repeated destroyed and reconstructed, and what is seen today was built during the Tongzhi reign (1862-1878) of the Qing.

(3) Zhiyuan Temple. The predecessor of this temple, situated to the east of the Huacheng Temple, was a nunnery of the same name built during the Jiajing reign (1522-1566) of the Ming. After repeated reconstructions and expansions it has eventually emerged as a three-courtyard affair. Its centerpiece, the Mahavira Hall, is graced with a golden-glazed roof. The road and ramp leading up to the front of the hall is paved with stone slabs engraved with lotus patterns. An awesome form of architecture and breathtaking ornamentation are perhaps reasons why the Zhiyuan Temple is regarded as the foremost Buddhist establishment of Mount Jiuhua.

(4) Tiantai Temple. The Tiantai Peak is the venue of the temple which is named after it but which is officially known as Ksitigarbha Bodhimandala. Construction of it began during the Ming, and it was rebuilt during the Guangxu reign (1875-1908) of the Qing. The buildings, including the Chamber of Ten Thousand Buddhas, the Hall of Ksitigarbha, and the Hall of Maitreya, are arranged in five rows laid out neatly one above the other along the contours of the mountain slope, so that in the distance the entire cluster looks like a titanic edifice. Numerous Buddhist figurines are carved into the walls and pillars of the temple. The place is a nice spot for enjoying watching the sunrise from underneath an ocean of clouds at the foot of the temple.

(5) Ganlu Temple. Standing half way up the Huacheng Mountain, the temple was originally known as Ganlu Nunnery or Ganlu Bodhimandala before it assumed its present name in 1667 in the Qing Dynasty at the suggestion of Yulin, a monk of Chan Buddhism who visited Mount Jiuhua and was impressed by the auspicious topography of the temple. Shortly afterwards, another

monk by the name of Dong'an raised money and expanded the temple which was later razed in war during the Xianfeng reign (1851-1861) of the Qing. The present building was erected in 1864. Its large size and august style of architecture rank it among the classic temples of Mount Jiuhua.

(6) Wannian Temple. This is a grand temple dating back to the Ming Dynasty that was rebuilt and renovated several times. It was expanded and given its present name in 1839 in the Qing Dynasty.

(7) Zhantan (Sandalwood) Temple. This once was a part of the Huacheng Temple and was rebuilt in 1896 in the Qing Dynasty by a monk by the name of Chanding. Housed in its halls, which evince the classic sanctity of a religious sanctuary, are horizontal nameboards, stone inscriptions and many other artifacts.

(8) Huiju Temple. The predecessor of this temple was the Huiju Nunnery dating back to the Qing Dynasty, and it assumed its present name in 1938. The temple features a complete collection of statues of the Buddha and bodhisattvas in lifelike images. Its posterior hall is a two-floor structure, with the second floor devoted to the Pavilion of Guanyin, and the ground floor occupied by the Hall of Ksitigarbha.

Mount Emei 峨眉山 (Éméi Shān)

Mount Emei Scenic Area, including Leshan Giant Buddha Scenic Area, was added as a World Cultural Heritage site to the UNESCO World Heritage List in 1996. Its highest peak, known as the Summit of Ten Thousand Buddhas, rises some 9,900 feet or 3,077 meters above sea level. A world of rocky eminences cocooned under a green blanket of trees, with a thicket of peaks emerging from the clouds and thrusting into the sky, Mount Emei is quite up to the saying, "No place under heaven is as beautiful as Mount Emei." Only by following a stone-paved path that begins at the foot of the mountain and winds its way around one peak after another for some 47 miles or 60 kilometers can one reach the summit of the mountain. The very diverse and rich vegetation on Mount Emei features some 3,200 species of trees and plants, of which 31 are under state protection. There are more than 500 species of flowers. Azalea alone boasts 29 types. Amidst this vegetation that covers 92 % of the mountain live some 2,300 kinds of animals, of which 157 are rare animals like the lesser panda which is on the verge of extinction. Some of these animals are under state protection; some live only on Mount Emei. Adjacent to Mount Emei is Lingyun Mountain where the colossal Leshan Giant Buddha was carved into a cliff face in 713 during the Tang Dynasty and with a sitting height of some 228 feet or 71 meters, the first and the largest of its kind in the world.

Buddhism found its way to Mount Emei probably during the Western and Eastern Jin dynasties (265-420) when the place was dominated by Daoism. Buddhism did not begin to thrive there until after the Tang and Song dynasties, and it was during the Song Dynasty that Mount Emei was formally declared as the domain of Samantabhadra. More than 100 temples were built on the mountain during the Ming and Qing dynasties. Buddhism went into decline here during the Republican years when many temples were left to fall into disrepair. The damp weather has taken its toll as well — as it has on the Leshan Giant Buddha. The Leshan Giant Buddha is not Sakyamuni, the founder of Buddhism, but his disciple Maitreya. According to historical records, the past dynasties all did something to maintain the Leshan Buddha. In modern times, the Buddha has experienced six periods of large-scale maintenance. By the time when the People's Republic was founded, only some 30 temples remained. The following is a brief introduction to some of the better known ones.

(1) Wannian (Ten Thousand Years) Temple. The exquisite bronze statue of Samantabhadra enshrined in the Wannian Temple is a priceless relic under state protection. The statue weighing 62 tons, honors Samantabhadra, Bodhisattva of Universal Benevolence. According to history books, in 968 during the Song Dynasty, the imperial court dispatched Zhang Chongjin, a palace attendant, to investigate repeated reports from Jiazhou Prefecture (present-day Jiading, Sichuan Province) about the discovery of auspicious signs of Samantabhadra. In 980, the imperial court had the statue cast and built a hall to enshrine this colossal sculpture some 23 feet or 7 meters high, thereby setting the beginnings of Mount Emei's history as the domain of Samantabhadra. The temple has

manicured gardens, ancient trees, majestic halls. A relatively old Buddhist establishment of Mount Emei, it was originally called the Puxian (Samantabhadra) Temple, which became the Baishui Temple during the Tang and Baishui Puxian Temple during the Song, and assumed the name of Shengshou Wannian Temple during the Wanli reign (1573-1620) of the Ming Dynasty when it was a colossal affair with seven courtyards. In 1946, a major fire reduced all the wooden structures to ashes, and only the brick halls built during the Ming survived. The present temple, reconstructed in 1953, has two courtyards, with the main hall housing the statues of Vairocana, Sakyamuni, and Amitabha. The front gate of the temple opens onto a forest. When night falls on a summer day, the place is taken over by a contingent of frogs native to Mount Emei with croaks evocative of the tones of a zither.

(2) Baoguo Temple. When it was first built at the foot of Mount Emei during the Wanli reign (1573-1620) of the Ming, it was known as Huizong Chamber. It assumed its present name during a major refurbishment during the Kangxi reign (1662-1722) of the Qing. The horizontal nameboard hung above its front gate is inscribed in the handwriting of Emperor Kangxi. The temple contains four main buildings with anterooms — the Maitreya Hall, the Mahavira Hall, the Seven-Buddha Hall, and the Tripitaka Pavilion — that are laid out in a descending order following the contours of the terrain. The Baoguo Temple is situated where people start climbing the mountain, and has quite a few fine artifacts on display. These include the cast-copper Huayan Pagoda, a masterpiece of foundry that is a 14-story structure with 4,700-odd Buddhist likenesses and the unabridged text of the *Garland Sutra* engraved in its walls. There is also an invaluable 2.4-meter-high color-glazed porcelain sculpture of the Buddha dating back to 1415 (13th year, Yongle reign, Ming Dynasty). The big bronze bell hung in front of the temple weighs 12,500 kg.

(3) Fuhu Temple. Nestling at the foot of Mount Emei down the road from the Baoguo Temple, the Fuhu Temple, meaning "Temple to Subdue Tigers," was first built during the Tang, and renamed Shenlong Chamber during the Song. At the time the place was terrorized by man-eating tigers, and the monks of the temple erected a victory-honoring dhvaju (a pillar with a silk stream fluttering atop it) to subdue them. (Another version asserts

that the name "Fuhu" stemmed from the mountain's tiger-like form.) The temple also had its fill of ups and downs in its history, and its last major repairs took place in 1651 during the Qing Dynasty. The temple was one of the largest Buddhist centers of Mount Emei, with its 13 major halls and chambers tucked away in the shade of a forest and arranged along a central axis. Although the temple buildings are under a canopy of trees, falling leaves seldom settle on its rooftops. This prompted Emperor Kangxi to name it "Dust-Free Garden," and inscribed the three characters on a horizontal board for the temple. During the War of Resistance against Japan (1937-1945), the temple became the school buildings of Sichuan University. In recent years, it has gradually been restored to its former scale and glory, with Buddhist statues being re-erected in its various halls.

(4) Qingyin Pavilion. Situated at the foot of the Niuxin Mountain, the Qingyin Pavilion used to be the Niuxin Temple during the Tang Dynasty. This is where two rivers converge, the Bailong (White Dragon) River in the east and the Heilong (Black Dragon) River in the west. Water tumbles down the two rivers from a height and plunges into the depth of a ravine, and in the process produces a peculiarly ringing sound. Hence the name of this site — "Twin Bridge Reverberated with a Ringing Sound" — one of the ten major scenic sights of Mount Emei. Just west of the Qingyin Pavilion is the sight known as "Strip of Sky," two vertical cliffs standing facing each other.

(5) Hongchunping Terrace. This is also the name of a temple on this terrace, with Chinese toon trees growing in front of it. The predecessor of this temple was the Thousand-Buddha Nunnery built during the Ming. It was rebuilt in 1790 (55th year of the Qianlong reign, Qing Dynasty), and its main hall is graced with a couplet in Emperor Qianlong's own handwriting. The treasure of the temple, however, is a lotus flower lantern nearly 6 feet or 2 meters in height and about 3 feet or 1 meter in diameter. Wrought towards the end of the Qing Dynasty, the lantern is carved with seven dragons and several hundred Buddhist statues in admirable craftsmanship.

(6) Xianfeng Temple, also known as Cave of Nine Old Men. Legend has it that this was where during a visit to Mount Emei the Yellow Emperor came across an old man and asked him how

many companions were with him. The old man answered nine. Such is the origin of the name of the Cave of Nine Old Men, which is known more popularly as Celestial Mansion of Nine Old Men. The cave is situated to the right of the temple. When the temple itself was built during the Wanli reign (1573-1620) of the Ming, it had four halls with roofs of cast-iron tiles, and the Ming court bestowed it with a collection of the *Tripitaka.* The buildings as they stand today were mostly repaired or rebuilt during the Qing. The temple is frequented by monkeys who will beg for food. Visitors to this place should make it a point to bring some food if they don't want to disappoint the monkeys.

(7) Xixiang (Elephant Bathing) Pool. This is a small affair known as Chuxi Convent when it was first built in 1368, the year the Ming Dynasty was founded. In 1699 in the Qing Dynasty it was expanded and became a temple. The tiny pool in front of the temple was said to be where Bodhisattva Samantabhadra bathed his elephant. The main hall, which enshrines the statues of three bodhisattvas — Guanyin (Avalokitesvara), Ksitigarbha, and Mahasthamaprapt, stands atop a mountain and is surrounded by firs. The place also teems with delightful monkeys.

(8) Golden Peak, the summit of Mount Emei. It is probably the best place to watch the sunrise. Because of its sheer height, in the past the temple halls on its slopes were often hit by lightening and burned down. New halls were built there a few years ago to accommodate those who come to marvel at the views.

Chapter 7

Chinese Buddhism: International Relations

The Mahayana branch of Buddhism advocates delivering the multitude of people from misery by benevolence, and admonishes people to perform good deeds during their lifetimes. Buddhists in China have all along maintained friendly cultural exchanges within its own regions and with counterparts in other Asian countries and beyond as Buddhism has made its way to the West. A recent example of such exchange was the return of a precious relic from the Sui Dynasty (581-618): The stone head of the Akshobhya Buddha statue, originally from the Simen (Four-Gate) Pagoda of the Shentong Temple in Shandong that was sawed off and stolen in 1997. The Buddha head was moved from place to place around the globe over a period of more than four years before coming into the possession Master Sheng Yen, founder of the Dharma Drum Mountain Foundation located in Peitou, Taipei as a donation to the foundation's Museum of Buddhist History and Culture.

"Returning this 1,300-year-old Buddhist relic to its historic roots and restoring it to its original dignified completeness is much more important than keeping it here," said Master Sheng, according to a November 30, 2002 Xinhua news report.

For centuries close neighbors of China — India, Sri Lanka, Nepal, Myanmar, Cambodia, Thailand, Indonesia, Korea and Japan — have engaged with China in goodwill exchanges. The following gives a brief account of Chinese Buddhist relations with these neighbors, starting with India and Nepal, the source of Buddhism.

India

Both China and India are among the most ancient civilizations in the world. Their territories are linked, but they have strikingly different cultural traditions. Buddhism, however, has played a major role in bridging that cultural gap and keeping the two great nations close together over the last several millennia.

One of the theories on how Buddhism came to China holds that 18 monks arrived in China during the reign of Qinshihuang or the First Emperor of Qin (221-210 BC) with Buddhist scriptures, including a monk named Sramana Srifang. No historical records exist to prove it, though the theory coincides with the historical fact that Asoka, the king of the Mayura Dynasty of India, was dispatching large numbers of Buddhist priests to neighboring countries during that time. In any case, at some point an avenue of Buddhist exchanges opened up between India and China: Indian Buddhists arrived in China to preach and translate scriptures, Chinese monks went on pilgrimages to India to search for more Buddhist scriptures and pay homage to holy landmarks of Buddhism. With this, it can be said that Buddhism provided the avenue for China and India to come close together. It is impossible for a book of this size to enumerate all the numerous monks who have come and gone between the two nations during the past 2,000 years. However, among the most prominent among the Indians who traveled to China are (See 3. The Scripture Translators, Chapter 1 and Appendices II: Who's Who in Han Buddhist History):

Kumarajiva (343-413). Born in Kuqa in a family of Indian descent, Kumarajiva began his religious life with his mother at the age of seven, went to Kubha to study the doctrines at nine, and, having excelled in his studies and shown verbal skill in debates, returned to Kuqa at 12. Before long he made a name for himself by his erudite knowledge of Mahayana and Hinayana classics. In 382 , he was captured by the Eastern Jin general Lü Guang dispatched by King Fu Jian of Former Qin (350-394) on an expedition against Kuqa, and brought to Liangzhou in present-day Wuwei, Gansu Province by the Chinese army. During the 17 years he spent in Liangzhou, Kumarajiva learned local customs and habits and the Chinese language and prepared himself for a career as a Buddhist scriptural translator. In 401, he arrived in Chang'an and won the respect of the emperor, Yao Xing. With his arrival, Chang'an became the Buddhist center of north China, and he became the leader of a team of Chinese and foreign scholars who translated large numbers of major scriptures, commandments and treatises into Chinese, thereby vastly replenishing the Buddhist literature in Chinese and opening up a new chapter in the development of Chinese Buddhism. For his tremendous contributions to the Sino-Indian cultural exchange, Kumarajiva is regarded as the foremost of the four major sutra translators in the history of Chinese Buddhism.

Paramartha (491-569). This Indian monk was preaching Buddhism in Funan (present-day Cambodia) before arriving in Nanhai in present-day Guangdong in 546. Two years later, he went to the capital of the Liang Dynasty (502-557) in present-day Nanjing, Jiangsu Province, and soon won the favor of Emperor Wu Xiao Yan. However, his life of settled peace and contentment was short lived with the outbreak of a mutiny launched by General Hou Jing. He became homeless, and had trouble making ends meet. Despite the hardships, he translated large numbers of Buddhist scriptures and treatises and became one of the four major translators of scriptures in the history of Chinese Buddhism.

Amoghavajra (705-774). Arriving in China as a child to receive his education in Chinese culture, Amoghavajra became a monk in China as well. He eventually rose to fame by rendering large numbers of Indian Buddhist scriptures in Chinese and becoming one of a major founder of the Esoteric School of Han Buddhism. (Amoghavajra was said to be a native of Sinhala. See Sri Lanka below).

Among the most prominent of the Chinese monks who made pilgrimages to India:

Faxian (336-422), a native of Wuyang (now Xiangqiu County, Shanxi Province) with the secular surname of Gong, he became a monk while a child, and making a pilgrimage to India had been a cherished dream since the time he was bestowed the commandments at the age of 20. In 399 during the Eastern Jin Dynasty, together with three companions, he set off from Chang'an (present-day Xi'an) to begin an arduous journey to India. The toughest part of the journey was in the desolate Gobi Desert.

He eventually arrived at Patuliputra, capital of Magadha. While there he studied and copied sutras and treatises for a while before traveling further south to Sinhala, the "Lion Country." He returned to China in 412. A year later, working together with the Indian monk Buddhabhadra (359-429), he translated six scriptures and treatises. Based on his travels to more than 30 countries, Faxian wrote the classic *Faxian's Pilgrimage to India.* At the time, quite a few Chinese went on pilgrimages to India, but because of the harsh conditions on the way, few were heard from again. Faxian, however, survived to be regarded in history as one of the most accomplished of all the pilgrims.

Xuanzang began his journey west in 629 during the Tang Dynasty. He stayed in the Nalanda Monastery for many years, where he established a high reputation throughout India. He eventually returned to China with a huge load of Sanskrit classics, some of which he translated into Chinese. He even translated Laozi's *Tao Te Jing* into Sanskrit, and the *Mahayana-sraddhotpada-sastra* by the Indian philosopher Asvaghosa from Sanskrit into Indian, thereby making historic contributions to Sino-Indian Buddhist exchanges.

Yijing (635-713), a native of Fanyang (present-day Zhuoxian, Hebei Province), was tonsured as a monk at the age of 15. His admiration of the noble deeds on behalf of Buddhism of Faxian and Xuanzang in journeying to India inspired him to make the same trip. In 671, he set off from Yangzhou and boarded a ship at Panyu, Guangdong, thereby beginning his solitary journey to India. Two years later he arrived in east India, where he first roamed the country to see famous Buddhist scenes and sights and then settled in the Nalanda Monastery as a student. Eleven years later, having studied various schools of Indian Buddhism and collected 400 or so Sanskrit versions of Buddhist literature, he began his journey home. In 695 during the reign of Empress Wu Zetian, he arrived at Luoyang to the personal welcome of the empress. His translations and works amounted to 239 volumes in 61 titles, second only to the achievements of Xuanzang.

The Buddhist ties between China and India went on continuously for more than 1,000 years, from the Han to the Song dynasties. It was not until the 12th century, when Buddhism was suppressed in India, that the two nations' exchanges in this field was interrupted.

In the early 20th century Indian Buddhism showed signs of revival. Buddhists from some Asian countries began to build temples in India. In the 1940s, Chinese Buddhists joined in the effort, hoping to restore the Sino-Indian Buddhist relations after an interruption of several centuries. In January 1940, a Chinese Buddhist delegation headed by Master Taixu visited India, and was accorded a warm welcome in Calcutta when they visited the Maha Bodhi Society, the Bangla Buddhist Association, and the International University founded by the celebrated poet Rabindranath Tagore (1861-1941). The visit laid a sound foundation for restoring the Buddhist relations between the two nations. In 1956, the Chinese Buddhist Association hosted an international Buddhist monks' delegation headed by India's Rev. Ananda Kusalyayana, and another Indian monk, Jagdis Kasyapa (1908-1976), was a member of the delegation. That same year a Chinese Buddhist and cultural delegation visited India. The Chinese Buddhist Association received the Indian Buddhist scholar Rahula in 1958, and another Indian Buddhist scholar Chandra Nanda in 1983. These mutual exchanges gradually brought the Buddhists of both countries close together again.

Nepal

A legend that is still popular in China has it that in remote antiquity, what is today's Napalese capital city of Cathmantu was a lake surrounded by mountains. It was Manjusri, the Bodhisattva of Wisdom, who wielded his sharp sword and slashed open the mountains to the south, draining the water and turning the lake into land. Whatever its origin, one thing is certain about this legend — it shows Nepal's close tie with China and Chinese Buddhism, for Manjusri is a major bodhisattva of Mahayana Buddhism, and his domain was Mount Wutai in China.

Moreover, ever since Buddhism was introduced into China in 1st century BC, Lumbini, Nepal, the birthplace of Sakyamuni, has been a mecca for Chinese Buddhist pilgrims. In 405 during the Eastern Jin Dynasty, the monk Faxian, who was studying in India (see above), paid a visit to Lumbini, becoming perhaps the first

Chinese to do so. *Faxian's Pilgrimage to India* gives a detailed account of his visit to Lumbini and Kapilavastu. While Faxian was studying Buddhism in India, Buddhabhadra, a well-known monk who belonged to the same caste as Sakyamuni, was preaching and translating Buddhist scriptures in China. One of his translations, the 60-volume *Buddhavatamsaka-mahavaipulya Sutra (Garland Sutra),* became a major scripture of Han Buddhism. After Faxian returned, Buddhabhadra joined him in the Daochang Monastery in present-day Nanjing, where they translated six major scriptures and commandments.

The celebrated Tang-dynasty monk Xuanzang also visited Lumbini and Kapilavastu. According to his eyewitness account in the *Records on the Western Regions of the Great Tang Empire*, the places were clustered with Buddhist establishments, and there were more than 2,000 monks devoted to the study of both Mahayana and Hinayana Buddhism.

In the 7th century, King Songtsan Gampo of Tibet married Princess Wencheng of the Tang imperial court and Princess Bhrikuti Devi of Nepalese royal family. As both princesses were Buddhist followers, they helped promote the exchanges between China and Nepal and open up a shortcut for Chinese pilgrims to go to India by way of Tibet and Nepal. It was precisely by this route that the 300 or so Chinese monks dispatched by the Northern Song court arrived in India to pursue Buddhist studies.

Meanwhile, during China's Yuan Dynasty, Nepalese craftsmen were invited to build a gold pagoda for Phags-pa in Tibet. One of them was the famed artisan Aniko, who later arrived in Dadu (Great Capital) of the Yuan, that is, present-day Beijing, where the imperial court entrusted him with the task of casting Buddhist statues and other projects. The famous White Dagoba of the Miaoying Temple in Beijing was designed and constructed under his supervision.

In the over half a century since the founding of the People's Republic, exchanges between Chinese and Nepalese Buddhists have included: In 1956, at the invitation of Ven. Amrita Nanda, a 15-member Chinese delegation with Shes-rab-rgya-tso as leader and Zhao Puchu as deputy leader attended the 4th session of the World Federation of Buddhists in Nepal. In 1959, the Chinese Buddhist Association invited a six-member delegation

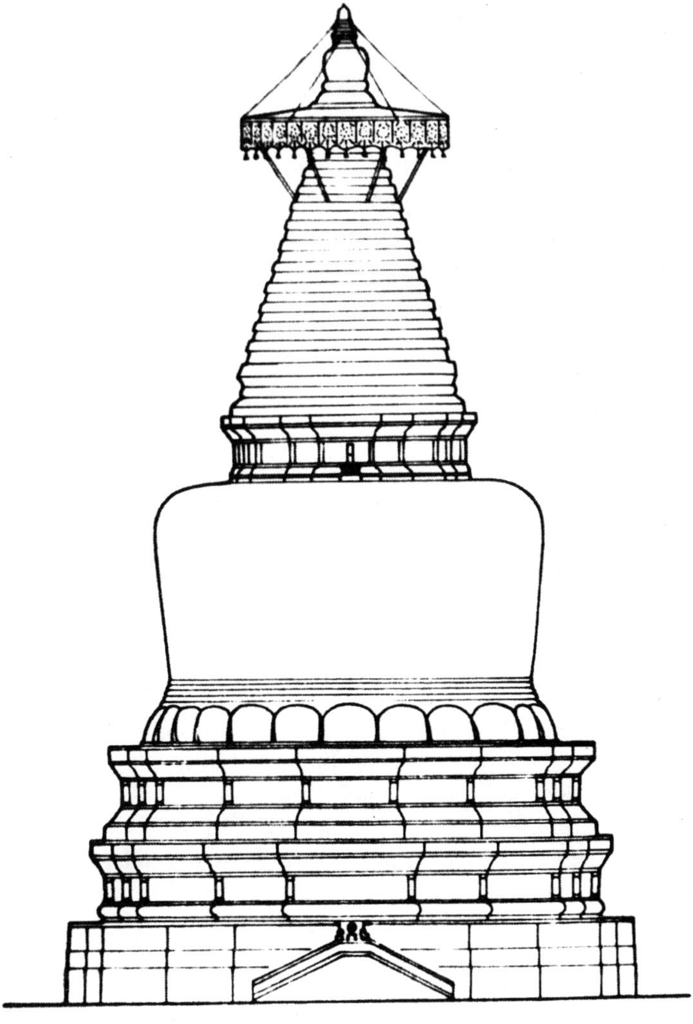

The model of the White Dagoba designed by the Nepalese architect Aniko for the Miaoying Temple in Dadu (now Beijing) of the Yuan Dynasty from Nepalese Society for the Rejuvenation of Buddhism headed by Ven. Amrita Nanda to pay a month-long visit to various parts of China, thereby greatly enhancing the understanding and friendship between Buddhists of both countries. Shortly after the Nepalese delegation returned home, the Chinese embassy in Katmandu donated a fund on behalf of the Chinese Buddhist Association to the Nepalese government for the construction of a science center. In 1997, five Nepalese *sramanerikas* were ordained to the *bhiksuni* commandments in Guangdong, China. To promote Sino-Nepalese friendship, the Chinese Buddhist Association built a Chinese-style monastery in Lumbini, which was completed and consecrated in a grand ceremony in 2000.

Sri Lanka

China and Sri Lanka started Buddhist exchanges as early as the Eastern Jin Dynasty (317-420). According to Volume 54 of *Book of Liang*, when the king of Sinhala, that is, present-day Sri Lanka, learned that the emperor of China worshipped the Buddha and his doctrines, the king dispatched an envoy to deliver a 3-foot or 1.38-meter-high jade statue of the Buddha by sea. It took the envoy 10 years to arrive at the Chinese capital of present-day Nanjing in 406. At about the same time, in 410, the Chinese monk Faxian left India and arrived in Sinhala. During his two-year stay there, he called on famous monks, collected Buddhist classics, and witnessed a grand parade in honor of the Buddha's tooth relic. By the time he left Sinhala and began his journey back to China in 412, Faxian had already cultivated a reputation for himself. Faxian today remains a household name in Sri Lanka, where there is the Faxian Cave, probably the former residence of the Chinese monk during his stay in the country.

During the Southern and Northern Dynasties (420-589), eight Sinhalese *bhiksunis* visited Nanjing, the capital of the Southern dynasties. Shortly afterwards, another group of 11 Sinhalese nuns headed by Tissara arrived in China to preside over a ceremony where Chinese nuns were to receive the commandments from two Nikayas of Sangha. Chinese Buddhists built a temple for the nuns from Sinhala and named it Tissara Temple, a legendary event among Sino-Sri Lanka Buddhist exchanges.

The Indian monk Amoghavajra (705-775) was said to be a native of Sinhala. In 742, he led a Chinese delegation on a journey to study in Sinhala. When he returned to Chang'an four years later, he organized a workshop to translate scriptures, and became the father of the Esoteric School of Chinese Buddhism.

During the Song Dynasty (960-1279), China retained a close Buddhist relationship with Sinhala. It was not until Western colonialists invaded that country were the frequent exchange of visits between monks from the two nations interrupted. The Sino-Sri Lanka Buddhist relations came into their own once again in the 1930s when Ven. Narada, abbot of the Vajrarama Monastery of Colombo, visited Shanghai, where he established wide contacts with local Buddhists and made the decision to accept five Chinese nuns to study in Ceylon. In 1940, the eminent monk Taixu headed a Chinese delegation on a visit to Ceylon, and talked to Dr. Gunapala Piyasena Malalasekera (1899-1973), leader of the Ceylon Buddhist Association, about ways and means to establish the World Federation of Buddhists. In 1942, Fafang, a disciple of Taixu, arrived in Ceylon to preach the doctrines of Mahayana Buddhism. In 1946, the Han-Tibetan Buddhist Academy of China and the Moha Bodhi Society of Ceylon reached an agreement, and as a result two Chinese students went to study in Ceylon and three Ceylonese students arrived in China. In 1950, Fafang was invited to Ceylon University as a lecturer on Chinese Buddhism.

The Sino-Sri Lanka Buddhist relationship became even closer after the founding of the People's Republic of China. In 1956, when the Ceylonese Buddhist circles launched a campaign to compile the English version of *Encyclopedia of Buddhism* to mark the 2,500th anniversary of the nirvana of Sakyamuni, the Chinese Buddhist Association responded by forming a panel of writers who contributed manuscripts on Chinese Buddhism. In 1961, at the request of Ceylon's Buddhist circles, the Chinese Buddhist Association escorted the Buddha's tooth relic all the way to Ceylon to be worshiped by local monks. In 1979, the visiting prime minister of Sri Lanka, Ranasinghe Premadasa, presented an imitation ancient statue of the Buddha to the Chinese Buddhist Association. Since then the two countries have exchanged visits to step up bilateral relationship in Buddhism. In 1986, five Chinese Buddhist Seminary students arrived in Sri Lanka, while Buddhist students from Sri Lanka were enrolled in Peking University. Thanks to the frequent exchanges, Sino-Sri Lanka friendship has been enhancing steadily.

Myanmar

Theravada Buddhism prevails over the religious life of Myanmar, but no conclusive historical evidence is extant to the exact time for the introduction of Buddhism into Myanmar. Legend has it that in the 3rd century BC, King Asoka of the Mayura dynasty in ancient India dispatched Buddhist preachers to neighboring countries and regions, including a so-called "Golden Region." But whether this is a reference to Myanmar is yet to be confirmed. Another theory has it that Buddhism spread into Myanmar from Sinhala during the 5th century. Both theories attest to the long history of Buddhism in Myanmar. In Volume 10 of his *Records on the Western Regions of the Great Tang Empire*, Xuanzang mentioned that in a country called Sriksetra, Buddhists were making a living by soliciting alms. *Biographies of Famous Tang Pilgrims to Western Regions* written by Yijing, who lived in an age slightly later than Xuanzang, said that a Chinese monk and a native of Jiangling (Jingzhou in present-day Hubei Province) by the name of Tanguang once visited the region of Arakan in western Myanmar, and he won the respect of the local king by offering him a substantial tribute.

In the 7th century Theravada Buddhism was introduced from Myanmar to the Dai-inhabited areas of Yunnan. In 792, the younger brother of the king of Burma, known at the time as the kingdom of Pyu, visited China and delivered Buddhist music scores to the Tang imperial court. Buddhism met its demise in Burma as a result of the Thai-Burmese war in the 12th century, but shortly afterwards, Theravada Buddhism once again found its way from Thailand into Yunnan by way of Burma. Historical records show that in the 18th century, the king of Burma dispatched an envoy and delivered to the emperor of China Buddhist statues and Buddhist scriptures in Burmese — highly likely the Pali language spelled in the Burmese alphabet.

The founding of the People's Republic of China in 1949 saw new developments in the growth of Sino-Burmese Buddhist relations. In 1955, a 10-member Chinese Buddhist Association delegation headed by Shes-rab-rgya-tso visited Burma at the invitation of the Burmese Buddhist circles. Most members of the delegation were well-known personages, who gave their Burmese friends quite a few gifts, including Buddhist bone relics, a Chinese edition of the *Tripitaka*, monastic habits in Han and Tibetan styles, alms bowls, and staffs. In September of the same year, a 12-member Burmese Buddhist delegation headed by U Thien Maung arrived in Beijing to escort a Buddha's tooth relic from Beijing's Lingguang Temple to Burma for public display. The Chinese Buddhist Association held a grand farewell summons ceremony in Guangji Temple, which was attended by more than 1,000 people from various walks of life, and appointed Zhao Puchu as the head of a Chinese delegation to go along with the Burmese delegation on the journey to Burma. When the airplane carrying with the Buddha's tooth relic arrived in Yangon, President Ba U and Premier U Nu were at the airport and personally carried the golden stupa enshrined with the relic from the airplane. When the float loaded with the relic drove through the city, the entire Yangon turned out into the streets to greet it. During the relic's eight-month display, more than one million people paid homage to it. To be able to take a look at the Buddha's tooth relic from China had been a dream cherished by the Burmese people for many generations, and when the dream came true at last shortly after the founding of the People's Republic of China, the consolation for them was immeasurable.

In May 1956, a delegation of the Chinese Buddhist Association arrived in Burma upon invitation for the closing ceremony of the 6th grand summons ceremony in commemoration of the 2,500th anniversary of the nirvana of Sakyamuni. (At this grand summons ceremony, taking place for only the sixth time in Buddhist history, an unprecedented number of 2,500 monks participated in proofreading and annotating the Pali edition of the *Tripitaka*.) When the Chinese delegation headed by Hubameng, a religious leader of ethnic Dai background, escorted the Buddha's tooth relic back to China, the Burmese government sent Khin

Maung Phyu, secretary-general of the Burmese government, and two others to accompany the delegation until the relic arrived in Kunming. In October 1958, the Chinese Buddhist Association presented an imitation of the Buddha's tooth relic to Burma at the request of the Burmese Buddhist Association. Later, a pagoda was erected in the region of Myitkyina in north Burma to enshrine the gift as a symbol of Sino-Burmese friendship.

China's policy of reform and opening up to the outside world has brought Buddhists of the two nations even more closely together. In 1994 and 1996 respectively, the Buddha's tooth relic was again publicly displayed in Myanmar, and the Chinese Buddhist Association dispatched a number of young monks to study Theravada Buddhism in Myanmar. In 2001, Myanmar government delegation headed by Minister of Religious Affairs U Aung Khin presented as a token of appreciation for the Chinese Buddhist Association's sharing of the tooth relic a 4-foot 6-inch tall jade Buddha that is now enshrined in the Jade Buddha Hall of Lingguang Temple in Beijing. (See 9. Major Han Buddhist Temples, Chapter 4) Obviously the Buddha's tooth relic has played a major role in the Sino-Burmese Buddhist relationship. The shared love of the relic has indeed been a bond to bring Buddhists of both countries close together.

Cambodia

Buddhist relations between China and Cambodia began during the Southern and Northern Dynasties in the 5th century when Cambodia was known as Funan. According to volume 58 of the *Book of Southern Qi*, an Indian monk by the name of Nagasena, who was living in China's Nanhai in present-day Guangdong, visited Funan by ship and talked to the king about the growth of Buddhism in China. The king in return entrusted Nagasena to bring a letter and gifts to Emperor Wu of the Southern Qi in 484. This event probably marked the first Buddhist contact between China and Cambodia. Shortly afterwards, Sanghapala (459-524), a Cambodian monk known in his country for his academic accomplishments, arrived in the Chinese capital in present-day Nanjing to settle down in the Zhengguan Temple. There, he joined the Indian monk Gunabhadra (394-468) in the study of Mahayana Buddhism. After the Southern Qi fell, Sanghapala went into hiding and lost all contact with society. After Emperor Wu of the Liang (502-557) converted to Buddhism, he began searching for talented Buddhists. In 503 another Cambodian monk, Mandra (5th-6th century), arrived in China to deliver many Sanskrit Buddhist scriptures and gifts to the Chinese emperor. In 506, Emperor Wu discovered the whereabouts of Sanghapala, brought him out of his hermitage, and had him resume his translation work of Buddhist sutras and treatises. It is said Sanghapala translated a total of 38 volumes in 11 (another theory puts it at 10) titles, a small number of which were probably done together with Mandra. In 519 and 539, the king of Cambodia twice paid tribute to Emperor Wu. When the emperor learned from one of the Cambodian envoys that Funan was in the possession of the Buddha's hair relics, he dispatched Monk Shi Baoyun to go along with the envoy back to Cambodian to ask the Cambodian king for a portion of the relics and invite a famous Cambodian *Tripitaka* expert to come preach in China. It happened that the famous Indian monk Paramartha was in Funan at the time, and with the consent of the Cambodian king, he was invited to China. Paramartha eventually emerged as one of the four major Buddhist translators in China. (See 3. The Scripture Translators, Chapter 1) After the Chen Dynasty (557-589) seized power from the Liang, more Cambodian Buddhists arrived in China as translators. Judging from the scriptures translated by Parmartha and others Cambodian monks in China, the same type of Mahayana Buddhism was dominating the religious life of Cambodia at the time.

During the 6th century, Funan was renamed Chenla. In Volume 10 of his *Records on the Western Regions of the Great Tang Empire*, Xuanzang mentioned Isana City as the capital of Chenla but was not able to give an eyewitness account of the place. In the early 9th century, the king of Chenla began construction of the Angkor City, which eventually assumed its present shape after several generations. Today, Angkor, with its central monastery of the same name, is the pride and emblem of the Cambodian people.

After the 12th century, Chenla became Cambodia, and due to influences from Thailand and Burma, the Cambodian people were gradually converted to Theravada Buddhism, which resulted in the disappearance of Mahayana Buddhism in that country.

Exchanges between Buddhists of China and Cambodia had been scanty over the last few centuries, but the situation improved somewhat after the founding of the Peoples' Republic of China. In May 1957, at the invitation of the Cambodian Buddhist circles, a Chinese delegation headed by Chisong arrived in Cambodia for a ceremony to mark the 2,500th anniversary of the nirvana of Sakyamuni. During the ceremony, members of the Chinese delegation came into wide contact with their hosts, including leaders of the two major local Buddhist sects. In June 1958, a Cambodian Buddhist delegation headed by Ven. Preah Huo Tat was warmly received by Chinese Buddhists when it visited China. Both events marked the restoration of Sino-Cambodian Buddhist relations after an interruption of several decades.

Thailand

According to Chinese history books, there were four countries in western Thailand — Lang-ya-hsiu, P'an-P'an, Ch'ih-t'u, and Dvaravati — in ancient times, and all of them had contacts with China. As early as the 5th century, Khmer monks inhabiting the Mekong Delta were coming to China to preach, while Chinese monks reciprocated by paying return visits. Some of the four countries held vital access to India for Chinese monks traveling by sea after the 7th century. This was the same route followed by the Chinese monks, Yilang of Yezhou, Yihui of Luoyang, Daolin of Jingzhou, on their way to India, according to the *Biographies of Famous Tang Pilgrims to Western Regions,* and they had all visited Lang-ya-hsiu. Yihui actually died there.

In 1387 in China's Ming Dynasty the kingdoms of Sien and Lavo were unified to create the new nation known as "Siam," a name that remained until it was changed to "Thailand" in the 20th century. Theravada Buddhism was introduced from Sri Lanka in the 13th-14th centuries, and that has remained the dominant religion in the area until today. After the founding of the People's Republic of China, Sino-Thai Buddhist relations progressed, particularly after 1975 with the establishment of diplomatic relations between China and Thailand. High-level exchanges and visits over recent years have taken place between religious circles of Thailand and the Chinese Buddhist Association. In June 1993, the Thai Sangharaja (patriarch) visited China upon invitation, and in 1995, the Buddha's finger relic was sent from China to Thailand to be worshipped by Thai Buddhists. Today, some Chinese monks are studying Theravada Buddhism in Thailand.

Indonesia

Indonesia is basically an Islamic country (87 percent of the population) with only some 1 percent of Indonesians identifying themselves as Buddhists, mostly in the Theravada tradition. In ancient times, however, Buddhism was popular in this island country, and this was particular so in Java and Sumatra where the relationship between Chinese and Indonesian Buddhists dates back to the 5th century. According to *Faxian's Pilgrimage to India,* an autobiographical account of the travels of the Chinese pilgrim monk Faxian to more than 30 countries in search of Buddhist doctrines, Brahamanism held sway in 412 when he stopped there for five months on his way back to China from Sinhala. It was not until the arrival of the Indian monk Gunavarman, who had been living in China, that Buddhism began to thrive there. According to legend, Gunavarman earned the respect of the royal family, and under the king's edict, the entire nation became Buddhist. In 424 at the time of Song of the Southern Dynasties, the well-known monks Huiguan and Huicong met Emperor Wen to suggest that Gunavarman be invited back to China to preach Buddhism. The emperor consented, and instructed the governor of Jiaozhou (now the northern part of Vietnam) to dispatch a ship to Java to fetch Gunavarman. Huiguan immediately sent Fazhang, Daochong, Daojun and some other monks to go along with a letter to the king of Java, asking for his permission to let go of Gunavarman. Before the Chinese mission arrived in Java, Gunavarman had already left the country and embarked on a journey aboard a merchant ship. A windstorm rose midway on the journey, sending the ship adrift to Guangzhou, where he landed. In 431 Gunavarman arrived in Jianye (present-day Nanjing in Jiangsu Province).

According to Volume 97 of the *Book of Song*, in 435 the king of Java sent a mission to China to deliver a letter of credentials, offer religious objects and solicit friendship. The letter of credentials received by the Chinese side contained a full account of the popularity of Buddhism in his country. During the 436-520 period, Java repeatedly sent missions to China to present gifts and seek friendly relations. During the Tang Dynasty (618-907), Sino-Indonesian Buddhist relations became even closer. Many Chinese monks on their way to India stopped over in Java or Sumatra, some of them to stay permanently. One of them was Yijing, who stayed in Srivijaya, a kingdom in Sumatra, for six months studying the Indian language before resuming his journey to India. Having studied in India for 11 years, Yijing visited Srivijaya once again, where he devoted himself to translation and writing for six years. It was not until 695 that he returned to China. During the Kaiyuan reign (713-741) of the Tang Dynasty, the Esoteric master Vajrabodhi (669-741) also stayed for a while in Srivijaya on his way from Sinhala to China. In 781 during the Tang Dynasty, the Java monk Bianhong arrived in Chang'an with religious gifts to Chinese monasteries. He settled down in the Qinglong Temple to study Tantrism from Monk Huiguo.

The Sino-Indonesian Buddhist ties continued uninterrupted during the Song Dynasty (960-1279). In 983, the Chinese monk Fayu stopped over in Srivijaya on his way back to China from a pilgrimage to India. When Fayu went to India again, the imperial court of the Song entrusted him with a letter of good will to the king of Srivijaya. After the 15th century, Islam became the major religion of Indonesia, and Buddhism went on a decline. The Buddhist ties between China and Indonesia faded as well. Buddhism still exists in Indonesia mainly among Chinese residents there.

Korea

Buddhist ties between China and Korea date back to the 4th century when the Korean Peninsular was composed of three countries, Koguryo, Shinla and Baekje. Individuals of each of these counters were sent or came on their own to China to learn Buddhism. Some of these people chose to stay after they finished their studies, while the others returned to preach Buddhism

Official records date Sino-Korean Buddhist relations back to 372 in the Eastern Jin Dynasty, when Fu Jian, who had made himself emperor of the Former Qin in Chang'an, sent envoys and monks to Kogurya with gifts of Buddhist statues and scriptures. The mission was warmly received, and the king of Kogurya sent an envoy to the Former Qin to express gratitude. This exchange triggered a constant stream of people from these three Korean countries to arrive in China to learn Buddhism. The arrivals reached an all-time high during the Sui and Tang dynasties.

During the Sui and Tang as different schools emerged in Han Buddhism, each of them acquired some following in Korea. In 628 during the Tang Dynasty, the Kogurya monk Todung arrived in Chang'an to study under Jizang, the patriarch of the Sanlun School. He ended up in Japan as a Sanlun preacher. Shinbang, a famed monk from Koguryo, distinguished himself in his study in China during the Tang Dynasty, and was summoned by the emperor to join Xuanzang's scripture translation workshop at the Hongfu Monastery. Another monk from Koguryo, Wonchik, a Vijnanavada scholar and disciple of Xuanzang, enjoyed the same prestige as another disciple of Xuanzang, Kuiji. In 638, the Koguryo monk Chachang arrived in Chang'an with a dozen or so disciples to study *vinaya* (monastic rules) and preach the commandments. The *Tripitaka* he brought back to his country was the first of its kind in the Korean history. In 661, another monk from Koguryo, Uisang, became a classmate of Fazang, the *de facto* father of the Huayan School, in the Zhixiang Temple at the Zhongnan Mountain. While there, both of them studied the *Garland Sutra.* After he returned to his country he became the patriarch of the Huayan School of the East Sea.

Quite a few Korean monks studied Esoteric Buddhism in China. In 632 (6th year, Zhenguan reign of Tang Dynasty), the Koguryo monk Myonglang arrived in China to study miscellaneous Tantrism. In 635 (9th year, Zhenguan reign), he returned to become the father of the Tong-hae-shin-in Sect. Many Koguryo monks studied Tantrism in China during the Kaiyuan reign (713-741) of the Tang Dynasty.

But even more Korean monks came to China to pursue Chan studies. According to history books, Pomlang arrived in the early

Tang to study under Daoxin, the fourth-generation patriarch of the Chan School. When Pomlang's disciple Shinhaeng came to China, he became a student of Zhikong, a disciple of Shengxiu. The *Quotations of Buddhists in Jingde Reign* mentions many Korean monks studying Chan Buddhism in China. Gim Kyokak, a scion of the imperial family of Shinla, arrived in China during the mid-Tang to settle down at Mount Jiuhua in present-day Qingyang County, Anhui Province. (See detailed description of Gim Kyokak under 5. Chan School, Chapter 3, and the Four Sacred Mountains of Buddhism, Chapter 6)

In late Tang Chinese Buddhism suffered a major setback at the hands of Emperor Wuzong. The crackdown was followed by endless war and turmoil during the Five Dynasties and Sixteen Kingdoms period, causing great losses to religious literature. Quite a few of the scriptures and treatises found their way to Korea. That is why after the Five Dynasties many precious works of Buddhist literature were retrieved from Korea, and in that sense Chinese Buddhists have a lot for which to thank their Korean counterparts.

The Sino-Korean Buddhist relations continued into the Song Dynasty. In 989, the king of Koguryo sent the monk Yoka to China to ask for an edition of the *Tripitaka*, a request that was readily granted by Emperor Taizong. The rulers of the Liao and the Jin dynasties also presented the *Khitan Tripitaka* to Koryo as gifts. Many monks in Koguryo were adept at copying Buddhist sutras in gold powder. This was not lost on the rulers of China. The Yuan court (1271-1368), for instance, twice sent scouts to that country to choose such copiers. On both occasions, a team of more than 100 copiers was put together and brought to China to copy the scriptures. It took about two years to finish copying the *Tripitaka* in gold. Unfortunately, these precious copies are nowhere to be found today.

After the Yuan Dynasty, Korean Buddhists developed a trend to practice both Chan and Jingtu (Pure Land) Buddhism at the same time, probably due to the influence of the Chinese Buddhist practice at the time. After the Japanese invasion of Korea, the Sino-Korean Buddhist relations were gradually torn apart.

After World War II, the Korean Peninsula divided into two countries. While Buddhist contacts across the boundary between

China and North Korea were sporadic at best, exchanges between China and the Republic of Korea were nonexistent. It was not until diplomatic relations were established between China and the Republic of Korea that Buddhists from both sides restored their contacts. The late president of the Chinese Buddhist Association, Zhao Puchu, visited the Republic of Korea, while major leaders of the Buddhist Religious Group Association and of the various Buddhist schools, paid repeated calls to China. Members of the Tiantai School in the Republic of Korea founded an ancestral memorial hall at the Guoqing Temple at Tiantai Mountain, Zhejiang Province. In 1995, a 33-member Buddhist delegation from the Republic of Korea attended a Sino-Korean Republic Conference on Friendly Buddhist Exchanges in Beijing. These activities helped close the ranks of Buddhists of both countries.

Japan

The Buddhist relations between China and Japan date back to the mid-6th century. In 552 during the Liang Dynasty, the king of Baekje had some Chinese editions of Buddhist scriptures and statues presented to Japan as gifts. The event marked the beginning of Buddhism in Japan. Since then Buddhists of China and Japan began to have direct contact with each other: Japanese came to China to study Buddhism while Chinese monks went to Japan to preach.

With the emergence of various schools, Buddhism reached its zenith during the Sui and Tang dynasties in China. This attracted many Japanese to China during the 593-628 period (from the 13th year of the Kaihuang reign of the Sui Dynasty to the 2nd year of the Zhenguan reign of the Tang Dynasty). In 607 in the Sui Dynasty Prince Shotoku of Japan, who advocated Buddhism and worshipped Chinese culture, dispatched an envoy to China to establish friendly relations. The following year he began sending people to China to learn Buddhism. More Japanese monks arrived in China later on, and their pursuits went beyond Buddhism to cover the entire Chinese culture.

In 625 during the Tang Dynasty, the Korguryo monk Keikan began his 1ectures in Japan on the Sanlun School but failed to establish it there. It was not until the return of some Japanese monks from studies in China that this school was founded in Japan. More Japanese returned from China, and as a result the Yogacara, Huayan, Chan ("Zen" in Japanese pronunciation), Pure Land, Tiantai, Esoteric Schools were established one after another. The one exception was the Vinaya School, which was founded in Japan by the Chinese monk Ganjin ("Jianzhen" in Chinese).

Ganjin (688-763), a native of Jiangyang (present-day Yangzhou, Jiangsu Province), was an expert in vinaya. During the Kaiyuan reign of Emperor Xuanzong of the Tang Dynasty, he set out on a journey to Japan to preach commandments with a 21-member entourage at the invitation of the Japanese monks Eiei and Fusho, but the journey fell through. His four other attempts failed too, due to natural causes in some cases and man-made hurdles as well in others. Towards the end of his 5th abortive attempt he lost his eyesight, but his determination to visit Japan remained undeterred. Finally, in 753, he embarked on his 6th journey at the age of 66 and succeeded. He was accorded a warm welcome in Japan and was put up in the Tadaiji Monastery in Nara, where it did not take long for him to begin preaching the commandments, his disciples including the Japanese emperor, members of the imperial family, as well as commoners. In 757, the emperor of Japan had the mansion of a deceased prince converted into a monastery and dedicated it to Ganjin. This is none other than the Tosho Daiji Temple in Nara, which became his domain. Shortly afterwards, he had altars established at the Yakushiji Temple in Shimotsuke and the Kannonji Temple in Tsukushi. These, along with the Tosho Daiji Temple, are known as the three major commandment altars of Japan. The statue of Ganjin enshrined in the Tosho Daiji Temple, made by one of his disciples, is regarded as a national treasure of Japan, and the man himself has been deified by the Japanese people as the "Blind Sage."

Among the Japanese monks who studied in China during the Tang Dynasty was the outstanding Kukai, who studied Esoteric Buddhism from Huiguo at the Qinglong Temple in Chang'an. In 806, he returned to Japan with 216 Buddhist classics and began spreading Esoteric Buddhism. He founded Japan's headquarters of the Esoteric School at Koyazan, and became the author of 150 or so books, thereby making a name for himself as a great master in disseminating the holy words of the Buddha.

Saicho and his disciple, Gishin, also rose to prominence in their studies of Buddhism in China. After the two of them arrived in China in 804, they first studied the Tiantai creed from their Chinese masters Daosui and Hangman and then received training in Esoteric Buddhism from Shunxiao at the Lingyan Monastery in present-day Shaoxing, Zhejiang Province. A year later they returned to Japan, bringing 230 Buddhist classics with them. Saicho was the author of 280 books, and extolled as a master preacher. Saicho's disciple, Enjin, arrived in China in 838 for visits and studies of Esoteric Buddhism, and he returned to Japan with 583 Buddhist classics in 847. It became a custom for Japanese visiting China to go home with some Buddhist books.

Most of the Buddhist scriptures and treatises were destroyed during Emperor Wuzong's suppression of Buddhism during the Huichang reign (841-846) of the Tang Dynasty, and even more losses were incurred during the war and turmoil of the Five Dynasties (907-960). Only the Chan School, which was passed on through mind-to-mind transmission without recourse to writings, survived the melee and became the only school of Han Buddhism to thrive after the Five Dynasties. In 1191 during the Southern Song time, the Japanese monk Eisai returned to Japan after being trained in the meditation practice of Chan Buddhism by the Chan monk Huaichan of the Linji branch, and established the Rinzai Sect in his own country. Eisai's disciple, Dogen, come to China in 1223 during the Southern Song Dynasty. Returning to Japan in 1227 from studies of the meditation practice of the Caodong Chan branch under the tutelage of Rujing at the Tiantong Temple in Ningbo, Zhejiang Province, he devoted himself to disseminating Chan Buddhism and established the Soto-shu Sect (Japan's version of Caodong) at the Eiheiji Temple. After the Song Dynasty, exchanges between monks of China and Japan continued to grow unabated.

In 1654 during the Qing Dynasty, the Chinese monk Yinyuan arrived in Japan to preach Chan Buddhism in Nagasaki and Uji. Yingyuan (1592-1673) was a native of Fuqing in Fujian Province, and the abbot of the Wanfu Temple of Huangbo Mountain. While in Japan, he built the Manfukuji Temple (named after the Wanfu Temple), established the Oboku-shu School (named after the Huangbo Mountain), and laid down the rule that the abbot of the Manfukuji Temple must be a monk from China, a rule that was terminated by the 13th abbot of the temple. The Manfukuji Temple transplanted the monastic systems and rituals from its Chinese counterparts, and some of these have remained unchanged to this day. In 1655, Mu'an arrived in Japan at the request of his master, Yinyuan, to assist the latter in running the Manfukuji Temple. He proved a great help to his master, and after he became the abbot of the temple, he expanded the temple into a colossal affair. The Oboku-Shu Sect headquartered in the Manfukuji Temple today still exerts a considerable influence on Japan's religious life.

Towards the end of the Qing Dynasty, Yang Wenhui, a lay Buddhist in China, took it upon himself to rejuvenate Buddhism by printing and publishing Buddhist scriptures. Many Japanese Buddhists helped him by collecting many scriptures and treatises that had been missing in China and sending them back to China.

After the founding of the People's Republic of China, Buddhist exchanges between China and Japan continued uninterrupted despite the fact that the two nations had had no diplomatic relations for more than two decades. During the Asian and Pacific Peace Conference held in 1952, Zhao v Puchu entrusted the Japanese delegates to bring a Buddhist statue to Japan as a token of peace and friendship. This gesture drew a warm response in Japan's Buddhist circles. This was the first exchange between Buddhists of the two nations after the end of World War II. Beginning from that year, friendly Japanese Buddhists worked to collect the remains of Chinese martyrs who had died in Japan and sent them back to China. In 1957, the Chinese Buddhist Association received a goodwill delegation formed by various Buddhist schools in Japan, and a joint communiqué was issued to mark the event. This opened a new chapter in friendly religious exchanges between the two nations. In 1963, Buddhists from China and Japan jointly commemorated the 1,200th anniversary of the death of Ganjin. In 1964, Japanese Buddhists sent a delegation to attend a ceremony held by the Chinese Buddhist Association to commemorate the 1,300th anniversary of the nirvana of Xuanzang and consecrate a stupa enshrined with the Buddha's tooth relic.

After the Sino-Japanese diplomatic relations returned to normal, Buddhists from both countries have stepped up their friendly exchanges. In 1980 the Toshodai Temple, founded by Ganjin, presented three Dunhuang manuscripts from its collection to the Chinese Buddhist Association. Further development is expected in Sino-Japanese Buddhist relations in the 21st century.

Appendices

I. Brief Chronology

Xia Dynasty ca. 2070-1600 BC

Shang Dynasty (ca. 1600-1046 BC)

Western Zhou Dynasty (1046-770 BC)

Eastern Zhou (770-221 BC)

Qin Dynasty (221-207 BC)

Han Dynasty (206 BC- 220 AD)

Introduction to China of Buddhism, estimated between the first century BC and first century AD. Chinese Buddhist circles in 1998 held a grand ceremony to celebrate the 2000th anniversary of the introduction of Buddhism to China, acknowledging 2 BC in the reign of Emperor Ai as the year when Buddhism found its way into China. Legend also has it that in 64 AD, Eastern Han Emperor Ming had a dream that inspired an imperial mission to India, resulting in the mission's return with monk-translators and the introduction of Buddhist sutras or teachings to China.

Three Kingdoms (220-280) and Jin (265-420) dynasties

More monks arrived from the Western Territory and India during the Three Kingdoms period, and many prominent monk-translators produced significant Buddhist works in China during the Jin period to develop the Han Buddhist *Tripitaka*, the Canon of Buddhism. Sutras and other Buddhist texts were hand-copied as the invention of printing was not to come until the Song Dynasty.

Southern Dynasties (420-589)

All the Southern dynasties emperors believed in or supported

Buddhism. The most ardent was Emperor Wu of the Liang Dynasty. He was originally a Daoist before announcing at a meeting of 2,000 monks and laymen in 504 his decision to give up Daoism for Buddhism. Devoting himself to the study of Buddhist philosophy, he had temples built and Buddhist statues sculpted and enshrined.

Northern Dynasties (386-581)

The world-famous Yungang and Longmen grottoes, and the unparalleled Yongning Monastery were built during this period. However, Buddhism suffered two campaigns of persecution that Buddhists refer to as "Disasters of the Dharma." Emperor Taiwu of the Northern Wei, launched a short-lived but devastating campaign to abolish Buddhism in 438. Emperor Wu of the Northern Zhou, also launched a short-lived but devastating campaign against Buddhism in 574.

Sui (581-618) and Tang dynasties (618-907)

The Height of Han Buddhism. The various schools of Han Buddhism emerged, and they all spread to Korea and Japan after many Japanese and Korean monks traveled to China for study. All Chinese emperors were supporters of Buddhism during the Tang Dynasty, with one significant exception — Emperor Wuzong who launched a crackdown on Buddhism in 842 during his 841-846 reign. Huge numbers of sutras were burned, monasteries were shut down, and monks were forced to return to secular life. Many schools ceased to exist as separate movements. Emperor Xuanzong resurrected Buddhism after he ascended the throne in 857. But although Buddhism survived Emperor Wuzong's crackdown, it never again enjoyed the kind of prosperity it had during the Sui and Early Tang period in China.

Song Dynasty (960-1279)

The invention of printing came in this era. During the Northern Song, Emperor Huizong (1101-1125) was at first opposed to Buddhism but later changed his views. Development of Buddhism during the Song was characterized by the prosperity of a single sect, the Chan, although the Tiantai sect gained as well. Otherwise, the different schools of Buddhism began to merge. The prevalent form of Buddhism in the Song Dynasty combined both the Chan (Zen) School's practice of meditation in a crossed-legged sitting posture and the Jingtu (Pure Land) School's practice of chanting the name of Amitabha.

Yuan Dynasty (1271-1368)

After Tibet became part of China during the Yuan Dynasty (1271-1368), the Yuan emperors were all pious followers of Tibetan Buddhism. Emperor Kublai Khan appointed the celebrated Lama Phags-pa of Tibet imperial tutor and entrusted him with the task of creating a written form of the Mongolian language. As a result, Buddhism reached its acme in Tibet, and Tibetan Buddhism spread throughout Mongolia. The religion fell out of favor in Ming Dynasty (1368-1644), but by the Qing (1644-1911), for political purposes, the imperial court again held Tibetan Buddhism in high esteem. One legacy of the Qing policies can be seen today in the Chengde Imperial Summer Resort and surrounding temples, Hebei Province. This vast Qing imperial garden includes Tibetan Buddhist temples featuring a replica of Lhasa's Potala Palace.

Ming (1368-1644) and Qing dynasties (1644-1911), and the Republican Period (1912-1949)

Han Buddhist temples today mostly house a Qing-dynasty Chinese version of the *Tripitaka*, known as the *Dragon Tripitaka,* earlier versions having been destroyed in previous dynasties. Many Buddhist temples today also are reconstructions from the Ming-Qing dynasties, or later. A number of eminent monks emerged during the Ming and Qing dynasties. Quite a few eminent Buddhist personages also emerged during the Republican years (1912-1949). These included the monks Dixian (1858-1935), Yuexia (1858-1917), Taixu (1889-1947), Hongyi (1880-1942), Xuyun (1840-1959), Yuanying (1878-1953), and Yinguang (1861-1940), and the lay Buddhists Yang Wenhui (1837-1911), Ouyang Jingwu (1871-1944), and Han Qingjing (1884-1949).

The People's Republic of China (Since 1949)

The Constitution of the People's Republic of China established freedom of religion, guaranteeing the right of Buddhist worship. In 1953, the Chinese Buddhist Association was established with headquarters in the Guangji Temple in Beijing. The association has helped establish cultural exchanges with Buddhists of foreign countries among its many activities, that also include operating the Chinese Buddhist Seminary at Fayuan Temple in Beijing. During the "cultural revolution" (1966-1976), many Buddhist sites were vandalized. Following that time, the state has invested considerable funds to the renovations of Buddhist sites. Today, with the opening up of China, Buddhist circles are thriving and welcoming visitors from all over the world.

II. Who's Who in Han Buddhist History (Eminent Monks in Alphabetical Order)

Amoghavajra 不空金刚 (705-774), one of the four major translators in Han Buddhist history and a founder of the Esoteric School of Han Buddhism. Said to have been born in present day Sri Lanka, he was an Indian of the Brahman caste who arrived in China as a child.

An Shigao 安世高, the first translator of Buddhist scriptures in China. He arrived in China in the mid-2nd century from Parthia, present-day Iran.

Bodhidharma 菩提达摩 (c. 520), recognized as bringing the Chan School philosophy from India as the 28th-generation disciple of Kasyapa, one of Sakyamuni's ten disciples. Legend associates him with the Shaolin Temple in Henan Province.

Daoxuan 道宣 (596-667), founder of the Vinaya (Disciplinary) School also called the "Vinaya School of the South Mountain." Born in Wuxing in present-day north Zhejiang, he settled at the Baiquan Temple on Zhongnan Mountain where he drew on the strengths of different schools of Buddhism to come up with his own understanding of the vinaya, the commandments or code of ethics for Buddhists.

Faxian 法显 (c.337-c.422), one of the most accomplished of the many early pilgrim monks. In 399, when he was 62, Faxian started off with a group of disciples from Chang'an (Xi'an) on an 11-year journey to more than 30 kingdoms in search of commandments and scriptures. He returned to China in 412. A year later, working together with the Indian monk Buddhabhadra (359-429), he translated six scriptures and treatises. Based on his travels in more than 30 countries, he wrote the classic *Faxian's Pilgrimage to India*. Faxian died at the age of 85 in Jiangling of Hubei Province.

Ganjin [Jianzhen] 鉴真 (688-763) both preached Buddhism and brought the culture of the high Tang Dynasty to Japan. A native of Jiangyang (present-day Yangzhou, Jiangsu Province), he succeeded in his determination to visit Japan in 753 after five previous failed attempts at age 66, after he had lost his eyesight. His disciples included the Japanese emperor, members of the imperial family, as well as commoners. In 757, the emperor of Japan had the mansion of a deceased prince converted into a monastery and dedicated it to Ganjin — the Tosho Daiji Temple in Nara, which became his domain. Shortly afterwards, he had altars established at the Yakushiji Temple in Shimotsuke and the Kannonji Temple in Tsukushi. These, along with the Tosho Daiji Monastery, are known as the three major commandment altars of Japan. The statue of Ganjin enshrined in the Tosho Daiji Monastery, made by one of his disciples, is regarded as a national treasure of Japan.

Gim Kyokak 金乔觉, who arrived in China from Korea during the mid-Tang and settled down at Mount Jiuhua in present-day Qingyang County, Anhui Province. It is said that three years after his death at age 99 in 803, his remains in a stone sarcophagus in a sitting posture were found in perfect condition, leading local Buddhists to believe Gim Kyokak to be the reincarnate of the bodhisattva Ksitigarbha. Thus Mount Jiuhua became one of the four major mountain sanctuaries of Chinese Buddhism and the mecca for tens of thousands of pilgrims from all over the world. His body is buried in a chamber underneath the Roushen Pagoda on the top of Shenguang Peak of Mount Jiuhua.

Huineng 慧能 (638-713), founder of the Chan (Zen) School of Han Buddhism. A highly accomplished monk of the Tang Dynasty, Huineng was the sixth Chan patriarch (Bodhidharma was the first) whose work established earlier Chan thinking into a formal school of thought. His many disciples also earned many followers to continue a religious tradition that has thrived to this day, spreading around the world.

Jizang 吉藏 (549-623) a founder of the Sanlun School of Han Buddhism. His lecturers in Chang'an (Xi'an) attracted people from all over the country. In 618, when Li Yuan entered Chang'an as the founding emperor of the Tang Dynasty, Jizang was one of the ten eminent monks the emperor invited to conduct Buddhist affairs for him. Most of Jizang's writings were on doctrines of the Sanlun School.

Kumarajiva 鸠摩罗什 (344-413), one of the four major translators of sutras in Han Buddhist history. He was born in Kuqa in today's Xinjiang Autonomous Region in the west of China in a family of Indian descent. His translations of the *Three Classics* helped found the Sanlun School.

Shandao 善导 (613-681), founder of the Jingtu or Pure Land School of Han Buddhism. A native of Linzi in present-day Zibo, Shandong Province, he came to believe that the most convenient and easily mastered of all Buddhist commandments was the Dharma Door for Reciting the Buddha's Name, the principle belief of the Jingtu School.

Tipitakacariya Paramartha 真谛 (491-569), one of the four major translators in Han Buddhist history. He was an Indian monk and scholar who preached Buddhism in what is present-day Cambodia before he arrived in present-day Guangdong in China in 546.

Xuanzang 玄奘 (602-664), founder of the Ci'en School of Buddhism and one of the four major translators in Han Buddhist history. His travels West — some 1373 years ago — in search of sutras inspired many myths and folk tales that were gathered some 400 years ago into *Journey to the West*, a book that became one of the great classics of Chinese literature. This eminent Tang Dynasty pilgrim monk and scholar is celebrated in both India and China for his many accomplishments.

Zhiyi 智义 (538-597), founder of the Tiantai School of Han Buddhism. The name of the Tiantai School of Buddhism in China honors Zhiyi, posthumously honored as Grand Master of Tiantai for the long years he spent practicing austerities on Mount Tiantai in present-day Tiantai County, Zhejiang. Zhiyi — who is said to have had double pupils in each of his eyes — synthesized various theories and practices that helped guide Han Buddhism into its own form, especially through his book *Insights into the Lotus Sutra.*

III. The Eight Ancestral Halls of Han Buddhism

- Ci'en Temple in the city of Xi'an, known as the birthplace of the Ci'en (Vinnanavada) school. North China.
- Great Xingshan Temple in the city of Xi'an, known as the birthplace of the Esoteric School of Han Buddhism. North China.
- Guoqing Temple, about 100 miles south of the city of Ningbo in Zhejiang Province, known as the birthplace of the Tiantai School of Han Buddhism. Southeast China.
- Huayan Temple in Chang'an County near the city of Xi'an, in Shaanxi Province, known as the birthplace of the Huayan School of Han Buddhism. North China.
- Longchang Temple on Baohua Mountain north of Jurong County and about 50 miles east of the city of Nanjing, Jiangsu Province, known as the birthplace of the Vinaya School of Han Buddhism. East China.
- Nanhua Temple in Qujiang County, Guangdong Province, known as the birthplace of the Chan School of Han Buddhism. South China.
- Qixia Temple in the Qixia Mountains in the suburbs of

Nanjing, Jiangsu Province, known as the birthplace of the Sanlun School of Han Buddhism. Southeast China.

- Xuanzhong Temple, nestled at the foot of Shibi Mountain in Jiaocheng County, Shanxi Province, known as the birthplace of the Jingtu (Pure Land) School of Han Buddhism. North China.

IV. United Nations World Cultural and Heritage Sites with Chinese Buddhist Ties

- Mogao Caves southeast of Dunhuang City in Gansu Province.
- Mount Taishan in central Shandong Province. One of the five sacred Daoist Mountains in China, it is home also to many Buddhist temples.
- Potala Palace in Lhasa, capital of Tibet.
- Chengde Imperial Summer Resort and surrounding temples, Hebei Province. This vast imperial garden built in the Qing Dynasty has Tibetan Buddhist temples that include a replica of Lhasa's Potala Palace.
- Giant Buddha of Leshan, Mount Emei in Sichuan Province. One of the four sacred Buddhist mountains in China.
- Mount Lushan in Jiangxi Province. In 391 Huiyuan, the founder of the Jingtu (Pure Land) School of Buddhism built Donglin Temple here that later became a Buddhist center for the whole of south China.
- Ancient city of Pingyao in Shanxi Province. First built over 2,700 years ago, this city retains the historical features of the Ming and Qing dynasties and includes Buddhist sculpture and architecture from that time.
- Dazu Stone Carvings near Chongqing City. The earliest sculpture dates from the late Tang Dynasty, an example of China's grotto art of the later period.

- Longmen Grottoes near Luoyang, Henan Province. Work here began in the Northern Wei Dynasty and continued over 400 years, leaving some 1,345 caves and niches, 3,600 inscribed tablets, over 50 pagodas and more than 100,000 statues.
- Yungang Grottoes, southern foot of Mount Wuzhou, west of Datong, a city in Shanxi Province. The oldest, most intact and largest-scale group of grottoes in China. The Gandhara and Quetta artistic styles originating in Indian Buddhism can be seen in the carvings here.

V. Buddhist Terms

Amita: Boundless, infinite.

Amitabha: The Buddha of Infinite Qualities, Boundless Light. An imaginary being unknown to ancient Buddhism, Amita Buddha became a favorite in China through the devotion of the Jingtu (Pure Land) School ("Jodo" in Japan) to chanting his name. Amitabha is closely associated with Avalokitesvara, also considered as Amitabha's incarnation. In the trinity of Amitabha, Avalokitesvara appears on his left and Mahasthamaprapta on his right.

Ananda: He is noted as the most learned disciple of the Buddha, known for hearing and remembering his teaching. Ananda is considered the second patriarch of Buddhism, second to Kasyapa.

Arhats: Worthy, enlightened, saintly Buddhists. The 16, 18 or 500 famous disciples appointed to witness to Buddha-truth and save the world.

Bodhi: Knowledge, understanding, perfect wisdom; the illuminated or enlightened mind. The tree under which Sakyamuni attained enlightenment is referred to as the bodhi tree.

Bodhisattva: Enlightened ones. People who have attained enlightenment but continue to live in the world to rescue others.

Buddha: Siddhartha Gautama of the Sakyas, a prince of a tribe in today's southern part of Nepal, went on a search for enlightenment after he had grown tired of luxury and material goods and a world in which existed old age, sickness and death. One evening he was sitting under a bodhi tree and fell into a deep meditation during which he achieved "enlightenment." He was given the title Buddha (the Awakened or Enlightened One) and was also known as Sakyamuni (the wise man of the sakya tribe). He died in ca. 480 BC.

Buddhist doctrine: The Buddha was an oral teacher. His doctrines were written down and codified by later followers. The essence of these doctrines is that all life is suffering, and people feel pain from the moment of birth to the moment of death. To overcome the suffering, people need to follow the Eightfold Path: right views, right intention, right speech, right action, right livelihood, right effort, right-mindedness and right contemplation.

Buddhism: The teachings of Buddha. The two major branches of Buddhism are Theravada, the Doctrine of the Elders, and Mahayana, the Great Vehicle. Theravada is more popularly known as Hinayana, the Lesser Vehicle, a term first coined as a pejorative by early Mahayana followers. In China, Han and Tibetan Buddhism are of the Mahayana Branch; Pali is of the Theravada branch.

Buddhists: Followers of Buddhism. They are estimated in the world at between 150 and 300 million. Some 70 million of those are in China.

Dagoba: See pagoda. The oldest extant large-scale dagoba is the White Dagoba in Beijing, built by a Nepalese architect named Aniko in 1297 during the Yuan Dynasty, at Miaoying Temple in Beijing.

Dharma: The doctrine or law, the teachings of Buddha.

Dhyana: Meditation. Also a name for the Chan or Zen School of Buddhism, which emphasizes meditation over words.

Eightfold Noble Path: The eight correct ways set forth by Sakyamuni the Buddha for a person of wisdom to achieve

Nirvana. They are: 1) Right view, understanding of the Four Noble Truths; 2.) Right thought or purpose; 3) Right speech — avoiding false and frivolous speech; 4) Right action or conduct; 5) Right livelihood or occupation; 6) Right effort or energy in uninterrupted progress toward the goal; 7) Right mindfulness and keeping the memory correct; 8) Right meditation.

Four Dogmas or Noble Truths: The fundamental doctrines of Sakyamuni that state the existence of suffering, that human desire is the cause of suffering, that the end of human desire can bring and end to suffering and that the way to destroy human desire is to lead a life of holiness. See Eightfold Noble Path.

Guanyin (Goddess of Mercy): The Buddhist deity of compassion, popular among worshippers for her power to alleviate suffering and especially popular in China. See also Avalokitesvara.

Hinayana Buddhism: Also called Theravada or Southern Buddhism, translated as the "Lesser Vehicle" as compared to the "Greater Vehicle" of Mahayana Buddhism. Hinayana is the orthodox school that developed after Sakyamuni's death until about the beginning of the Christian era, when Mahayana doctrines were introduced. Hinayana has the concept of the Buddha as a spiritual doctor, less interested in philosophy than in a remedy to human suffering. The term Hinayana was coined by Mahayana followers to emphasize Mahayana's goal of universal salvation over the narrower goal of personal salvation of Hinayana. Hinayana Buddhism is prevalent in Dai-inhabited areas of China like Yunnan Province as well as in Sri Lanka, Burma and Thailand. Pali is the general literary language of the surviving forms of Hinayana Buddhism.

Kasyapa (Mahakasyapa): One of the principal disciples of Sakyamuni and after his death became leader of the disciples. The first compiler of the Buddhist canon and the first patriarch.

Lokapalas: Heavenly kings, the four guardians of the world and of the Buddhist faith.

Mahayana Buddhism: Also called Northern Buddhism, translated as the "Greater Vehicle" as compared to the "Lesser Vehicle" or Hinayana Buddhism. Mahayana is the Buddhism prevalent in China, Mongolia, Nepal, Korea and Japan. It has a concept of an Eternal Buddha and Universal Salvation with a pantheon of deities who have achieved nirvana as well as bodhisattvas, beings who deny themselves final nirvana until they have first saved all living beings. Sanskrit is the general literary language of Mahayana.

Nirvana: The extinction of suffering, or delusion, transport across the bitter sea of mortality. The goal of Buddhist belief.

Pagoda: The Chinese pagoda evolved from the Indian stupa, religious monuments that in their most basic form were mounds of brick-faced earth that served as repositories for relics. In East and Southeast Asia, the stupa evolved into the pagoda, a multi-storied or pavilion-shaped structure that served several purposes because of its height. Although originally designed as tombs for Buddhist relics, pagodas do not always include relics. Nearly all pagodas in China are associated with Buddhism. The inverted-bowl-style pagoda of Tibetan Buddhism is called a dagoba.

Sakyamuni: The historic Buddha, the Buddha revealed, the saint of the Sakya tribe. His death is estimated at around 483-487 BC, a few years before that of Confucius in 479. The image of Sakyamuni the Buddha takes the central place in the major hall in most Han Buddhist temples.

Samadhi: Sanskrit for deep concentration, state of one-pointedness.

Samsara: Birth and death, rebirth and redeath, ever-recurring samsara or transmigrations.

Sangha: Community of monks and nuns, novices, and lay believers who observe Buddhist vows.

Sutra: Traditional teachings and sermons of the Buddha.

Tiratana: The "Three Treasures" of Buddhism: Buddha, Dharma, and Sangha.

Tripitaka: The Buddhist Canon; literally, the three "baskets" — the teachings or sutras, the disciplinary rules or vinaya, and abstract philosophical treatises or sastras.

Trilokya: Three Realms. This represents the world outlook of the Mahayana Buddhism, which classifies the world into three realms, that is, kamadhatu (Realm of Desire), rupadhatu (Material Realm), and arupadhatu (Immaterial Realm). Each realm has its own multitude of people who need the guidance and education of Buddhism.

Vairocana: The First of the Dhyani or Celestial Buddhas, the essence of wisdom or bodhi and absolute purity.

VI. The Chinese Buddhist Association

The Chinese Buddhist Association is the national organization representing Buddhists of all ethnic backgrounds across China. It was founded in 1953 after prominent Buddhist personages gathered in Beijing for the First National Buddhist Congress. Some 140 delegates attended the congress, and elected Dharmacarya (Master of the Law) Yuanying (1878-1953) president. When Yuanying died in autumn of that year, he was succeeded by Shes-rab-rgya-tso (1884-1968), a prominent Tibetan Buddhist scholar. Zhao Puchu served as president from 1980 until his death in 2000 at the age of 93. Among those present to pay final tribute to Zhao Puchu at services at the Beijing Babaoshan Cemetery was Chinese President Jiang Zemin.

The Chinese Buddhist Association assists the government in carrying out the policy of freedom of religious belief and serves as a bridge between Buddhists and the government. Abroad, it carries out friendly cultural exchanges with Buddhists of foreign countries on behalf of Chinese Buddhists. The association has also done much to promote Buddhism by repairing temples and monasteries, training monks and publishing books and periodicals. An example of its charitable activities is its donation of some one million yuan when the worst floods in a hundred years struck some regions in China.

With headquarters in the Guangji Temple in Beijing, the Chinese Buddhist Association also operates the Buddhist Seminary at the

Fayuan Temple in Beijing, with branches in Qixia Mountain of Nanjing and in the Lingyan Mountain of Suzhou. Student monks live the same community life as monks in a large temple. They devote two hours to studies, and spend the rest of the day chanting incantations or meditating, and they are obliged to maintain the decorum and etiquette of a monk. The students are asked to foster a monastic lifestyle so that they can become role models in observing Buddhist discipline and set a good example in their conduct. Students study for a term of four years in the seminary, which enrolls students once in two years. Only senior middle school graduates and those with the same level of education are eligible for enrolment. Outstanding undergraduates have the opportunity to apply for postgraduate courses. Buddhist studies comprise 70 percent of the curricula, while literature, history, philosophy and foreign languages (English and Japanese) account for 30 percent. There are also some 20 or so elementary and secondary seminaries in various provinces, municipalities and autonomous regions, in which thousands of monks and nuns receive training.

In 1981, the Chinese Buddhist Association launched the journal, *Fayin* (*Voice of the Law*). In recent years, the Chinese Buddhist Culture Research Institute affiliated with the Chinese Buddhist Association created the periodical *Buddhist Culture*. More than 20 other Buddhist periodicals are being published in China, undoubtedly a result of the policy of reform and opening up to the outside world. After the founding of the People's Republic of China, some personages in Buddhist circles began to put together a monthly journal to publicize cultural knowledge associated with Buddhism. With the approval of the People's Government, the *Modern Buddhist Studies* was created in September 1950, and this publication became the voice of the Chinese Buddhist Association after the association was formed in 1953. However, in 1964, after 15 years of circulation, *Modern Buddhist Studies* went out of operation.

The Sutra Engraving Center in Nanjing, Jiangsu Province is also run by the Chinese Buddhist Association. The center is in the possession of a hundred thousand wood blocks, and supplies Buddhist circles at home and abroad with close to 200 titles of scriptures. Towards the end of the Qing Dynasty, a lay Buddhist by the name of Yang Renshan founded the Jinling Sutra Engraving Center in Nanjing, Jiangsu Province, and soon the center made a name for itself at home and abroad. Even the great man of letters, Lu Xun (1881-1936), donated money to it for the engraving of the *Sutra of One Hundred Parables*. After Yang died, his student, Ouyang Jian, took over. After a period of thriving business, the center gradually went downhill during the 1937-1945 War of Resistance against Japan. It was all but closed down on the eve of liberation in 1949. In the early post-liberation years, with the support of the People's Government, farsighted personages in the Chinese Buddhist circles restored the center, and shipped wood blocks engraved with texts of Buddhist scriptures from across the country to it, in an effort to preserve the heritage of Chinese Buddhism. In 1957, the Sutra Engraving Center came under the direct leadership of the Chinese Buddhist Association. However, during the catastrophe of the ten-year "cultural revolution" of 1966-1976, the center fell prey to cultural vandalism. Its houses were put to other uses, and its engraved wood blocks were messed up and became piles of waste materials. It was only after Premier Zhou Enlai intervened in the 1970s that things returned to normal.

During its early days, the goal of the association was to "unite with all the Buddhists of the country under the leadership of the People's Government to participate in the movement to love and protect the motherland and world peace, assist the People's Government in carrying out the policy of freedom of religious belief, and rally the efforts of Buddhists across the land to carry forward the fine sects of Buddhism," according to the Constitution of the Chinese Buddhist Association, *Modern Buddhist Studies*, issue No. 6, 1953. The Constitution of the Chinese Buddhist Association has been revised at various periods of time. For instance, the Constitution adopted at the Sixth National Congress (See the revised version of the Constitution of the Chinese Buddhist Association, *Fayin*, issue No. 12, 1993) added to the association's original goal:

"The goal of this association is to assist the People's Government in carrying out the policy of freedom of religious belief and safeguard the lawful rights and interests of the Buddhists; disseminate the doctrines of Buddhism, carry forward the fine schools of Buddhism, step up the building of Buddhism itself, and develop Buddhist undertakings; unite Buddhists of various ethnic backgrounds to participate in economic development and promoting socialist culture and ethics, and contribute to reform and opening up to the outside world, economic growth, the reunification of the motherland, and world peace."

Local Buddhist associations have been established in various provinces, municipalities and autonomous regions. There are also Buddhist associations in many counties as well. These local associations are not affiliated to the Chinese Buddhist Association, but they are connected in religious work. Leaders of local associations are almost without exception council members or standing council members of the Chinese Buddhist Association. And the local associations have basically the same goals and tasks as the national association. The Charity Society of the Southern Putuo Monastery of Xiamen, Fujian Province is a staunch force in helping people in distress and danger. In 1998, the society donated 4.5 million yuan and built 10 "Hope Project" primary schools for disaster stricken areas. Some wealthy monasteries operate hospitals or clinics to treat low-income patients or those having financial difficulties free or at a minimum rate. The Puji Hospital of the Putuo Mountain, Zhejiang Province is an example.

In some large cities there are also laymen's associations that provide venues for lay Buddhists to hold meetings or meditation sessions at regular intervals. Leaders of such organizations are elected at laymen's congresses. These people meditate on their own on a regular basis, and they also invite monks to preach for them.

VII. Suggested Readings (Books in English)

Ancient Pagodas in China, by Luo Zhewen, Foreign Languages Press, 1994.

Cultural Flow Between China and the Outside World Throughout History, by Shen Fuwei, Foreign Languages Press, Beijing, 1996. (Includes information on the early Chinese translator monks.)

Religion in China Today, by Foster Stockwell, New World Press, Beijing, 1993.

Chinese Tea Culture, by Wang Ling, Foreign Languages Press, 2002.
(The Chan or Zen School of Buddhism is especially associated with the practice of drinking tea, but tea culture also flourished in Tibet's monasteries. This book includes information on the relationship between Daoism and tea as well as Chinese Buddhism and tea.)

Xi'an: China's Ancient Capital, by Cao Lei, Foreign Languages Press, 1990.
(Xi'an, known in ancient times as Chang'an and an early center of Buddhism, is the site today of many important Buddhist historical sites.)

An Intellectual History of China, Foreign Languages Press, 1991.

The Origin of Chinese Deities, by Cheng Manchao, Foreign Languages Press, 1991.
(Most of the Chinese deities in this book are Daoist, but the book also contains information on Avalokitesvara or Guanyin, the popular Buddhist deity.)

Journey to the West (3 Volumes), by Wu Cheng'en, translated by W. J. F. Jenner, Foreign Languages Press, Beijing.
(This Chinese classic is based on the myths and folktales that sprung up about the Buddhist monk Xuanzang as he traveled West in the Tang Dynasty in search of Buddhist sutras.)

The Realm of Tibetan Buddhism, text by Li Jicheng; photos by Gu Shoukang and Kang Song; translation by Wang Wenjiong, Foreign Languages Press, 1999.
(Written by a researcher at the Institute of World Religions of the Chinese Academy of Social Sciences and illustrated with some 159 color photographs of Tibetan monasteries, cultural relics and art.)

A Guide to Chinese Martial Arts, Foreign Languages Press,
(The modern martial arts master Li Tianji (1914-1996) includes a section in this book on the Shaolin Buddhist Temple in Henan Province and its history.)

Beijing, China Travel Kit Series, by Xu Mingqiang, Foreign Languages Press, Beijing, 1997.

(Illustrated with photos, maps and charts, this book includes information on the temples, mosques and churches in Beijing. It includes tips for visitors to temples, bus routes, opening times, and a layout map of a typical Chinese Buddhist temple.)

World Cultural and Natural Heritage Sites, by Luo Zhewen, 2002.
(Part of the FLP's "Culture of China" series, this book includes Buddhist sites in its brief descriptions and color photographs of China's UNESCO Cultural and Natural Heritage sites.)

China, A New History, by John King Fairbank, the Belknap Press of Harvard University Press, 1992.

Sui-Tang Chang'an — A Study in the Urban History of Medieval China, by Victor Cunrui Xiong, the Center for Chinese Studies, the University of Michigan, Ann Arbor, 2000.

A Dictionary of Chinese Buddhist Terms, compiled by William Edward Soothill and Lewis Hodous; published by Kegan Paul, Trench, Trubner & Co., Ltd, London. (c. 1939)

Index

图书在版编目（CIP）数据

中国旅游—佛教 / 郑立新 著.
—北京：外文出版社，2004
ISBN 7-119-03334 -4
I. 中…　II. 郑…　III. 佛教-概况-中国-英文
IV. B947. 2

中国版本图书馆 CIP 数据核字（2003）第 036286 号

英文翻译： 凌　原
英文定稿 李振国
英文编辑： 葛璐珊　郁　苓
责任编辑： 吴灿飞　胡开敏
美编设计： 蔡　荣

中国旅游——佛教

郑立新 著

*

外文出版社出版
（中国北京百万庄大街 24 号）
邮政编码　100037
外文出版社网址 http://www.flp.com.cn
外文出版社电子信箱: info@flp.com.cn
sales@flp.com.cn
三河市汇鑫印务有限公司印刷
中国国际图书贸易总公司发行
（中国北京车公庄西路 35 号）
北京邮政信箱第 399 号　邮政编码　100044
2004 年(28 开)第 1 版
2004 年第 1 版第 1 次印刷
（英）
ISBN 7-119-03334-4/G · 575（外）
06000
7-E-3493P